CONFESSIONS

OF

AN ENGLISH OPIUM-EATER,

BEING AN EXTRACT FROM

THE LIFE OF A SCHOLAR.

FROM THE AUTHOR, TO THE AMERICAN EDITOR OF HIS WORKS.

THESE papers I am anxious to put into the hands of your house, and, so far as regards the U. S., of *your* house exclusively; not with any view to further emolument, but as an acknowledgment of the services which you have already rendered me; namely, first, in having brought together so widely scattered a collection — a difficulty which in my own hands by too painful an experience I had found from nervous depression to be absolutely insurmountable; secondly, in having made me a participator in the pecuniary profits of the American edition, without solicitation or the shadow of any expectation on my part, without any legal claim that I could plead, or equitable warrant in established usage, solely and merely upon your own spontaneous motion. Some of these new papers, I hope, will not be without their value in the eyes of those who have taken an interest in the original series. But at all events, good or bad, they are now tendered to the appropriation of your individual house, the Messrs. TICKNOR & FIELDS, according to the amplest extent of any power to make such a transfer that I may be found to possess by law or custom in America.

I wish this transfer were likely to be of more value. But the veriest trifle, interpreted by the spirit in which I offer it, may express my sense of the liberality manifested throughout this transaction by your honorable house.

Ever believe me, my dear sir,

Your faithful and obliged,

THOMAS DE QUINCEY.

FROM THE AUTHOR TO THE READER.

I HERE present you, courteous reader, with the record of a remarkable period of my life; according to my application of it, I trust that it will prove, not merely an interesting record, but, in a considerable degree, useful and instructive. In *that* hope it is that I have drawn it up; and *that* must be my apology for breaking through that delicate and honorable reserve, which, for the most part, restrains us from the public exposure of our own errors and infirmities. Nothing, indeed, is more revolting to English feelings, than the spectacle of a human being obtruding on our notice his moral ulcers, or scars, and tearing away that "decent drapery" which time, or indulgence to human frailty, may have drawn over them: accordingly, the greater part of *our* confessions (that is, spontaneous and extra-judicial confessions) proceed from demireps, adventurers, or swindlers; and for any such acts of gratuitous self-humiliation from those who can be supposed in sympathy with the decent and self-respecting part of society, we must look to French literature, or to that part of the German which is tainted with the spurious and defective sensibility of the French. All this I feel so forcibly, and so nervously am I alive to reproach of this tendency, that I have for many months hesitated about the propriety of allowing this, or any part of my narrative, to come before the public eye, until after my death (when, for many reasons, the whole will be published): and it is not without an anxious review of the reasons for and against this step, that I have, at last, concluded on taking it.

Guilt and misery shrink, by a natural instinct, from public notice: they court privacy and solitude; and, even in the choice of a grave, will sometimes sequester themselves from the general population of the church-yard, as if declining to claim fellowship with the great family of man, and wishing (in the affecting language of Mr. Wordsworth)

——Humbly to express
A penitential loneliness.

It is well, upon the whole, and for the interest of us

all, that it should be so; nor would I willingly, in my own person, manifest a disregard of such salutary feelings; nor in act or word do anything to weaken them. But, on the one hand, as my self-accusation does not amount to a confession of guilt, so, on the other, it is possible that, if it did, the benefit resulting to others, from the record of an experience purchased at so heavy a price, might compensate, by a vast over-balance, for any violence done to the feelings I have noticed, and justify a breach of the general rule. Infirmity and misery do not, of necessity, imply guilt. They approach, or recede from, the shades of that dark alliance, in proportion to the probable motives and prospects of the offender, and the palliations, known or secret, of the offence; in proportion as the temptations to it were potent from the first, and the resistance to it, in act or in effort, was earnest to the last. For my own part, without breach of truth or modesty, I may affirm, that my life has been, on the whole, the life of a philosopher: from my birth I was made an intellectual creature; and intellectual in the highest sense my pursuits and pleasures have been, even from my school-boy days. If opium-eating be a sensual pleasure, and if I am bound to confess that I have indulged in it to an excess, not yet *recorded** of any other man, it is no less true, that I have struggled against this fascinating enthralment with a religious zeal, and have at length accomplished what I never yet heard attributed to any other man — have untwisted, almost to its final links, the accursed chain which fettered me. Such a self-conquest may reasonably be set off in counterbalance to any kind or degree of self-indulgence. Not to insist that, in my case, the self-conquest was unquestionable, the self-indulgence open to doubts of casuistry, according as that name shall be extended to acts aiming at the bare relief of pain, or shall be restricted to such as aim at the excitement of positive pleasure.

Guilt, therefore, I do not acknowledge; and, if I did, it is possible that I might still resolve on the present act of confession, in consideration of the service which I may thereby render to the whole class of opium-eaters. But who are they? Reader, I am sorry to say, a very numerous class indeed. Of this I became convinced, some years ago, by computing, at that time, the number of those in one small class of English society (the class of men

* "Not yet *recorded*," I say; for there is one celebrated man of the present day, who, if all be true which is reported of him, has greatly exceeded me in quantity.

distinguished for talent, or of eminent station) who were known to me, directly or indirectly, as opium-eaters; such, for instance, as the eloquent and benevolent ——; the late Dean of ——; Lord ——; Mr. ——, the philosopher; a late under-secretary of state (who described to me the sensation which first drove him to the use of opium, in the very same words as the Dean of ——, namely, "that he felt as though rats were gnawing and abrading the coats of his stomach"); Mr. ——; and many others, hardly less known, whom it would be tedious to mention. Now, if one class, comparatively so limited, could furnish so many scores of cases (and that within the knowledge of one single inquirer), it was a natural inference, that the entire population of England would furnish a proportionable number. The soundness of this inference, however, I doubted, until some facts became known to me, which satisfied me that it was not incorrect. I will mention two: 1. Three respectable London druggists, in widely remote quarters of London, from whom I happened lately to be purchasing small quantities of opium, assured me that the number of *amateur* opium-eaters (as I may term them) was, at this time, immense; and that the difficulty of distinguishing these persons, to whom habit had rendered opium necessary from such as were purchasing it with a view to suicide, occasioned them daily trouble and disputes. This evidence respected London only. But, 2 (which will possibly surprise the reader more), some years ago, on passing through Manchester, I was informed by several cotton manufacturers that their work-people were rapidly getting into the practice of opium-eating; so much so, that on a Saturday afternoon the counters of the druggists were strewed with pills of one, two, or three grains, in preparation for the known demand of the evening. The immediate occasion of this practice was the lowness of wages, which, at that time, would not allow them to indulge in ale or spirits; and, wages rising, it may be thought that this practice would cease: but, as I do not readily believe that any man, having once tasted the divine luxuries of opium, will afterwards descend to the gross and mortal enjoyments of alcohol, I take it for granted

> That those eat now who never ate before ;
> And those who always ate now eat the more.

Indeed, the fascinating powers of opium are admitted, even by medical writers who are its greatest enemies : thus, for instance, Awsiter, apothecary to Greenwich Hospital, in his "Essay on the Effects of Opium" (published in the year 1763), when attempting to explain why Mead had not been sufficiently explicit on the properties, counter-agents, &c., of this drug, expresses himself in the following mysterious terms (φονοντια συνετοισι): "Perhaps he thought the subject of too delicate a nature to be made common; and as many people might then indiscriminately use it, it would take from that necessary fear and caution, which should prevent their experiencing the extensive power of this drug; *for there are many properties in it, if universally known, that would habituate the use, and make it more in request with us than the Turks themselves;* the result of which knowledge," he adds, "must prove a general misfortune." In the necessity of this conclusion I do not altogether concur; but upon that point I shall have occasion to speak at the close of my Confessions, where I shall present the reader with the *moral* of my narrative.

PRELIMINARY CONFESSIONS.

THESE preliminary confessions, or introductory narrative of the youthful adventures which laid the foundation of the writer's habit of opium-eating in after life, it has been judged proper to premise, for three several reasons:

1. As forestalling that question, and giving it a satisfactory answer, which else would painfully obtrude itself in the course of the Opium Confessions — "How came any reasonable being to subject himself to such a yoke of misery, voluntarily to incur a captivity so servile, and knowingly to fetter himself with such a seven-fold chain? —" a question which, if not somewhere plausibly resolved, could hardly fail, by the indignation which it would be apt to raise as against an act of wanton folly, to interfere with that degree of sympathy which is necessary in any case to an author's purposes.

2. As furnishing a key to some parts of that tremendous scenery which afterwards peopled the dreams of the opium-eater.

3 As creating some previous interest of a personal sort in the confessing subject, apart from the matter of the confessions, which cannot fail to render the

confessions themselves more interesting. If a man "whose talk is of oxen" should become an opium-eater, the probability is, that (if he is not too dull to dream at all) he will dream about oxen: whereas, in the case before him, the reader will find that the opium-eater boasteth himself to be a philosopher; and accordingly, that the phantasmagoria of *his* dreams (waking or sleeping, day dreams or night dreams) is suitable to one who, in that character,

Humani nihil a se alienum putat.

For amongst the conditions which he deems indispensable to the sustaining of any claim to the title of philosopher, is not merely the possession of a superb intellect in its *analytic* functions (in which part of the pretension, however, England can for some generations show but few claimants; at least, he is not aware of any known candidate for this honor who can be styled emphatically *a subtle thinker*, with the exception of *Samuel Taylor Coleridge*, and, in a narrower department of thought, with the recent illustrious exception *

* A third exception might perhaps have been added: and my reason for not adding that exception is chiefly because it was only in his juvenile efforts that the writer whom I allude to expressly addressed himself to philosophical themes; his riper powers have been dedicated (on very excusable and very intelligible grounds, under the present direction of the popular mind in England) to criticism and the fine arts. This reason apart, however, I doubt whether he is not rather to be considered an acute thinker than a subtle one. It is, besides, a great drawback on his mastery over philosophical subjects, that he has obviously not had the advantage of a regular scholastic education: he has not read Plato in his youth (which most likely was only his misfortune), but neither has he read Kant in his manhood (which is his fault).

of *David Ricardo*), — but also on such a constitution of the *moral* faculties as shall give him an inner eye and power of intuition for the vision and mysteries of human nature: that constitution of faculties, in short, which (amongst all the generations of men that from the beginning of time have deployed into life, as it were, upon this planet) our English poets have possessed in the highest degree — and Scottish * professors in the lowest.

I have often been asked how I first came to be a regular opium-eater; and have suffered, very unjustly, in the opinion of my acquaintance, from being reputed to have brought upon myself all the sufferings which I shall have to record, by a long course of indulgence in this practice, purely for the sake of creating an artificial state of pleasurable excitement. This, however, is a misrepresentation of my case. True it is, that for nearly ten years I did occasionally take opium, for the sake of the exquisite pleasure it gave me; but, so long as I took it with this view, I was effectually protected from all material bad consequences, by the necessity of interposing long intervals between the several acts of indulgence, in order to renew the pleasurable sensations. It was not for the purpose of creating pleasure, but of mitigating pain in the severest degree, that I first began to use opium as an article of daily diet. In the twenty-eighth year of my age, a most painful affection of the stomach, which I had first experienced about ten years before, attacked me in great strength. This affection had originally been caused by the extrem-

* I disclaim any allusion to existing professors, of **whom**, indeed, I know only one.

2

ties of hunger, suffered in my boyish days. During the season of hope and redundant happiness which succeeded (that is, from eighteen to twenty-four) it had slumbered: for the three following years it had revived at intervals; and now, under unfavorable circumstances, from depression of spirits, it attacked me with violence that yielded to no remedies but opium. As the youthful sufferings which first produced this derangement of the stomach were interesting in themselves and in the circumstances that attended them, I shall here briefly retrace them.

My father died when I was about seven years old, and left me to the care of four guardians. I was sent to various schools, great and small; and was very early distinguished for my classical attainments, especially for my knowledge of Greek. At thirteen I wrote Greek with ease; and at fifteen my command of that language was so great, that I not only composed Greek verses in lyric metres, but would converse in Greek fluently, and without embarrassment — an accomplishment which I have not since met with in any scholar of my times, and which, in my case, was owing to the practice of daily reading off the newspapers into the best Greek I could furnish *extempore;* for the necessity of ransacking my memory and invention for all sorts and combinations of periphrastic expressions, as equivalents for modern ideas, images, relations of things, &c., gave me a compass of diction which would never have been called out by a dull translation of moral essays, &c. "That boy," said one of my masters, pointing the attention of a stranger to me, "that boy could harangue an Athenian mob better than you or I could address an English one." He who honored me with this eulogy was a scholar, "and a ripe and good one," and, of all my tutors, was the only one whom I loved or reverenced. Unfortunately for me (and, as I afterwards learned, to this worthy man's great indignation), I was transferred to the care, first of a blockhead, who was in a perpetual panic lest I should expose his ignorance; and, finally, to that of a respectable scholar, at the head of a great school on an ancient foundation. This man had been appointed to his situation by —— College, Oxford; and was a sound, well-built scholar, but (like most men whom I have known from that college) coarse, clumsy, and inelegant. A miserable contrast he presented, in my eyes, to the Etonian brilliancy of my favorite master; and, besides, he could not disguise from my hourly notice the poverty and meagreness of his understanding. It is a bad thing for a boy to be, and know himself, far beyond his tutors, whether in knowledge or in power of mind. This was the case, so far as regarded knowledge at least, not with myself only; for the two boys who jointly with myself composed the first form were better Grecians than the head-master, though not more elegant scholars, nor at all more accustomed to sacrifice to the graces. When I first entered, I remember that we read Sophocles; and it was a constant matter of triumph to us, the learned triumvirate of the first form, to see our "Archididascalus" (as he loved to be called) conning our lesson before we went up, and laying a regular train, with lexicon and grammar, for blowing up and blasting (as it were) any difficulties he found in the choruses; whilst *we* never condescended to open our books, until the moment of going up, and were generally employed in writing epigrams upon his wig, or some such important matter. My two class-fellows were poor, and dependent, for their future prospects at the university, on the recommendation of the head-master; but I, who had a small patrimonial property, the income of which was sufficient to support me at college, wished to be sent thither immediately. I made earnest representations on the subject to my guardians, but all to no purpose. One, who was more reasonable, and had more knowledge of the world than the rest, lived at a distance; two of the other three resigned all their authority into the hands of the fourth; and this fourth, with whom I had to negotiate, was a worthy man, in his way, but haughty, obstinate, and intolerant of all opposition to his will. After a certain number of letters and personal interviews, I found that I had nothing to hope for, not even a compromise of the matter, from my guardian: unconditional submission was what he demanded; and I prepared myself, therefore, for other measures. Summer was now coming on with hasty steps, and my seventeenth birth-day was fast approaching; after which day I had sworn within myself that I would no longer be numbered amongst school-boys. Money being what I chiefly wanted, I wrote to a woman of high rank, who, though young herself, had known me from a child, and had latterly treated me with great distinction, requesting that she would "lend" me five guineas. For upwards of a week no answer came; and I was beginning to despond, when, at length, a servant put into my hands a double letter, with a coronet on the seal. The letter was kind and obliging;

the fair writer was on the sea-coast, and in that way the delay had arisen; she enclosed double of what I had asked, and good-naturedly hinted, that if I should *never* repay her, it would not absolutely ruin her. Now, then, I was prepared for my scheme: ten guineas, added to about two that I had remaining from my pocket money, seemed to me sufficient for an indefinite length of time; and at that happy age, if no *definite* boundary can be assigned to one's power, the spirit of hope and pleasure makes it virtually infinite.

It is a just remark of Dr. Johnson's (and, what cannot often be said of his remarks, it is a very feeling one) that we never do anything consciously for the last time (of things, that is, which we have long been in the habit of doing), without sadness of heart. This truth I felt deeply when I came to leave ——, a place which I did not love, and where I had not been happy. On the evening before I left —— forever, I grieved when the ancient and lofty school-room resounded with the evening service, performed for the last time in my hearing; and at night, when the muster-roll of names was called over, and mine (as usual) was called first, I stepped forward, and passing the head-master, who was standing by, I bowed to him, and looking earnestly in his face, thinking to myself, "He is old and infirm, and in this world I shall not see him again." I was right; I never *did* see him again, nor never shall. He looked at me complacently, smiled good-naturedly, returned my salutation (or rather my valediction), and we parted (though he knew it not) forever. I could not reverence him intellectually; but he had been uniformly kind to me, and had allowed me many indulgences; and I grieved at the thought of the mortification I should inflict upon him.

The morning came, which was to launch me into the world, and from which my whole succeeding life has, in many important points, taken its coloring. I lodged in the head-master's house, and had been allowed, from my first entrance, the indulgence of a private room, which I used both as a sleeping room and as a study. At half after three I rose, and gazed with deep emotion at the ancient towers of ——, "drest in earliest light,' and beginning to crimson with the radiant lustre of a cloudless July morning. I was firm and immovable in my purpose, but yet agitated by anticipation of uncertain danger and troubles; and if I could have foreseen the hurricane, and perfect hail-storm of affliction, which soon fell upon me, well might I have been agitated. To this agitation the deep peace of the morning presented an affecting contrast, and in some degree a medicine. The silence was more profound than that of midnight: and to me the silence of a summer morning is more touching than all other silence, because, the light being broad and strong, as that of noon-day at other seasons of the year, it seems to differ from perfect day chiefly because man is not yet abroad; and thus, the peace of nature, and of the innocent creatures of God, seems to be secure and deep, only so long as the presence of man, and his restless and unquiet spirit, are not there to trouble its sanctity. I dressed myself, took my hat and gloves, and lingered a little in the room. For the last year and a half this room had been my "pensive citadel:" here I had read and studied through all the hours of night; and, though true it was, that, for the latter part of this time, I, who was framed for love and gentle affections, had lost my gayety and happiness, during the strife and fever of contention with my guardian, yet, on the other hand, as a boy so passionately fond of books, and dedicated to intellectual pursuits, I could not fail to have enjoyed many happy hours in the midst of general dejection. I wept as I looked round on the chair, hearth, writing-table, and other familiar objects, knowing too certainly that I looked upon them for the last time. Whilst I write this, it is eighteen years ago; and yet, at this moment, I see distinctly, as if it were but yesterday, the lineaments and expressions of the object on which I fixed my parting gaze: it was a picture of the lovely ——, which hung over the mantel-piece; the eyes and mouth of which were so beautiful, and the whole countenance so radiant with benignity and divine tranquillity, that I had a thousand times laid down my pen, or my book, to gather consolation from it, as a devotee from his patron saint. Whilst I was yet gazing upon it, the deep tones of —— clock proclaimed that it was four o'clock. I went up to the picture, kissed it, and then gently walked out, and closed the door forever!

* * * * * *

So blended and intertwisted in this life are occasions of laughter and of tears, that I cannot yet recall, without smiling, an incident which occurred at that time, and which had nearly put a stop to the immediate execution of my plan. I had a trunk of immense weight; for, besides my clothes, it contained nearly all my library. The difficulty was to get this removed to a carrier's: my room was at an aërial elevation in the house, and (what was worse) the staircase which communicated with this angle of the building was accessible only by a gallery, which passed the head-master's chamber-door. I was a favorite with all the servants; and knowing that any of them would screen me, and act confidentially, I communicated my embarrassment to a groom of the head-master's. The groom swore he would do anything I wished; and, when the time arrived, went up stairs to bring the trunk down. This I feared was beyond the strength of any one man: however, the groom was a man

> Of Atlantean shoulders, fit to bear
> The weight of mightiest monarchies;

and had a back as spacious as Salisbury Plains. Accordingly he persisted in bringing down the trunk alone, whilst I stood waiting at the foot of the last flight, in anxiety for the event. For some time I heard him descending with slow and firm steps; but, unfortunately, from his trepidation, as he drew near the dangerous quarter, within a few steps of the gallery his foot slipped; and the mighty burden, falling from his shoulders, gained such increase of impetus at each step of the descent, that, on reaching the bottom, it trundled, or rather leaped, right across, with the noise of twenty devils, against the very bed-room door of the archididascalus. My first thought was, that all was lost; and that my only chance for executing a retreat was to sacrifice my baggage. However, on reflection, I determined to abide the issue. The groom was in the utmost alarm, both on his own account and on mine: but, in spite of this, so irresistibly had the sense of the ludicrous, in this unhappy *contretems*, taken possession of his fancy, that he sang out a long, loud, and canorous peal of laughter, that might have wakened the Seven Sleepers. At the sound of this resonant merriment, within the very ears of insulted authority, I could not forbear joining in it; subdued to this, not so much by the unhappy *etourderie* of the trunk, as by the effect it had upon the groom. We both expected, as a matter of course, that Dr. —— would sally out of his room; for, in general, if but a mouse stirred, he sprang out like a mastiff from his kennel. Strange to say, however, on this occasion, when the noise of laughter had ceased, no sound, or rustling even, was to be heard in the bed-room. Dr. —— had a painful complaint, which sometimes keeping him awake, made him sleep, perhaps, when it did come, the deeper. Gathering courage from the silence, the groom hoisted his burden again, and accomplished the remainder of his descent without accident. I waited until I saw the trunk placed on a wheelbarrow, and on its road to the carrier's: then, "with Providence my guide," I set off on foot, carrying a small parcel, with some articles of dress under my arm: a favorite English poet in one pocket; and a small 12mo. volume, containing about nine plays of Euripides, in the other.

It had been my intention, originally, to proceed to Westmoreland, both from the love I bore to that county, and on other personal accounts. Accident, however, gave a different direction to my wanderings, and I bent my steps towards North Wales.

After wandering about for some time in Denbighshire, Merionethshire, and Caernarvonshire, I took lodgings in a small neat house in B——. Here I might nave staid with great comfort for many weeks; foi provisions were cheap at B——, from the scarcity ot other markets for the surplus products of a wide agri‐cultural district. An accident, however, in which, perhaps, no offence was designed, drove me out to wander again. I know not whether my reader may have remarked, but I have often remarked, that the proudest class of people in England (or, at any rate, the class whose pride is most apparent) are the families of bishops. Noblemen, and their children, carry about with them, in their very titles, a sufficient notification of their rank. Nay, their very names (and this applies also to the children of many untitled houses) are often, to the English ear, adequate exponents of high birth, or descent. Sackville, Manners, Fitzroy, Paulet, Caven-dish, and scores of others, tell their own tale. Such persons, therefore, find everywhere a due sense of their claims already established, except among those who are ignorant of the world, by virtue of their own obscurity; "Not to know *them* argues one's self un-known." Their manners take a suitable tone and coloring; and, for once that they find it necessary to impress a sense of their consequence upon others, they meet with a thousand occasions for moderating and tempering this sense by acts of courteous condescension. With the families of bishops it is otherwise; with them it is all up-hill work to make known their pretensions; for the proportion of the episcopal bench taken from noble families is not at any time very large; and the succession to these dignities is so rapid, that the public ear seldom has time to become familiar with them unless where they are connected with some literary reputation. Hence it is that the children of bishops carry about with them an austere and repulsive air, indicative of claims not generally acknowledged,—a sort of *noli me tangere* manner, nervously apprehensive of too familiar approach, and shrinking with the sensitiveness of a gouty man, from all contact with the οἱ πολλοί. Doubtless, a powerful understanding, or unusual goodness of nature, will preserve a man from such weakness; but, in general, the truth of my representation will be acknowledged; pride, if not of deeper root in such families, appears, at least, more upon the surface of their manners. This spirit of manners naturally communicates itself to their domestics, and other dependants. Now, my landlady had been a lady's maid, or a nurse, in the family of the Bishop of ——; and had but lately married away and "settled" (as such people express it) for life. In a little town like B——, merely to have lived in the bishop's family conferred some distinction; and my good landlady had rather more than her share of the pride I have noticed on that score. What "my lord" said, and what "my lord" did,—how useful he was in parliament, and how indispensable at Oxford,—formed the daily burden of her talk. All this I bore very well; for I was too good-natured to laugh in anybody's face, and I could make an ample allowance for the garrulity of an old servant. Of necessity, however, I must have appeared in her eyes very inadequately impressed with the bishop's importance; and, perhaps to punish me for my indifference, or, possibly, by accident, she one day repeated to me a conversation in which I was indirectly a party concerned. She had been to the palace to pay her respects to the family and, dinner being over, was summoned into the dining room. In giving an account of her household economy, she happened to mention that she had let her apartments. Thereupon the good bishop (it seemed) had taken occasion to caution her as to her selection of inmates; "for," said he, "you must recollect, Betty, that this place is in the high road to the Head; so that *multitudes of Irish swindlers*, running away from their debts into England, and of English swindlers, running away from their debts to the Isle of Man, are likely to take this place in their route." This advice was certainly not without reasonable grounds, but rather fitted to be stored up for Mrs. Betty's private meditations, than specially reported to me. What followed, however, was somewhat worse: — "O, my lord," answered my landlady (according to her own representation of the matter), "I really don't think this young gentleman is a swindler; because ——." "You don't *think* me a swindler?" said I, interrupting her, in a tumult of indignation; "for the future, I shall spare you the trouble of thinking about it." And without delay I prepared for my departure. Some concessions the good woman seemed disposed to make; but a harsh and contemptuous expression, which I fear that I applied to the learned dignitary himself, roused *her* indignation in turn; and reconciliation then became impossible. I was, indeed, greatly irritated at the bishop's having suggested any grounds of suspicion, however remotely, against a person whom he had never seen; and I thought of letting him know my mind in Greek; which, at the same time that it would furnish some presumption that I was no swindler, would also (I hoped) compel the bishop to reply in the same language; in which case, I doubted not to make it appear, that if I was not so rich as his lordship, I was a far better Grecian. Calmer thoughts, however, drove this boyish design out of my mind: for I considered that the bishop was in the right to counsel an old servant; that he could not have designed that his advice should be reported to me; and that the same coarseness of mind which had led Mrs. Betty to repeat the advice at all might have colored it in a way more agreeable to her own style of thinking than to the actual expressions of the worthy bishop.

I left the lodging the very same hour; and this turned out a very unfortunate occurrence for me, because, living henceforward at inns, I was drained of my money very rapidly. In a fortnight I was reduced to short allowance; that is, I could allow myself only one meal a day. From the keen appetite produced by constant exercise and mountain air, acting on a youthful stomach, I soon began to suffer greatly on this slender regimen; for the single meal which I could venture to order was coffee or tea. Even this, however, was at length withdrawn; and, afterwards, so long as I remained in Wales, I subsisted either on blackberries, hips, haws, &c., or on the casual hospitalities which I now and then received, in return for such little services as I had an opportunity of rendering. Sometimes I wrote letters of business for cottagers who happened to have relatives in Liverpool or in London; more often I wrote love-letters to their sweethearts for young women who had lived as servants in Shrewsbury, or other towns on the English border. On all such occasions I gave great satisfaction to my humble friends, and was generally treated with hospitality; and once, in particular, near the village of Llan-y-styndwr (or some such name), in a sequestered part of Merionethshire, I was entertained for upwards of three days by a family of young people, with an affectionate and fraternal kindness that left an impression upon my heart not yet impaired. The family consisted, at that time, of four sisters and three brothers, all grown up, and remarkable for elegance and delicacy of manners. So much beauty, and so much native good breeding and refinement, I do not remember to have seen before or since in any cottage, except once or twice in Westmoreland and Devonshire. They spoke English; an accomplishment not often met with in so many members of one family, especially in villages remote from the high road. Here I wrote, on my first introduction, a letter about prize-money, for one of the brothers, who had served on board an English man-of-war; and, more privately, two love-letters for two of the sisters. They were both interesting looking girls, and one of uncommon loveliness. In the midst of their confusion and blushes, whilst dictating, or rather giving me general instructions, it did not require any great penetration to discover that what they wished was that their letters should be as kind as was consistent with proper maidenly pride. I contrived so to temper my expressions as to reconcile the gratification of both feelings; and they were much pleased with the way in which I had expressed their thoughts, as (in their simplicity) they were astonished at my having so readily discovered them. (The reception one meets with from the women of a family generally determines the tenor of one's whole entertainment.) In this case I had dis charged my confidential duties as secretary so much to the general satisfaction, perhaps also amusing them with my conversation, that I was pressed to stay with a cordiality which I had little inclination to resist. I slept with the brothers, the only unoccupied bed standing in the apartment of the young women: but in all other points they treated me with a respect not usually paid to purses as light as mine; as if my scholarship were sufficient evidence that I was of "gentle blood." Thus I lived with them for three days, and great part of a fourth; and, from the undiminished kindness which they continued to show me, I believe I might have staid with them up to this time, if their power had corresponded with their wishes. On the last morning, however, I perceived upon their countenances, as they sate at breakfast, the expression of some unpleasant communication which was at hand; and soon after, one of the brothers explained to me, that their parents had gone, the day before my arrival, to an annual meeting of Methodists, held at Caernarvon, and were that day expected to return; "and if they should not be so civil as they ought to be," he begged, on the part of all the young people, that I would not take it amiss. The parents returned with churlish faces, and "*Dym Sassenach*" (*no English*) in answer to all my addresses. I saw how matters stood; and so, taking an affectionate leave of my kind and interesting young hosts, I went my way. For, though they spoke warmly to their parents in my behalf, and often excused the manner of the old people, by saying that it was "only their way," yet I easily understood that my talent for writing love-letters would do as little to recommend me with two grave sexagenarian Welsh Methodists as my Greek Sapphics or Alcaics; (and what had been hospitality, when offered to me with the gracious courtesy of my young friends, would become charity, when connected with the harsh demeanor of these old people.) Certainly, Mr. Shelley is right in his notions about old age; (unless powerfully counteracted by all sorts of opposite agencies, it is a miserable corrupter and blighter to the genial charities of the human heart.)

Soon after this, I contrived, by means which I must omit for want of room, to transfer myself to London. And now began the latter and fiercer stage of my long sufferings; without using a disproportionate expression, I might say, of my agony. For I now suffered, for upwards of sixteen weeks, the physical anguish of hunger in various degrees of intensity; but as bitter, perhaps, as ever any human being can have suffered who has survived it. I would not needlessly harass my reader's feelings by a detail of all that I endured; for extremities such as these, under any circumstances of heaviest misconduct or guilt, cannot be contemplated, even in description, without a rueful pity that is painful to the natural goodness of the human heart. Let it suffice, at least on this occasion, to say, that a few fragments of bread from the breakfast-table of one individual (who supposed me to be ill, but did not know of my being in utter want), and these at uncertain intervals, constituted my whole support. During the former part of my sufferings (that is, generally in Wales, and always for the first two months in London), I was houseless, and very seldom slept under a roof. To this constant exposure to the open air I ascribe it mainly, that I did not sink under my torments. Latterly, however, when cold and more inclement weather came on, and when, from the length of my sufferings, I had begun to sink into a more languishing condition, it was, no doubt, fortunate for me, that the same person to whose breakfast-table I had access allowed me to sleep in a large, unoccupied house, of which he was tenant. Unoccupied, I call it, for there was no household or establishment in it; nor any furniture, indeed, except a table and a few chairs. But I found, on taking possession of my new quarters, that the house already contained one single inmate, a poor, friendless child, apparently ten years old; but she seemed hunger-bitten; and sufferings of that sort often make children look older than they are. From this forlorn child I learned, that she had slept and lived there alone, for some time before I came; and great joy the poor creature expressed, when she found that I was in future to be her companion through the hours of darkness. The house was large; and, from the want of furniture, the noise of the rats made a prodigious echoing on the spacious staircase and hall; and, amidst the real fleshly ills of cold, and, I fear, hunger, the forsaken child had found leisure to suffer still more (it appeared) from the self-created one of ghosts. I promised her protection against all ghosts whatsoever; but, alas! I could offer her no other assistance. We lay upon the floor, with a bundle of cursed law papers for a pillow, but with no other covering than a sort of large horseman's cloak; afterwards, however, we discovered, in a garret, an old sofa-cover, a small piece of rug, and some fragments of other articles, which added a little to our warmth. The poor child crept close to me for warmth, and for security against her ghostly enemies. When I was not more than usually ill, I took her into my arms, so that, in general, she was tolerably warm, and often slept when I could not; for, during the last two months of my sufferings, I slept much in the daytime, and was apt to fall into transient dozings at all hours. But my sleep distressed me more than my watching; for, besides the tumultuousness of my dreams (which were only not so awful as those which I shall have to describe hereafter as produced by opium), my sleep was never more than what is called *dog-sleep;* so that I could hear myself moaning, and was often, as it seemed to me, awakened suddenly by my own voice; and, about this time, a hideous sensation began to haunt me as soon as I fell into a slumber, which has since returned upon me, at different periods of my life, namely, a sort of twitching (I know not where, but apparently about the region of the stomach), which compelled me violently to throw out my feet for the sake of relieving it. This sensation coming on as soon as I began to sleep, and the effort to relieve it constantly awaking me, at length I slept only from exhaustion; and, from increasing weakness (as I said before), I was constantly falling asleep, and constantly awaking. Meantime, the master of the house sometimes came in upon us suddenly, and very early; sometimes not till ten o'clock; sometimes not at all. He was in constant fear of bailiffs; improving on the plan of Cromwell, every night he slept in a different quarter of London; and I observed that he never failed to examine, through a private window, the appearance of those who knocked at the door, before he would allow it to be opened. He breakfasted alone; indeed, his tea equipage would hardly have admitted of his hazarding an invitation to a second person, any more than the quantity of esculent *material*, which, for the most part, was little more than a roll, or a few biscuits, which he had bought on his road from the place where he had slept. Or, if he *had* asked a party, as I once learnedly and facetiously observed to him, the several members of it must have *stood* in the relation to each other (not *sate* in any relation whatever) of succession, as the metaphysicians have it, and not of coëxistence; in the relation of parts of time, and not of the parts of space. During his breakfast, I generally contrived a reason for lounging in; and, with an air of as much indifference as I could assume, took up such fragments as he had left, — sometimes, indeed, there were none at all. In doing this, I committed no robbery, except upon the man himself, who was thus obliged (I believe), now and then, to send out at noon for an extra biscuit; for, as to the poor child, *she* was never admitted into his study (if I may give that name to his chief depository of parchments, law writings, &c.); that room was to her the Blue-beard room of the house, being regularly locked on his departure to dinner, about six o'clock, which usually was his final departure for the night. Whether this child was an illegitimate daughter of Mr. ——, or only a servant, I could not ascertain; she did not herself know; but certainly she was treated altogether as a menial servant. No sooner did Mr. —— make his appearance, than she went below stairs, brushed his shoes, coat, &c.; and, except when she was summoned to run an errand, she never emerged from the dismal Tartarus of the kitchens, to the upper air, until my welcome knock at night called up her little trembling footsteps to the front door. Of her life during the daytime, however, I knew little but what I gathered from her own account at night; for, as soon as the hours of business commenced, I saw that my absence would be acceptable; and, in general, therefore, I went off and sate in the parks, or elsewhere, until night-fall.

But who, and what, meantime, was the master of the house, himself? Reader, he was one of those anomalous practitioners in lower departments of the law, who, — what shall I say? — who, on prudential reasons, or from necessity, deny themselves all the indulgence in the luxury of too delicate a conscience (a periphrasis which might be abridged considerably, but *that* I leave to the reader's taste); in many walks of life, a conscience is a more expensive incumbrance than a wife or a carriage; and just as people talk of "laying down" their carriages, so I suppose my friend, Mr. ——, had "laid down" his conscience for a time; meaning, doubtless, to resume it as soon as he could afford it. The inner economy of such a man's daily life would present a most strange picture, if I could allow myself to amuse the reader at his expense. Even with my limited opportunities for observing what went on, I saw many scenes of London intrigues, and complex chicanery, "cycle and epicycle, orb in orb," at which I sometimes smile to this day, and at which I smiled then, in spite of my misery. My situation, however, at that time, gave me little experience, in my own person, of any qualities in Mr. ——'s character but such as did him honor; and of his whole strange composition, I must forget everything but that towards me he was obliging, and, to the extent of his power, generous.

That power was not, indeed, very extensive. However, in common with the rats, I sate rent free; and as Dr. Johnson has recorded that he never but once in his life had as much wall-fruit as he could eat, so let me be grateful that, on that single occasion, I had as large a choice of apartments in a London mansion as I could possibly desire. Except the Blue-beard room, which the poor child believed to be haunted, all others, from the attics to the cellars, were at our service. "The world was all before us," and we pitched our tent for the night in any spot we chose. This house I have already described as a large one. It stands in a conspicuous situation, and in a well-known part of London. Many of my readers will have passed it, I doubt not, within a few hours of reading this. For myself, I never fail to visit it when business draws me to London. About ten o'clock this very night, August 15, 1821, being my birth-day, I turned aside from my evening walk, down Oxford-street, purposely to take a glance at it. It is now occupied by a respectable family, and, by the lights in the front drawing-room, I observed a domestic party, assembled, perhaps, at tea, and apparently cheerful and gay; — marvellous contrast, in my eyes, to the darkness, cold, silence, and desolation, of that same house eighteen years ago, when its nightly occupants were one famishing scholar and a neglected child. Her, by the by, in after years, I vainly endeavored to trace. Apart from her situation, she was not what would be called an interesting child. She was neither pretty, nor quick in understanding, nor remarkably pleasing in manners But, thank God! even in those years I needed not the embellishments of novel accessories to conciliate my affections. Plain human nature, in its humblest and most homely apparel, was enough for me; and I loved the child because she was my partner in wretchedness. If she is now living, she is probably a mother, with children of her own; but, as I have said, I could never trace her.

This I regret; but another person there was, at that time, whom I have since sought to trace, with far deeper earnestness, and with far deeper sorrow at my failure. This person was a young woman, and one of that unhappy class who subsist upon the wages of prostitution. I feel no shame, nor have any reason to feel it, in avowing, that I was then on familiar and friendly terms with many women in that unfortunate condition. The reader needs neither smile at this avowal, nor frown; for, not to remind my classical readers of the old Latin proverb, "*Sine Cerere,*" &c., it may well be supposed that in the existing state of my purse my connection with such women could not have been an impure one. But the truth is, that at no time of my life have I been a person to hold myself polluted by the touch or approach of any creature that wore a human shape. On the contrary, from my very earliest youth, it has been my pride to converse familiarly, *more Socratico,* with all human beings,—man, woman, and child,—that chance might fling in my way: a practice which is friendly to the knowledge of human nature, to good feelings, and to that frankness of address which becomes a man who would be thought a philosopher; for a philosopher should not see with the eyes of the poor limitary creature calling himself a man of the world, and filled with narrow and self-regarding prejudices of birth and education, but should look upon himself as a catholic creature, and as standing in an equal relation to high and low, to educated and uneducated, to the guilty and the innocent. Being myself, at that time, of necessity, a peripatetic, or a walker of the streets, I naturally fell in, more frequently, with those female peripatetics, who are technically called street-walkers. Many of these women had occasionally taken my part against watchmen who wished to drive me off the steps of houses where I was sitting. But one amongst them, — the one on whose account I have at all introduced this subject, — yet no! let me not class thee, oh noble-minded Ann ——, with that order of women; — let me find, if it be possible, some gentler name to designate the condition of her to whose bounty and compassion — ministering to my necessities when all the world had forsaken me — I owe it that I am at this time alive. For many weeks, I had walked, at nights, with this poor friendless girl, up and down Oxford-street, or had rested with her on steps and under the shelter of porticoes. She could not be so old as myself: she told me, indeed, that she had not completed her sixteenth year. By such questions as my interest about her prompted, I had gradually drawn forth her simple history. Hers was a case of ordinary occurrence (as I have since had reason to think), and one in which, if London beneficence had better adapted its arrangements to meet it, the power of the law might oftener be interposed to protect and to avenge. But the stream of London charity flows in a channel which, though deep and mighty, is yet noiseless and under ground; — not obvious or readily accessible to poor, houseless wanderers and it cannot be denied that the outside air and framework of London society is harsh, cruel, and repulsive In any case, however, I saw that part of her injuries might easily have been redressed; and I urged her often and earnestly to lay her complaint before a magistrate. Friendless as she was, I assured her that she would meet with immediate attention; and that English justice, which was no respecter of persons, would speedily and amply avenge her on the brutal ruffian who had plundered her little property. She promised me often that she would; but she delayed taking the steps I pointed out, from time to time; for she was timid and dejected to a degree which showed how deeply sorrow had taken hold of her young heart; and perhaps she thought justly that the most upright judge and the most righteous tribunals could do nothing to repair her heaviest wrongs. Something, however, would perhaps have been done; for it had been settled between us, at length, — but, unhappily, on the very last time but one that I was ever to see her, — that in a day or two we should speak on her behalf. This little service it was destined, however, that I should never realize. Meantime, that which she rendered to me, and which was greater than I could ever have repaid her, was this: — One night, when we were pacing slowly along Oxford-street, and after a day when I had felt unusually ill and faint, I requested her to turn off with me into Soho-square. Thither we went; and we sate down on the steps of a house, which, to this hour,

I never pass without a pang of grief, and an inner act of homage to the spirit of that unhappy girl, in memory of the noble act which she there performed. Suddenly, as we sate, I grew much worse. I had been leaning my head against her bosom, and all at once I sank from her arms and fell backwards on the steps. From the sensations I then had, I felt an inner conviction of the liveliest kind, that without some powerful and reviving stimulus I should either have died on the spot, or should, at least, have sunk to a point of exhaustion from which all reäscent, under my friendless circumstances, would soon have become hopeless. Then it was, at this crisis of my fate, that my poor orphan companion, who had herself met with little but injuries in this world, stretched out a saving hand to me. Uttering a cry of terror, but without a moment's delay, she ran off into Oxford-street, and in less time than could be imagined returned to me with a glass of port-wine and spices, that acted upon my empty stomach (which at that time would have rejected all solid food) with an instantaneous power of restoration; and for this glass the generous girl, without a murmur, paid out of her own humble purse, at a time, be it remembered, when she had scarcely wherewithal to purchase the bare necessaries of life, and when she could have no reason to expect that I should ever be able to reïmburse her. O, youthful benefactress! how often, in succeeding years, standing in solitary places, and thinking of thee with grief of heart and perfect love, — how often have I wished that, as in ancient times the curse of a father was believed to have a supernatural power, and to pursue its object with a fatal necessity of self-fulfilment, — even so the benediction of a heart oppressed with gratitude might have a like prerogative; might have power given to it from above to chase, to haunt, to waylay, to overtake, to pursue thee into the central darkness of a London brothel, or (if it were possible) into the darkness of the grave, there to awaken thee with an authentic message of peace and forgiveness, and of final reconciliation!

I do not often weep; for not only do my thoughts on subjects connected with the chief interests of man daily, nay, hourly, descend a thousand fathoms "too deep for tears;" not only does the sternness of my habits of thought present an antagonism to the feelings which prompt tears, — wanting, of necessity, to those who, being protected usually by their levity from any tendency to meditative sorrow, would, by that same levity, be made incapable of resisting it on any casual access of such feelings; but also, I believe, that all minds which have contemplated such objects as deeply as I have done, must, for their own protection from utter despondency, have early encouraged and cherished some tranquillizing belief as to the future balances and the hieroglyphic meanings of human sufferings. On these accounts I am cheerful to this hour; and, as I have said, I do not often weep. Yet some feelings, though not deeper or more passionate, are more tender than others; and often, when I walk, at this time, in Oxford street, by dreamy lamp-light, and hear those airs played on a barrel-organ which years ago solaced me and my dear companion (as I must always call her), I shed tears, and muse with myself at the mysterious dispensation which so suddenly and so critically separated us forever. How it happened, the reader will understand from what remains of this introductory narration.

Soon after the period of the last incident I have recorded, I met, in Albemarle-street, a gentleman of his late Majesty's household. This gentleman had received hospitalities, on different occasions, from my family; and he challenged me upon the strength of my family likeness. I did not attempt any disguise; I answered his questions ingenuously, and, on his pledging his word of honor that he would not betray me to my guardians, I gave him an address to my friend, the attorney. The next day I received from him a ten-pound bank note. The letter enclosing it was delivered, with other letters of business, to the attorney; but, though his look and manner informed me that he suspected its contents, he gave it up to me honorably, and without demur.

This present, from the particular service to which it was applied, leads me naturally to speak of the purpose which had allured me up to London, and which I had been (to use a forensic word) *soliciting* from the first day of my arrival in London, to that of my final departure.

In so mighty a world as London, it will surprise my readers that I should not have found some means of staving off the last extremities of penury; and it will strike them that two resources, at least, must have been open to me, namely, either to seek assistance from the friends of my family, or to turn my youthful talents and attainments into some channel of pecuniary emolument. As to the first course, I may observe, generally, that what I dreaded beyond all other evils was the chance of being reclaimed by my guardians; not doubting that whatever power the law gave them would have been enforced against me to the utmost; that is, to the extremity of forcibly restoring me to the school which I had quitted; a restoration which as it would, in my eyes, have been a dishonor, even if submitted to voluntarily, could not fail, when extorted from me in contempt and defiance of my own wishes and efforts, to have been a humiliation worse to me than death, and which would, indeed, have terminated in death. I was, therefore, shy enough of applying for assistance even in those quarters where I was sure of receiving it, at the risk of furnishing my guardians with any clue for recovering me. But, as to London in particular, though doubtless my father had in his lifetime had many friends there, yet (as ten years had passed since his death) I remembered few of them even by name; and never having seen London before, except once for a few hours, I knew not the address of even those few. To this mode of gaining help, therefore, in part the difficulty, but much more the paramount fear which I have mentioned, habitually indisposed me. In regard to the other mode, I now feel half inclined to join my reader in wondering that I should have overlooked it. As a corrector of Greek proofs (if in no other way), I might, doubtless, have gained enough for my slender wants. Such an office as this I could have discharged with an exemplary and punctual accuracy that would soon have gained me the confidence of my employers. But it must not be forgotten that, even for such an office as this, it was necessary that I should first of all have an introduction to some respectable publisher; and this I had no means of obtaining. To say the truth, however, it had never once occurred to me to think of literary labors as a source of profit. No mode sufficiently speedy of obtaining money had ever occurred to me, but that of borrowing it on the strength of my future claims and expectations. This mode I sought by every avenue to compass; and amongst other persons I applied to a Jew named D——.*

---

* To this same Jew, by the way, some eighteen months afterwards, I applied again on the same business; and, dating at that time from a respectable college, I was fortunate enough to gain his serious attention to my proposals. My necessities had not arisen from any extravagance, or youthful levities (these, my habits and the nature of my pleasures raised me far above), but simply from the vindictive malice of my guardian, who, when he found himself no longer able to prevent me from going to the university, had, as a parting token of his good nature, refused to sign an order for granting me a shilling beyond the allowance made to me at school, namely, one hundred pounds per annum. Upon this sum, it was, in my time, barely possible to have lived in college; and not possible to a man, who, though above the paltry affectation of ostentatious disregard for money, and without any expensive tastes, confided, nevertheless, rather too much in servants, and did not delight in the petty details of minute economy. I soon, therefore, became embarrassed; and, at length, after a most voluminous negotiation with the Jew (some parts of which, if I had leisure to rehearse them, would greatly amuse my readers), I was put in possession of the sum I asked for, on the "regular" terms of paying the Jew seventeen and a half per cent. by way of annuity on all the money furnished; Israel, on his part, graciously resuming no more than about ninety guineas of the said money, on account of an attorney's bill (for what services, to whom rendered, and when, — whether at the siege of Jerusalem, at the building of the Second Temple, or on some earlier occasion, — I have not yet been able to discover). How many perches this bill measured I really forget; but I still keep it in a cabinet of natural curiosities, and some time or other I believe I shall present it to the British Museum.

To this Jew, and to other advertising money-lenders (some of whom were, I believe, also Jews), I had introduced myself, with an account of my expectations; which account, on examining my father's will at Doctor's Commons, they had ascertained to be correct. The person there mentioned as the second son of —— was found to have all the claims (or more than all) that I had stated: but one question still remained, which the faces of the Jews pretty significantly suggested, — was I that person? This doubt had never occurred to me as a possible one; I had rather feared, whenever my Jewish friends scrutinized me keenly, that I might be too well known to be that person, and that some scheme might be passing in their minds for entrapping me and selling me to my guardians. It was strange to me to find my own self, *materialiter* considered (so I expressed it, for I doted on logical accuracy of distinctions), accused, or at least suspected, of counterfeiting my own self, *formaliter* considered. However, to satisfy their scruples, I took the only course in my power. Whilst I was in Wales, I had received various letters from young friends: these I produced, — for I carried them constantly in my pocket, — being, indeed, by this time, almost the only relics of my personal incumbrances (excepting the clothes I wore), which I had not in one way or other disposed of. Most of these letters were from the Earl of ——, who was, at that time, my chief (or rather only) confidential friend. These letters were dated from Eton. I had also some from the Marquis of ——, his father, who, though absorbed in agricultural pursuits, yet having been an Etonian himself, and as good a scholar as a nobleman needs to be, still retained an affection for classical studies.

and for youthful scholars. He had, accordingly, from the time that I was fifteen, corresponded with me; sometimes upon the great improvements which he had made, or was meditating, in the counties of M—— and Sl——, since I had been there; sometimes upon the merits of a Latin poet; at other times, suggesting subjects to me on which he wished me to write verses.

On reading the letters, one of my Jewish friends agreed to furnish two or three hundred pounds on my personal security, provided I could persuade the young earl, — who was, by the way, not older than myself, — to guarantee the payment on our coming of age: the Jew's final object being, as I now suppose, not the trifling profit he could expect to make by me, but the prospect of establishing a connection with my noble friend, whose immense expectations were well known to him. In pursuance of this proposal on the part of the Jew, about eight or nine days after I had received the ten pounds, I prepared to go down to Eton. Nearly three pounds of the money I had given to my money-lending friend, on his alleging that the stamps must be bought, in order that the writings might be prepared whilst I was away from London. I thought in my heart that he was lying; but I did not wish to give him any excuse for charging his own delays upon me. A smaller sum I had given to my friend the attorney (who was connected with the money-lenders as their lawyer), to which, indeed, he was entitled for his unfurnished lodgings. About fifteen shillings I had employed in reëstablishing (though in a very humble way) my dress. Of the remainder, I gave one-quarter to Ann, meaning, on my return, to have divided with her whatever might remain

These arrangements made, soon after six o'clock, on a dark winter evening, I set off, accompanied by Ann, towards Piccadilly; for it was my intention to go down as far as Salt Hill on the Bath or Bristol mail. Our course lay through a part of the town which has now all disappeared, so that I can no longer retrace its ancient boundaries: Swallow-street, I think it was called. Having time enough before us, however, we bore away to the left, until we came into Golden-square: there, near the corner of Sherrard-street, we sat down, not wishing to part in the tumult and blaze of Piccadilly. I had told her of my plans some time before; and now I assured her again that she should share in my good fortune, if I met with any; and that I would never forsake her, as soon as I had power to protect her. This I fully intended, as much from inclination as from a sense of duty; for, setting aside gratitude, which, in any case, must have made me her debtor for life, I loved her as affectionately as if she had been my sister; and at this moment with seven-fold tenderness, from pity at witnessing her extreme dejection. I had, apparently, most reason for dejection, because I was leaving the saviour of my life; yet I, considering the shock my health had received, was cheerful and full of hope. She, on the contrary, who was parting with one who had had little means of serving her, except by kindness and brotherly treatment, was overcome by sorrow; so that, when I kissed her at our final farewell, she put her arms about my neck, and wept, without speaking a word. I hoped to return in a week at furthest, and I agreed with her that on the fifth night from that, and every night afterwards, she should wait for me, at six o'clock, near the bottom of Great Titchfield-street, which had been our customary haven, as it were, of rendezvous, to prevent our missing each other in the great Mediterranean of Oxford-street. This, and other measures of precaution, I took: one, only, I forgot. She had either never told me, or (as a matter of no great interest) I had forgotten, her surname. It is a general practice, indeed, with girls of humble rank in her unhappy condition, not (as novel-reading women of higher pretensions) to style themselves *Miss Douglass*, *Miss Montague*, &c., but simply by their Christian names, *Mary*, *Jane*, *Frances*, &c. Her surname, as the surest means of tracing her, I ought now to have inquired; but the truth is, having no reason to think that our meeting could, in consequence of a short interruption, be more difficult or uncertain than it had been for so many weeks, I had scarcely for a moment adverted to it as necessary, or placed it amongst my memoranda against this parting interview; and my final anxieties being spent in comforting her with hopes, and in pressing upon her the necessity of getting some medicine for a violent cough and hoarseness with which she was troubled, I wholly forgot it until it was too late to recall her.

It was past eight o'clock when I reached the Gloucester Coffee-House, and the Bristol Mail being on the point of going off, I mounted on the outside. The fine fluent motion* of this mail soon laid me asleep. It is somewhat remarkable that the first easy or refreshing

* The Bristol Mail is the best appointed in the kingdom, owing to the double advantage of an unusually good road, and of an extra sum for expenses subscribed by the Bristol merchants.

sleep which I had enjoyed for some months was on the outside of a mail-coach, — a bed which, at this day, I find rather an uneasy one. Connected with this sleep was a little incident which served, as hundreds of others did at that time, to convince me how easily a man, who has never been in any great distress, may pass through life without knowing, in his own person, at least, anything of the possible goodness of the human heart, or, as I must add with a sigh, of its possible vileness. So thick a curtain of *manners* is drawn over the features and expression of men's natures, that, to the ordinary observer, the two extremities, and the infinite field of varieties which lie between them, are all confounded, — the vast and multitudinous compass of their several harmonies reduced to the meagre outline of differences expressed in the gamut or alphabet of elementary sounds. The case was this: for the first four or five miles from London, I annoyed my fellow-passenger on the roof, by occasionally falling against him when the coach gave a lurch to his side; and, indeed, if the road had been less smooth and level than it is, I should have fallen off, from weakness. Of this annoyance he complained heavily, as, perhaps, in the same circumstances, most people would. He expressed his complaint, however, more morosely than the occasion seemed to warrant; and if I had parted with him at that moment, I should have thought of him (if I had considered it worth while to think of him at all) as a surly and almost brutal fellow. However, I was conscious that I had given him some cause for complaint, and, therefore, I apologized to him, and assured him I would do what I could to avoid falling asleep for the future, and at the same time, in as few words as possible, I explained to him that I was ill, and in a weak state from long suffering, and that I could not afford, at that time, to take an inside place. The man's manner changed, upon hearing this explanation, in an instant; and when I next woke for a minute, from the noise and lights of Hounslow (for, in spite of my wishes and efforts, I had fallen asleep again within two minutes from the time I had spoken to him), I found that he had put his arm round me to protect me from falling off; and for the rest of my journey he behaved to me with the gentleness of a woman, so that, at length, I almost lay in his arms; and this was the more kind, as he could not have known that I was not going the whole way to Bath or Bristol. Unfortunately, indeed, I *did* go rather further than I intended; for so genial and refreshing was my sleep, that the next time, after leaving Hounslow, that I fully awoke, was upon the sudden pulling up of the mail (possibly at a post-office), and, on inquiry, I found that we had reached Maidenhead, six or seven miles, I think, ahead of Salt Hill. Here I alighted; and for the half-minute that the mail stopped, I was entreated by my friendly companion (who, from the transient glimpse I had of him in Piccadilly, seemed to me to be a gentleman's butler, or person of that rank), to go to bed without delay. This I promised, though with no intention of doing so; and, in fact, I immediately set forward, or, rather, backward, on foot. It must then have been nearly midnight; but so slowly did I creep along, that I heard a clock in a cottage strike four before I turned down the lane from Slough to Eton. The air and the sleep had both refreshed me; but I was weary, nevertheless. I remember a thought (obvious enough, and which has been prettily expressed by a Roman poet) which gave me some consolation, at that moment, under my poverty. There had been, some time before, a murder committed on or near Hounslow Heath. I think I cannot be mistaken when I say that the name of the murdered person was *Steele*, and that he was the owner of a lavender plantation in that neighborhood. Every step of my progress was bringing me nearer to the heath; and it naturally occurred to me that I and the accursed murderer, if he were that night abroad, might, at every instant, be unconsciously approaching each other through the darkness; in which case, said I, supposing I — instead of being (as, indeed, I am) little better than an outcast,

> Lord of my learning, and no land beside —

were, like my friend Lord ——, heir, by general repute, to £70,000 per annum, what a panic should I be under, at this moment, about my throat! Indeed, it was not likely that Lord —— should ever be in my situation; but, nevertheless, the spirit of the remark remains true, that vast power and possessions make a man shamefully afraid of dying; and I am convinced that many of the most intrepid adventurers, who, by fortunately being poor, enjoy the full use of their natural courage, would, if, at the very instant of going into action, news were brought to them that they had unexpectedly succeeded to an estate in England of £50,000 a year, feel their dislike to bullets considerably sharpened,* and their efforts at perfect equanimity and self-possession proportionably difficult. So true it is, in the language of a wise man, whose own experience had made him acquainted with both fortunes, that riches are better fitted

> To slacken virtue, and abate her edge,
> Than tempt her to do aught may merit praise.
>
> *Paradise Regained.*

I dally with my subject, because, to myself, the remembrance of these times is profoundly interesting. But my reader shall not have any further cause to complain; for I now hasten to its close. In the road between Slough and Eton I fell asleep; and, just as the morning began to dawn, I was awakened by the voice of a man standing over me and surveying me. I know not what he was. He was an ill-looking fellow, but not, therefore, of necessity, an ill-meaning fellow; or, if he were, I suppose he thought that no person sleeping out-of-doors in winter could be worth robbing. In which conclusion, however, as it regarded myself, I beg to assure him, if he should be among my readers, that he was mistaken. After a slight remark, he passed on. I was not sorry at his disturbance, as it enabled me to pass through Eton before people were generally up. The night had been heavy and lowering, but towards the morning it had changed to a slight frost, and the ground and the trees were now covered with rime. I

* It will be objected that many men, of the highest rank and wealth, have, in our own day, as well as throughout our history, been amongst the foremost in courting danger in battle. True but this is not the case supposed. Long familiarity with power has, to them, deadened its effect and its attractions.

slipped through Eton unobserved; washed myself, and, as far as possible, adjusted my dress, at a little public house in Windsor; and, about eight o'clock, went down towards Pote's. On my road I met some junior boys, of whom I made inquiries. An Etonian is always a gentleman, and, in spite of my shabby habiliments, they answered me civilly. My friend, Lord ——, was gone to the University of ——. "Ibi omnis effusus labor!" I had, however, other friends at Eton; but it is not to all who wear that name in prosperity that a man is willing to present himself in distress. On recollecting myself, however, I asked for the Earl of D——, to whom (though my acquaintance with him was not so intimate as with some others) I should not have shrunk from presenting myself under any circumstances. He was still at Eton, though, I believe, on the wing for Cambridge. I called, was received kindly, and asked to breakfast.

Here let me stop, for a moment, to check my reader from any erroneous conclusions. Because I have had occasion incidentally to speak of various patrician friends, it must not be supposed that I have myself any pretensions to rank or high blood. I thank God that I have not. I am the son of a plain English merchant, esteemed, during his life, for his great integrity, and strongly attached to literary pursuits (indeed, he was himself, anonymously, an author). If he had lived, it was expected that he would have been very rich; but, dying prematurely, he left no more than about £30,000 amongst seven different claimants. My mother I may mention with honor, as still more highly gifted; for, though unpretending to the name and honors of a *lite-*

rary woman, I shall presume to call her (what many literary women are not) an *intellectual* woman; and I believe that if ever her letters should be collected and published, they would be thought generally to exhibit as much strong and masculine sense, delivered in as pure "mother English," racy and fresh with idiomatic graces, as any in our language, — hardly excepting those of Lady M. W. Montague. These are my honors of descent; I have no others; and I have thanked God sincerely that I have not, because, in my judgment, a station which raises a man too eminently above the level of his fellow-creatures, is not the most favorable to moral or to intellectual qualities.

Lord D—— placed before me a most magnificent breakfast. It was really so; but in my eyes it seemed trebly magnificent, from being the first regular meal, the first "good man's table," that I had sat down to for months. Strange to say, however, I could scarcely eat anything. On the day when I first received my ten-pound bank-note, I had gone to a baker's shop and bought a couple of rolls; this very shop I had two months or six weeks before surveyed with an eagerness of desire which it was almost humiliating to me to recollect. I remembered the story about Otway; and feared that there might be danger in eating too rapidly. But I had no need for alarm; my appetite was quite sunk, and I became sick before I had eaten half of what I had bought. This effect, from eating what approached to a meal, I continued to feel for weeks; or, when I did not experience any nausea, part of what I ate was rejected, sometimes with acidity, sometimes immediately and without any acidity. On the present occasion, at Lord

D——'s table, I found myself not at all better than usual; and, in the midst of luxuries, I had no appetite I had, however, unfortunately, at all times a craving for wine; I explained my situation, therefore, to Lord D——, and gave him a short account of my late sufferings, at which he expressed great compassion, and called for wine. This gave me a momentary relief and pleasure; and on all occasions, when I had an opportunity, I never failed to drink wine, which I worshipped then as I have since worshipped opium. I am convinced, however, that this indulgence in wine continued to strengthen my malady, for the tone of my stomach was apparently quite sunk; but, by a better regimen, it might sooner, and, perhaps, effectually, have been revived. I hope that it was not from this love of wine that I lingered in the neighborhood of my Eton friends; I persuaded myself *then* that it was from reluctance to ask of Lord D——, on whom I was conscious I had not sufficient claims, the particular service in quest of which I had come to Eton. I was, however, unwilling to lose my journey, and,—I asked it. Lord D——, whose good nature was unbounded, and which, in regard to myself, had been measured rather by his compassion perhaps for my condition, and his knowledge of my intimacy with some of his relatives, than by an over-rigorous inquiry into the extent of my own direct claims, faltered, nevertheless, at this request. He acknowledged that he did not like to have any dealings with money-lenders, and feared lest such a transaction might come to the ears of his connections. Moreover, he doubted whether *his* signature, whose expectations were so much more bounded than those of ——, would avail with my unchristian friends. However, he did not wish, as it seemed, to mortify me by an absolute refusal; for, after a little consideration, he promised, under certain conditions, which he pointed out, to give his security. Lord D—— was at this time not eighteen years of age; but I have often doubted, on recollecting, since, the good sense and prudence which on this occasion he mingled with so much urbanity of manner (an urbanity which in him wore the grace of youthful sincerity), whether any statesman — the oldest and the most accomplished in diplomacy — could have acquitted himself better under the same circumstances. Most people, indeed, cannot be addressed on such a business, without surveying you with looks as austere and unpropitious as those of a Saracen's head.

Recomforted by this promise, which was not quite equal to the best, but far above the worst, that I had pictured to myself as possible, I returned in a Windsor coach to London three days after I had quitted it. And now I come to the end of my story. The Jews did not approve of Lord D——'s terms; whether they would in the end have acceded to them, and were only seeking time for making due inquiries, I know not; but many delays were made, — time passed on, — the small fragment of my bank-note had just melted away, and before any conclusion could have been put to the business, I must have relapsed into my former state of wretchedness. Suddenly, however, at this crisis, an opening was made, almost by accident, for reconciliation with my friends. I quitted London in haste, for a remote part of England; after some time, I proceeded to the university; and it was not until many months had passed away, that I had it in my power again to revisit the ground which had become so interesting to me, and to this day remains so, as the chief scene of my youthful sufferings.

Meantime, what had become of poor Ann? For her I have reserved my concluding words; according to our agreement, I sought her daily, and waited for her every night, so long as I stayed in London, at the corner of Titchfield-street. I inquired for her of every one who was likely to know her; and during the last hours of my stay in London, I put into activity every means of tracing her that my knowledge of London suggested, and the limited extent of my power made possible. The street where she had lodged I knew, but not the house; and I remembered, at last, some account which she had given of ill treatment from her landlord, which made it probable that she had quitted those lodgings before we parted. She had few acquaintances; most people, besides, thought that the earnestness of my inquiries arose from motives which moved their laughter or their slight regard; and others, thinking that I was in chase of a girl who had robbed me of some trifles, were naturally and excusably indisposed to give me any clue to her, if, indeed, they had any to give. Finally, as my despairing resource, on the day I left London, I put into the hands of the only person who (I was sure) must know Ann by sight, from having been in company with us once or twice, an address to —— in ——shire, at that time the residence of my family. But, to this hour, I have never heard a syllable about her. This, amongst such troubles as most men meet with in this life, has been my heaviest affliction. If she lived, doubtless we must have been sometimes in search of each other, at the very same moment, through the mighty labyrinths of London; perhaps even within a few feet of each other, — a barrier no wider, in a London street, often amounting in the end to a separation for eternity! During some years, I hoped that she *did* live; and I suppose that, in the literal and unrhetorical use of the word *myriad*, I may say, that on my different visits to London, I have looked into many, many myriads of female faces, in the hope of meeting her. I should know her again amongst a thousand, if I saw her for a moment; for, though not handsome, she had a sweet expression of countenance, and a peculiar and graceful carriage of the head. I sought her, I have said, in hope. So it was for years; but now I should fear to see her; and her cough, which grieved me when I parted with her, is now my consolation. I now wish to see her no longer, but think of her, more gladly, as one long since laid in the grave; — in the grave, I would hope, of a Magdalen; — taken away, before injuries and cruelty had blotted out and transfigured her ingenuous nature, or the brutalities of ruffians had completed the ruin they had begun.

So then, Oxford-street, stony-hearted stepmother, thou that listenest to the sighs of orphans, and drinkest the tears of children, at length I was dismissed from thee! — the time was come, at last, that I no more should pace in anguish thy never-ending terraces; no more should dream, and wake in captivity to the pangs of hunger. Successors, too many, to myself and Ann, have, doubtless, since then trodden in our footsteps; inheritors of our calamities; other orphans than Ann have sighed; tears have been shed by other children, and thou, Oxford-street, hast since echoed to the groans of innumerable hearts. For myself, however, the storm which I had outlived seemed to have been the pledge of a long fair weather; the premature sufferings which I had paid down, to have been accepted as a ransom for many years to come, as a price of long immunity from sorrow; and if again I walked in London, a solitary and contemplative man (as oftentimes I did), I walked for the most part in serenity and peace of mind. And, although it is true that the calamities of my novitiate in London had struck root so deeply in my bodily constitution that afterwards they shot up and flourished afresh, and grew into a noxious umbrage that has overshadowed and darkened my latter years, yet these second assaults of suffering were met with a fortitude more confirmed, with the resources of a maturer intellect, and with alleviations from sympathizing affection, how deep and tender!

Thus, however, with whatsoever alleviations, years that were far asunder were bound together by subtile links of suffering derived from a common root. And herein I notice an instance of the short-sightedness of human desires, — that oftentimes, on moonlight nights, during my first mournful abode in London, my consolation was (if such it could be thought) to gaze from Oxford-street up every avenue in succession which pierces through the heart of Mary-le-bone to the fields and the woods; for *that*, said I, travelling with my eyes up the long vistas which lay part in light and part in shade, "*that* is the road to the north, and, therefore, to ——; and if I had the wings of a dove, *that* way I would fly for comfort." Thus I said, and thus I wished in my blindness; yet, even in that very northern region it was, in that very valley, nay, in that very house to which my erroneous wishes pointed, that this second birth of my sufferings began, and that they again threatened to besiege the citadel of life and hope. There it was that for years I was persecuted by visions as ugly, and as ghastly phantoms, as ever haunted the couch of an Orestes; and in this unhappier than he,—that sleep, which comes to all as a respite and a restoration, and to him especially as a blessed balm for his wounded heart and his haunted brain, visited me as my bitterest scourge. Thus blind was I in my desires; yet, if a veil interposes between the dim-sightedness of man and his future calamities, the same vale hides from him their alleviations; and a grief which had not been feared is met by consolations which had not been hoped. I, therefore, who participated, as it were, in the troubles of Orestes (excepting only in his agitated conscience), participated no less in all his supports; my Eumenides, like his, were at my bed-feet, and stared in upon me through the curtains; but, watching by my pillow, or defrauding herself of sleep to bear me company through the heavy watches of the night, sat my Electra; for thou, beloved M., dear companion of my later years, thou wast my Electra! and neither in nobility of mind nor in long-suffering affection wouldst permit that a Grecian sister should excel an English wife. For thou thoughtest not much to stoop to humble offices of kindness, and to servile ministrations of tenderest affection; to wipe away for years the unwholesome dews upon the forehead, or to refresh the lips when parched and baked with fever; nor even when thy own peaceful slumbers had by long sympathy become infected with the spectacle of my dread contest with phantoms and shadowy enemies, that oftentimes bade me "sleep no more!" — not even then didst thou utter a complaint or any murmur, nor withdraw thy angelic smiles, nor shrink from thy service of love, more than Electra did of old. For she, too, though she was a Grecian woman, and the daughter of the king* of men, yet wept sometimes, and hid her face † in her robe.

But these troubles are past, and thou wilt read these records of a period so dolorous to us both as the legend of some hideous dream that can return no more. Meantime I am again in London; and again I pace the terraces of Oxford-street by night; and oftentimes, — when I am oppressed by anxieties that demand all my philosophy and the comfort of thy presence to support, and yet remember that I am separated from thee by three hundred miles, and the length of three dreary months, — I look up the streets that run northward from Oxford-street, upon moonlight nights, and recollect my youthful ejaculation of anguish; and remem-

---

* Agamemnon.

† *Ομμα θεις εισω πεπλων.* The scholar will know that throughout this passage I refer to the early scenes of the Orestes, — one of the most beautiful exhibitions of the domestic affections which even the dramas of Euripides can furnish. To the English reader, it may be necessary to say, that the situation at the opening of the drama is that of a brother attended only by his sister during the demoniacal possession of a suffering conscience (or, in the mythology of the play, haunted by the furies), and in circumstances of immediate danger from enemies, and of desertion or cold regard from nominal friends.

bering that thou art sitting alone in that same valley, and mistress of that very house to which my heart turned in its blindness nineteen years ago, I think that, though blind indeed, and scattered to the winds of late, the promptings of my heart may yet have had reference to a remoter time, and may be justified if read in another meaning; and if I could allow myself to descend again to the impotent wishes of childhood, I should again say to myself, as I look to the north, "O that I had the wings of a dove!" and with how just a confidence in thy good and gracious nature might I add the other half of my early ejaculation, — "And *that* way I would fly for comfort!"

THE PLEASURES OF OPIUM.

It is so long since I first took opium, that if it had been a trifling incident in my life, I might have forgotten its date: but cardinal events are not to be forgotten; and, from circumstances connected with it, I remember that it must be referred to the autumn of 1804. During that season I was in London, having come thither for the first time since my entrance at college. And my introduction to opium arose in the following way: From an early age I had been accustomed to wash my head in cold water at least once a day; being suddenly seized with tooth-ache, I attributed it to some relaxation caused by an accidental intermission of that practice; jumped out of bed, plunged my head into a basin of cold water, and, with hair thus wetted, went to sleep. The next morning, as I need hardly say, I awoke with excruciating rheumatic pains of the head and face, from which I had hardly any respite for about twenty days. On the twenty-first day I think it was, and on a Sunday, that I went out into the streets; rather to run away, if possible, from my torments, than with any distinct purpose. By accident, I met a college acquaintance, who recommended opium. Opium! dread agent of unimaginable pleasure and pain! I had heard of it as I had heard of manna or of ambrosia, but no further; how unmeaning a sound was it at that time! what solemn chords does it now strike upon my heart! what heart-quaking vibrations of sad and happy remembrances! Reverting for a moment to these, I feel a mystic importance attached to the minutest circumstances connected with the place, and the time, and the man (if man he was), that first laid open to me the paradise of opium-eaters. It was a Sunday afternoon, wet and cheerless; and a duller spectacle this earth of ours has not to show than a rainy Sunday in London. My road homewards lay through Oxford-street; and near "the *stately* Pantheon" (as Mr. Wordsworth has obligingly called it) I saw a druggist's shop. The druggist (unconscious minister of celestial pleasures!), as if in sympathy with the rainy Sunday, looked dull and stupid, just as any mortal druggist might be expected to look on a Sunday; and when I asked for the tincture of opium, he gave it to me as any other man might do; and, furthermore, out of my shilling returned to me what seemed to be a real copper half-penny, taken out of a real wooden drawer. Nevertheless, in spite of such indications of humanity, he has ever since existed in my mind as a beatific vision of an immortal druggist, sent down to earth on a special mission to myself. And it confirms me in this way of considering him, that when I next came up to London, I sought him near the stately Pantheon, and found him not; and thus to me, who knew not his name (if, indeed, he had one), he seemed rather to have vanished from Oxford-street than to have removed to any bodily fashion. The reader may choose to think of him as, possibly, no more than a sublunary druggist: it may be so, but my faith is better: I believe him to have evanesced,* or evaporated. So, unwillingly, would I connect any mortal remembrances with that hour, and place, and creature, that first brought me acquainted with the celestial drug.

Arrived at my lodgings, it may be supposed that I lost not a moment in taking the quantity prescribed. I was necessarily ignorant of the whole art and mystery of opium-taking; and what I took, I took under every disadvantage. But I took it; and in an hour, — oh heavens! what a revulsion! what an upheaving, from its lowest depths, of the inner spirit! what an apocalypse of the world within me! That my pains had vanished was now a trifle in my eyes; this negative effect was swallowed up in the immensity of those positive effects which had opened before me, in the abyss of divine enjoyment thus suddenly revealed. Here was a panacea, a φαρμακον νεπενθες, for all human woes; here was the secret of happiness, about which philosophers had disputed for so many ages, at once discovered; happiness might now be bought for a penny, and

* *Evanesced:* — this way of going off from the stage of life appears to have been well known in the 17th century, but at that time to have been considered a peculiar privilege of blood royal and by no means to be allowed to druggists. For, about the year 1686, a poet of rather ominous name (and who, by the by, did ample justice to his name), namely, Mr. FLAT-MAN, in speaking of the death of Charles II., expresses his surprise that any prince should commit so absurd an act as dying; because, says he,

> Kings should disdain to die, and only *disappear;*
> They should *abscond*, that is, into the other world.

carried in the waistcoat-pocket; portable ecstasies might be had corked up in a pint-bottle; and peace of mind could be sent down in gallons by the mail-coach. But, if I talk in this way, the reader will think I am laughing; and I can assure him that nobody will laugh long who deals much with opium: its pleasures even are of a grave and solemn complexion; and, in his happiest state, the opium-eater cannot present himself in the character of *L'Allegro;* even then, he speaks and thinks as becomes *Il Penseroso.* Nevertheless, I have a very aprehensible way of jesting, at times, in the midst or my own misery; and, unless when I am checked by some more powerful feelings, I am afraid I shall be guilty of this indecent practice even in these annals of suffering or enjoyment. The reader must allow a little to my infirm nature in this respect; and, with a few indulgences of that sort, I shall endeavor to be as grave, if not drowsy, as fits a theme like opium, so anti-mercurial as it really is, and so drowsy as it is falsely reputed.

And, first, one word with respect to its bodily effects; for upon all that has been hitherto written on the subject of opium, whether by travellers in Turkey (who may plead their privilege of lying as an old immemorial right) or by professors of medicine, writing *ex cathedra* I have but one emphatic criticism to pronounce, — Lies! lies! lies! I remember once, in passing a book stall, to have caught these words from a page of some satiric author: "By this time I became convinced that the London newspapers spoke truth at least twice a week, namely, on Tuesday and Saturday, and might safely be depended upon for — the list of bankrupts."

In like manner, I do by no means deny that some truths have been delivered to the world in regard to opium; thus, it has been repeatedly affirmed, by the learned, that opium is a dusky brown in color, — and this, take notice, I grant; secondly, that it is rather dear, which also I grant, — for, in my time, East India opium has been three guineas a pound, and Turkey, eight; and, thirdly, that if you eat a good deal of it, most probably you must do what is particularly disagreeable to any man of regular habits, namely, — die.* These weighty propositions are, all and singular, true; I cannot gainsay them; and truth ever was, and will be, commendable. But, in these three theorems, I believe we have exhausted the stock of knowledge as yet accumulated by man on the subject of opium. And, therefore, worthy doctors, as there seems to be room for further discoveries, stand aside, and allow me to come forward and lecture on this matter.

First, then, it is not so much affirmed as taken for granted, by all who ever mention opium, formally or incidentally, that it does or can produce intoxication. Now, reader, assure yourself, *meo periculo*, that no quantity of opium ever did, or could, intoxicate. As to the tincture of opium (commonly called laudanum), *that* might certainly intoxicate, if a man could bear to take enough of it; but why? because it contains so

* Of this, however, the learned appear latterly to have doubted; for, in a pirated edition of Buchan's Domestic Medicine, which I once saw in the hands of a farmer's wife, who was studying it for the benefit of her health, the doctor was made to say, — "Be particularly careful never to take above five-and-twenty *ounces* of laudanum at once." The true reading being probably five-and-twenty *drops*, which are held to be equal to about one grain of crude opium

much proof spirit, and not because it contains so much opium. But crude opium, I affirm peremptorily, is incapable of producing any state of body at all resembling that which is produced by alcohol; and not in *degree* only incapable, but even in *kind;* it is not in the quantity of its effects merely, but in the quality, that it differs altogether. The pleasure given by wine is always mounting, and tending to a crisis, after which it declines; that from opium, when once generated, is stationary for eight or ten hours: the first, to borrow a technical distinction from medicine, is a case of acute, the second of chronic, pleasure; the one is a flame, the other a steady and equable glow. But the main distinction lies in this, that whereas wine disorders the mental faculties, opium, on the contrary (if taken in a proper manner), introduces amongst them the most exquisite order, legislation, and harmony. Wine robs a man of his self-possession; opium greatly invigorates it. Wine unsettles and clouds the judgment, and gives a preternatural brightness, and a vivid exaltation, to the contempts and the admirations, to the loves and the hatreds, of the drinker; opium, on the contrary, communicates serenity and equipoise to all the faculties, active or passive; and, with respect to the temper and moral feelings in general, it gives simply that sort of vital warmth which is approved by the judgment, and which would probably always accompany a bodily constitution of primeval or antediluvian health. Thus, for instance, opium, like wine, gives an expansion to the heart and the benevolent affections; but, then, with this remarkable difference, that in the sudden development of kind-heartedness which accompanies inebriation, there is always more or less of a maudlin character which exposes it to the contempt of the bystander Men shake hands, swear eternal friendship, and shed tears, — no mortal knows why; and the sensual creature is clearly uppermost. But the expansion of the benigner feelings, incident to opium, is no febrile access, but a healthy restoration to that state which the mind would naturally recover upon the removal of any deep-seated irritation of pain that had disturbed and quarrelled with the impulses of a heart originally just and good. True it is, that even wine, up to a certain point, and with certain men, rather tends to exalt and to steady the intellect; I myself, who have never been a great wine-drinker, used to find that half a dozen glasses of wine advantageously affected the faculties, brightened and intensified the consciousness, and gave to the mind a feeling of being "ponderibus librata suis;" and certainly it is most absurdly said, in popular language, of any man, that he is *disguised* in liquor; for, on the contrary, most men are disguised by sobriety; and it is when they are drinking (as some old gentleman says in Athenæus) that men display themselves in their true complexion of character; which surely is not disguising themselves. But still, wine constantly leads a man to the brink of absurdity and extravagance: and, beyond a certain point, it is sure to volatilize and to disperse the intellectual energies; whereas opium always seems to compose what had been agitated, and to concentrate what had been distracted. In short, to sum up all in one word, a man who is inebriated, or tending to inebriation, is, and feels that he is, in a condition which calls up into supremacy the merely human too often the brutal, part of his nature; but the opium-eater (I speak of him who is not suffering from any disease, or other remote effects of opium) feels that the diviner part of his nature is paramount; that is, the moral affections are in a state of cloudless serenity; and over all is the great light of the majestic intellect.

This is the doctrine of the true church on the subject of opium: of which church I acknowledge myself to be the only member, — the alpha and omega; but then it is to be recollected, that I speak from the ground of a large and profound personal experience, whereas most of the unscientific* authors who have at all treated of

*Amongst the great herd of travellers, &c., who show sufficiently by their stupidity that they never held any intercourse with opium, I must caution my readers specially against the brilliant author of "*Anastasius.*" This gentleman, whose wit would lead one to presume him an opium-eater, has made it impossible to consider him in that character, from the grievous misrepresentation which he has given of its effects, at page 215–217, of vol. I. Upon consideration, it must appear such to the author himself; for, waiving the errors I have insisted on in the text, which (and others) are adopted in the fullest manner, he will himself admit that an old gentleman with a snow-white beard," who eats "ample doses of opium," and is yet able to deliver what is meant and received as very weighty counsel on the bad effects of that practice, is but an indifferent evidence that opium either kills people prematurely, or sends them into a mad-house. But, for my part, I see into this old gentleman and his motives; the fact is, he was enamored of "the little golden receptacle of the pernicious drug," which Anastasius carried about him; and no way of obtaining it so safe and so feasible occurred, as that of frightening its owner out of his wits (which, by the by, are none of the strongest). This commentary throws a new light upon the case, and greatly improves it as a story; for the old gentleman's speech, considered as a lecture on pharmacy, is highly absurd; but, considered as a hoax on Anastasius, it reads excellently.

opium, and even of those who have written expressly on the *materia medica*, make it evident, from the horror they express of it, that their experimental knowledge of its action is none at all. I will, however, candidly acknowledge that I have met with one person who bore evidence to its intoxicating power, such as staggered my own incredulity; for he was a surgeon, and had himself taken opium largely. I happened to say to him, that his enemies (as I had heard) charged him with talking nonsense on politics, and that his friends apologized for him by suggesting that he was constantly in a state of intoxication from opium. Now, the accusation, said I, is not *prima facie*, and of necessity, an absurd one; but the defence *is*. To my surprise, however, he insisted that both his enemies and his friends were in the right. "I will maintain," said he. "that I *do* talk nonsense; and secondly, I will maintain that I do not talk nonsense upon principle, or with any view to profit, but solely and simply," said he "solely and simply, — solely and simply (repeating it three times over), because I am drunk with opium; and that daily." I replied, that as to the allegation of his enemies, as it seemed to be established upon such respectable testimony, seeing that the three parties concerned all agreed in it, it did not become me to question it; but the defence set up I must demur to. He proceeded to discuss the matter, and to lay down his reasons; but it seemed to me so impolite to pursue an argument which must have presumed a man mistaken in a point belonging to his own profession, that I did not press him even when his course of argument seemed open to objection; not to mention that a man who talks nonsense, even though "with no view to profit," is not altogether the most agreeable partner in a dispute, whether as opponent or respondent. I confess, however, that the authority of a surgeon, and one who was reputed a good one, may seem a weighty one to my prejudice; but still I must plead my experience, which was greater than his greatest by seven thousand drops a day; and though it was not possible to suppose a medical man unacquainted with the characteristic symptoms of vinous intoxication, yet it struck me that he might proceed on a logical error of using the word intoxication with too great latitude, and extending it generically to all modes of nervous excitement, instead of restricting it as the expression for a specific sort of excitement, connected with certain diagnostics. Some people have maintained, in my hearing, that they had been drunk upon green tea; and a medical student in London, for whose knowledge in his profession I have reason to feel great respect, assured me, the other day, that a patient, in recovering from an illness, had got drunk on a beef-steak.

Having dwelt so much on this first and leading error in respect to opium, I shall notice very briefly a second and a third; which are, that the elevation of spirits produced by opium is necessarily followed by a proportionate depression, and that the natural and even immediate consequence of opium is torpor and stagnation, animal and mental. The first of these errors I shall content myself with simply denying; assuring my reader, that for ten years, during which I took opium at intervals, the day succeeding to that on which I allowed myself this luxury was always a day of unusually good spirits.

With respect to the torpor supposed to follow, or rather (if we were to credit the numerous pictures of Turkish opium-eaters) to accompany, the practice of opium-eating, I deny that also. Certainly, opium is classed under the head of narcotics, and some such effect it may produce in the end; but the primary effects of opium are always, and in the highest degree, to excite and stimulate the system: this first stage of its action always lasted with me, during my novitiate, for upwards of eight hours; so that it must be the fault of the opium-eater himself, if he does not so time his exhibition of the dose (to speak medically) as that the whole weight of its narcotic influence may descend upon his sleep. Turkish opium-eaters, it seems, are absurd enough to sit, like so many equestrian statues, on logs of wood as stupid as themselves. But, that the reader may judge of the degree in which opium is likely to stupefy the faculties of an Englishman, I shall (by way of treating the question illustratively, rather than argumentatively) describe the way in which I myself often passed an opium evening in London, during the period between 1804 and 1812. It will be seen, that at least opium did not move me to seek solitude, and much less to seek inactivity, or the torpid state of self-involution ascribed to the Turks. I give this account at the risk of being pronounced a crazy enthusiast or visionary; but I regard that little. I must desire my reader to bear in mind, that I was a hard student, and at severe studies for all the rest of my time; and certainly I had a right occasionally to relaxations as well as other people: these, however, I allowed myself but seldom.

The late Duke of —— used to say, "Next Friday, by the blessing of Heaven, I purpose to be drunk;" and in like manner I used to fix beforehand how often, within a given time, and when, I would commit a debauch of opium. This was seldom more than once in three weeks; for at that time I could not have ventured to call every day (as I did afterwards) for "*a glass of laudanum negus, warm, and without sugar.*" No; as I have said, I seldom drank laudanum, at that time, more than once in three weeks: this was usually on a Tuesday or a Saturday night; my reason for which was this. In those days, Grassini sang at the opera, and her voice was delightful to me beyond all that I had ever heard. I know not what may be the state of the opera-house now, having never been within its walls for seven or eight years; but at that time it was by much the most pleasant place of resort in London for passing an evening. Five shillings admitted one to the gallery, which was subject to far less annoyance than the pit of the theatres; the orchestra was distinguished, by its sweet and melodious grandeur, from all English orchestras, the composition of which, I confess, is not acceptable to my ear, from the predominance of the clangorous instruments, and the almost absolute tyranny of the violin. The choruses were divine to hear; and when Grassini appeared in some interlude, as she often did, and poured forth her passionate soul as Andromache, at the tomb of Hector, &c., I question whether any Turk, of all that ever entered the paradise of opium-eaters, can have had half the pleasure I had. But, indeed, I honor the barbarians too much by supposing them capable of any pleasures approaching to the intellectual ones of an Englishman. For music is an intellectual or a sensual pleasure, according to the temperament of him who hears it. And, by the by, with the exception of the fine extravaganza on that subject in Twelfth Night, I do not recollect more than one thing said adequately on the subject of music in all literature; it is a passage in the *Religio Medici** of Sir T. Brown, and, though chiefly remarkable for its sublimity, has also a philosophic value, inasmuch as it points to the true theory of musical effects. The mistake of most people is, to suppose that it is by the ear they communicate with music, and therefore that they are purely passive to its effects. But this is not so; it is by the reäction of the mind upon the notices of the ear (the *matter* coming by the senses, the *form* from the mind) that the pleasure is constructed; and therefore it is that people of equally good ear differ so much in this point from one another. Now opium, by greatly increasing the activity of the mind, generally increases, of necessity, that particular mode of its activity by which we are able to construct out of the raw material of organic sound an elaborate intellectual pleasure. But, says a friend, a succession of musical sounds is to me like a collection of Arabic characters: I can attach no ideas to them. Ideas! my good sir? there is no occasion for them; all that class of ideas which can be available in such a case has a language of representative feelings. But this is a sub-

* I have not the book at this moment to consult; but I think the passage begins, "And even that tavern music, which makes one man merry, another mad, in me strikes a deep fit of devotion;" &c.

ject foreign to my present purposes; it is sufficient to say, that a chorus, &c., of elaborate harmony, displayed before me, as in a piece of arras-work, the whole of my past life, — not as if recalled by an act of memory, but as if present and incarnated in the music; no longer painful to dwell upon, but the detail of its incidents removed, or blended in some hazy abstraction, and its passions exalted, spiritualized, and sublimed. All this was to be had for five shillings. And over and above the music of the stage and the orchestra, I had all around me, in the intervals of the performance, the music of the Italian language talked by Italian women, — for the gallery was usually crowded with Italians, — and I listened with a pleasure such as that with which Weld, the traveller, lay and listened, in Canada, to the sweet laughter of Indian women; for the less you understand of a language, the more sensible you are to the melody or harshness of its sounds. For such a purpose, therefore, it was an advantage to me that I was a poor Italian scholar, reading it but little, and not speaking it at all, nor understanding a tenth part of what I heard spoken.

These were my opera pleasures; but another pleasure I had, which, as it could be had only on a Saturday night, occasionally struggled with my love of the opera; for, at that time, Tuesday and Saturday were the regular opera nights. On this subject I am afraid I shall be rather obscure, but, I can assure the reader, not at all more so than Marinus in his life of Proclus, or many other biographers and auto-biographers of fair reputation. This pleasure, I have said, was to be had only on a Saturday night. What, then, was Saturday night to me, more than any other night? I had no labors that

I rested from; no wages to receive; what needed I to care for Saturday night, more than as it was a summons to hear Grassini? True, most logical reader; what you say is unanswerable. And yet so it was and is, that whereas different men throw their feelings into different channels, and most are apt to show their interest in the concerns of the poor chiefly by sympathy, expressed in some shape or other, with their distresses and sorrows, I, at that time, was disposed to express my interest by sympathizing with their pleasures. The pains of poverty I had lately seen too much of, — more than I wished to remember; but the pleasures of the poor, their consolations of spirit, and their reposes from bodily toil, can never become oppressive to contemplate. Now, Saturday night is the season for the chief regular and periodic return of rest to the poor; in this point the most hostile sects unite, and acknowledge a common link of brotherhood; almost all Christendom rests from its labors. It is a rest introductory to another rest; and divided by a whole day and two nights from the renewal of toil. On this account I feel always, on a Saturday night, as though I also were released from some yoke of labor, had some wages to receive, and some luxury of repose to enjoy. For the sake, therefore, of witnessing, upon as large a scale as possible, a spectacle with which my sympathy was so entire, I used often, on Saturday nights, after I had taken opium, to wander forth, without much regarding the direction or the distance, to all the markets, and other parts of London, to which the poor resort on a Saturday night, for laying out their wages. Many a family party, consisting of a man, his wife, and sometimes one or two of his children, have I listened to, as they stood consulting on their ways and means, or the strength of their exchequer, or the price of household articles. Gradually I became familiar with their wishes, their difficulties, and their opinions. Sometimes there might be heard murmurs of discontent; but far oftener expressions on the countenance, or uttered in words, of patience, hope, and tranquillity. And, taken generally, I must say, that, in this point, at least, the poor are far more philosophic than the rich; that they show a more ready and cheerful submission to what they consider as irremediable evils, or irreparable losses. Whenever I saw occasion, or could do it without appearing to be intrusive, I joined their parties, and gave my opinion upon the matter in discussion, which, if not always judicious, was always received indulgently. If wages were a little higher, or expected to be so, or the quartern loaf a little lower, or it was reported that onions and butter were expected to fall, I was glad; yet, if the contrary were true, I drew from opium some means of consoling myself. For opium (like the bee, that extracts its materials indiscriminately from roses and from the soot of chimneys) can overrule all feelings into a compliance with the master-key. Some of these rambles led me to great distances; for an opium-eater is too happy to observe the motion of time. And sometimes, in my attempts to steer homewards, upon nautical principles, by fixing my eye on the pole-star, and seeking ambitiously for a north-west passage, instead of circumnavigating all the capes and head-lands I had doubled in my outward voyage, I came suddenly upon such knotty problems of alleys, such enigmatical entries, and such sphinx's riddles of streets without thoroughfares, as must, I conceive, baffle the audacity of porters, and confound the intellects of hackney-coachmen. I could almost have believed, at times, that I must be the first discoverer of some of these *terræ incognitæ*, and doubted whether they had yet been laid down in the modern charts of London. For all this, however, I paid a heavy price in distant years, when the human face tyrannized over my dreams, and the perplexities of my steps in London came back and haunted my sleep, with the feeling of perplexities moral or intellectual, that brought confusion to the reason, or anguish and remorse to the conscience.

Thus I have shown that opium does not, of necessity, produce inactivity or torpor; but that, on the contrary, it often led me into markets and theatres. Yet, in candor, I will admit that markets and theatres are not the appropriate haunts of the opium-eater, when in the divinest state incident to his enjoyment. In that state, crowds become an oppression to him; music, even, too sensual and gross. He naturally seeks solitude and silence, as indispensable conditions of those trances, or profoundest reveries, which are the crown and consummation of what opium can do for human nature. I, whose disease it was to meditate too much and to observe too little, and who, upon my first entrance at college, was nearly falling into a deep melancholy, from brooding too much on the sufferings which I had witnessed in London, was sufficiently aware of the tendencies of my own thoughts to do all I could to counteract them. I was, indeed, like a person who, according to the old legend, had entered the cave of

Trophonius; and the remedies I sought were to force myself into society, and to keep my understanding in continual activity upon matters of science. But for these remedies, I should certainly have become hypochondriacally melancholy. In after years, however, when my cheerfulness was more fully reëstablished, I yielded to my natural inclination for a solitary life. And at that time I often fell into these reveries upon taking opium; and more than once it has happened to me, on a summer night, when I have been at an open window, in a room from which I could overlook the sea at a mile below me, and could command a view of the great town of L——, at about the same distance, that I have sat from sunset to sunrise, motionless, and without wishing to move.

I shall be charged with mysticism, Behmenism, quietism, &c.; but that shall not alarm me. Sir H. Vane, the younger, was one of our wisest men; and let my readers see if he, in his philosophical works, be half as unmystical as I am. I say, then, that it has often struck me that the scene itself was somewhat typical of what took place in such a reverie. The town of L—— represented the earth, with its sorrows and its graves left behind, yet not out of sight, nor wholly forgotten. The ocean, in everlasting but gentle agitation, and brooded over by dove-like calm, might not unfitly typify the mind, and the mood which then swayed it. For it seemed to me as if then first I stood at a distance, and aloof from the uproar of life; as if the tumult, the fever, and the strife, were suspended; a respite granted from the secret burdens of the heart; a sabbath of repose; a resting from human labors. Here were the hopes which blossom in the paths of life, reconciled with the peace which is in the grave; motions of the intellect as unwearied as the heavens, yet for all anxieties a halcyon calm; a tranquillity that seemed no product of inertia, but as if resulting from mighty and equal antagonisms; infinite activities, infinite repose.

O just, subtile, and mighty opium! that to the hearts of poor and rich alike, for the wounds that will never heal, and for "the pangs that tempt the spirit to rebel," bringest an assuaging balm; — eloquent opium! that with thy potent rhetoric stealest away the purposes of wrath, and, to the guilty man, for one night givest back the hopes of his youth, and hands washed pure from blood; and, to the proud man, a brief oblivion for

> Wrongs unredressed, and insults unavenged;

that summonest to the chancery of dreams, for the triumphs of suffering innocence, false witnesses, and confoundest perjury, and dost reverse the sentences of unrighteous judges; — thou buildest upon the bosom of darkness, out of the fantastic imagery of the brain, cities and temples, beyond the art of Phidias and Praxiteles, — beyond the splendor of Babylon and Hekatompylos; and, "from the anarchy of dreaming sleep," callest into sunny light the faces cf long-buried beauties, and the blessed household countenances, cleansed from the "dishonors of the grave." Thou only givest these gifts to man; and thou hast the keys of Paradise, oh just, subtile, and mighty opium!

INTRODUCTION

TO

THE PAINS OF OPIUM.

Courteous, and, I hope, indulgent reader (for all my readers must be indulgent ones, or else, I fear, I shall shock them too much to count on their courtesy), having accompanied me thus far, now let me request you to move onwards, for about eight years; that is to say, from 1804 (when I said that my acquaintance with opium first began) to 1812. The years of academic life are now over and gone, — almost forgotten; the student's cap no longer presses my temples; if my cap exists at all, it presses those of some youthful scholar, I trust, as happy as myself, and as passionate a lover of knowledge. My gown is, by this time, I dare to say, in the same condition with many thousands of excellent books in the Bodleian, namely, diligently perused by certain studious moths and worms; or departed, however (which is all that I know of its fate), to that great reservoir of *somewhere*, to which all the tea-cups, tea-caddies, tea-pots, tea-kettles, &c.,

have departed (not to speak of still frailer vessels, such as glasses, decanters, bed-makers, &c.), which occasional resemblances in the present generation of teacups, &c., remind me of having once possessed, but of whose departure and final fate, I, in common with most gownsmen of either university, could give, I suspect, but an obscure and conjectural history. The persecutions of the chapel-bell, sounding its unwelcome summons to six o'clock matins, interrupts my slumbers no longer; the porter who rang it, upon whose beautiful nose (bronze, inlaid with copper) I wrote, in retaliation, so many Greek epigrams whilst I was dressing, is dead, and has ceased to disturb anybody; and I, and many others who suffered much from his tintinnabulous propensities, have now agreed to overlook his errors, and have forgiven him. Even with the bell I am now in charity; it rings, I suppose, as formerly, thrice a day; and cruelly annoys, I doubt not, many worthy gentlemen, and disturbs their peace of mind; but, as to me, in this year 1812, I regard its treacherous voice no longer (treacherous I call it, for, by some refinement of malice, it spoke in as sweet and silvery tones,as if it had been inviting one to a party); its tones have no longer, indeed, power to reach me let the wind sit as favorable as the malice of the bel. itself could wish; for I am two hundred and fifty miles away from it, and buried in the depth of mountains. And what am I doing amongst the mountains? Taking opium. Yes, but what else? Why, reader, in 1812, the year we are now arrived at, as well as for some years previous, I have been chiefly studyir.g German metaphysics, in the writings of Kant, Fichte,

Schelling, &c. And how, and in what manner, do I live? in short, what class or description of men do I belong to? I am at this period, namely, in 1812, living in a cottage; and with a single female servant (*honi soit qui mal y pense*), who, amongst my neighbors, passes by the name of my "house-keeper." And, as a scholar and a man of learned education, and in that sense a gentleman, I may presume to class myself as an unworthy member of that indefinite body called *gentlemen.* Partly on the ground I have assigned, perhaps, — partly because, from my having no visible calling or business, it is rightly judged that I must be living on my private fortune, — I am so classed by my neighbors; and, by the courtesy of modern England, I am usually addressed on letters, &c., *Esquire*, though having, I fear, in the rigorous construction of heralds, but slender pretensions to that distinguished honor; — yes, in popular estimation, I am X. Y. Z., Esquire, but not Justice of the Peace, nor Custos Rotulorum. Am I married? Not yet. And I still take opium? On Saturday nights. And, perhaps, have taken it unblushingly ever since "the rainy Sunday," and "the stately Pantheon," and "the beatific druggist" of 1804? Even so. And how do I find my health after all this opium-eating? in short, how do I do? Why, pretty well, I thank you, reader; in the phrase of ladies in the straw, "as well as can be expected." In fact, if I dared to say the real and simple truth (it must not be forgotten that, hitherto I thought, to satisfy the theories of medical men, I ought to be ill), I was never better in my life than in the spring of 1812; and I hope sincerely, that the quantity of claret, port, or "particular Madeira," which, in all probability, you, good reader, have taken and design to take, for every term of eight years, during your natural life, may as little disorder your health as mine was disordered by opium I had taken for the eight years between 1804 and 1812. Hence you may see again the danger of taking any medical advice from *Anastasius;* in divinity, for aught I know, or law, he may be a safe counsellor, but not in medicine. No; it is far better to consult Dr. Buchan, as I did; for I never forgot that worthy man's excellent suggestion, and I was "particularly careful not to take above five-and-twenty ounces of laudanum." To this moderation and temperate use of the article I may ascribe it, I suppose, that as yet, at least (that is, in 1812), I am ignorant and unsuspicious of the avenging terrors which opium has in store for those who abuse its lenity. At the same time, I have been only a *dilettante* eater of opium; eight years' practice, even, with the single pre caution of allowing sufficient intervals between every indulgence, has not been sufficient to make opium necessary to me as an article of daily diet. But now comes a different era. Move on, if you please, reader, to 1813. In the summer of the year we have just quitted, I had suffered much in bodily health from distress of mind connected with a very melancholy event. This event, being no ways related to the subject now before me, further than through bodily illness which it produced, I need not more particularly notice. Whether this illness of 1812 had any share in that of 1813, I know not; but so it was, that, in the latter year, I was attacked by a most appalling irritation of the stomach, in all respects the same as that which had caused me so much suffering in youth, and accompanied by a revival of all the old dreams. This is the point of my narrative on which, as respects my own self-justification, the whole of what follows may be said to hinge. And here I find myself in a perplexing dilemma: — Either, on the one hand, I must exhaust the reader's patience, by such a detail of my malady, and of my struggles with it, as might suffice to establish the fact of my inability to wrestle any longer with irritation and constant suffering; or, on the other hand, by passing lightly over this critical part of my story, I must forego the benefit of a stronger impression left on the mind of the reader, and must lay myself open to the misconstruction of having slipped by the easy and gradual steps of self-indulging persons, from the first to the final stage of opium-eating (a misconstruction to which there will be a lurking predisposition in most readers, from my previous acknowledgments). This is the dilemma, the first horn of which would be sufficient to toss and gore any column of patient readers, though drawn up sixteen deep, and constantly relieved by fresh men; consequently *that* is not to be thought of. It remains, then, that I *postulate* so much as is necessary for my purpose. And let me take as full credit for what I postulate as if I had demonstrated it, good reader, at the expense of your patience and my own. Be not so ungenerous as to let me suffer in your good opinion through my own forbearance and regard for your comfort: No; believe all that I ask of you, namely, that I could resist no longer, — believe it liberally, and as an act of grace, or else in mere prudence; for, if not, then, in the next edition of my Opium Confessions revised and enlarged, I will make you believe, and tremble; and, *a force d'ennuyer*, by mere dint of pandiculation, I will terrify all readers of mine from ever again questioning any postulate that I shall think fit to make.

This, then, let me repeat: I postulate that, at the time I began to take opium daily, I could not have done otherwise. Whether, indeed, afterwards, I might not have succeeded in breaking off the habit, even when it seemed to me that all efforts would be unavailing, and whether many of the innumerable efforts which I *did* make might not have been carried much further, and my gradual re-conquests of ground lost might not have been followed up much more energetically,—these are questions which I must decline. Perhaps I might make out a case of palliation; but—shall I speak ingenuously?—I confess it, as a besetting infirmity of mine, that I am too much of an Eudæmonist; I hanker too much after a state of happiness, both for myself and others; I cannot face misery, whether my own or not, with an eye of sufficient firmness; and am little capable of encountering present pain for the sake of any reversionary benefit. On some other matters, I can agree with the gentlemen in the cotton trade* at Manchester in affecting the Stoic philosophy; but not in this. Here I take the liberty of an Eclectic philosopher, and I look out for some courteous and considerate sect that will condescend more to the infirm condition of an

*A handsome news-room, of which I was very politely made free in passing through Manchester, by several gentlemen of that place, is called, I think, *The Porch;* whence I, who am a stranger in Manchester, inferred that the subscribers meant to profess themselves followers of Zeno. But I have been since assured that this is a mistake.

opium-eater; that are "sweet men," as Chaucer says, "to give absolution," and will show some conscience in the penances they inflict, and the efforts of abstinence they exact from poor sinners like myself. An inhuman moralist I can no more endure, in my nervous state, than opium that has not been boiled. At any rate, he who summons me to send out a large freight of self-denial and mortification upon any cruising voyage of moral improvement, must make it clear to my understanding that the concern is a hopeful one. At my time of life (six-and-thirty years of age), it cannot be supposed that I have much energy to spare; in fact, I find it all little enough for the intellectual labors I have on my hands; and, therefore, let no man expect to frighten me by a few hard words into embarking any part of it upon desperate adventures of morality.

Whether desperate or not, however, the issue of the struggle in 1813 was what I have mentioned; and from this date the reader is to consider me as a regular and confirmed opium-eater, of whom to ask whether on any particular day he had or had not taken opium, would be to ask whether his lungs had performed respiration, or the heart fulfilled its functions. You understand now, reader, what I am; and you are by this time aware, that no old gentleman, "with a snow-white beard," will have any chance of persuading me to surrender "the little golden receptacle of the pernicious drug." No: I give notice to all, whether moralists or surgeons, that whatever be their pretensions and skill in their respective lines of practice, they must not hope for any countenance from me, if they think to begin by any savage proposition for a Lent or Ramadam of abstinence from opium. This, then, being all fully understood between us, we shall in future sail before the wind. Now, then, reader, from 1813, where all this time we have been sitting down and loitering, rise up, if you please, and walk forward about three years more. Now draw up the curtain, and you shall see me in a new character.

If any man, poor or rich, were to say that he would tell us what had been the happiest day in his life, and the why and the wherefore, I suppose that we should all cry out, Hear him! hear him! As to the happiest day, that must be very difficult for any wise man to name; because any event, that could occupy so distinguished a place in a man's retrospect of his life, or be entitled to have shed a special felicity on any one day, ought to be of such an enduring character, as that (accidents apart) it should have continued to shed the same felicity, or one not distinguishably less, on many years together. To the happiest *lustrum*, however, or even to the happiest *year*, it may be allowed to any man to point without discountenance from wisdom. This year, in my case, reader, was the one which we have now reached; though it stood, I confess, as a parenthesis between years of a gloomier character. It was a year of brilliant water (to speak after the manner of jewellers), set, as it were, and insulated, in the gloom and cloudy melancholy of opium. Strange as it may sound, I had a little before this time descended suddenly, and without any considerable effort, from three hundred and twenty grains of opium (that is, eight* thou-

* I here reckon twenty-five drops of laudanum as equivalent to one grain of opium, which, I believe, is the common estimate

sand drops of laudanum) per day, to forty grains, or one-eighth part. Instantaneously, and as if by magic, the cloud of profoundest melancholy which rested upon my brain, like some black vapors that I have seen roll away from the summits of mountains, drew off in one day; passed off with its murky banners as simultaneously as a ship that has been stranded, and is floated off by a spring tide, —

> That moveth altogether, if it move at all.

Now, then, I was again happy: I now took only one thousand drops of laudanum per day, — and what was that? A latter spring had come to close up the season of youth: my brain performed its functions as healthily as ever before. I read Kant again, and again I under stood him, or fancied that I did. Again my feelings of pleasure expanded themselves to all around me; and, if any man from Oxford or Cambridge, or from neither, had been announced to me in my unpretending cottage, I should have welcomed him with as sumptuous a reception as so poor a man could offer. Whatever else was wanting to a wise man's happiness, of laudanum I would have given him as much as he wished, and in a golden cup. And, by the way, now that I speak of giving laudanum away, I remember, about this time, a little incident, which I mention, because,

---

However, as both may be considered variable quantities (the crude opium varying much in strength, and the tincture still more), I suppose that no infinitesimal accuracy can be had in such a calculation. Tea-spoons vary as much in size as opium in strength. Small ones hold about one hundred drops: so that eight thousand drops are about eighty times a tea-spoonful. The reader sees how much I kept within Dr. Buchan's indulgent allowance.

trifling as it was, the reader will soon meet it again in my dreams, which it influenced more fearfully than could be imagined. One day a Malay knocked at my door. What business a Malay could have to transact amongst English mountains, I cannot conjecture; but possibly he was on his road to a seaport about forty miles distant.

The servant who opened the door to him was a young girl, born and bred amongst the mountains, who had never seen an Asiatic dress of any sort: his turban, therefore, confounded her not a little; and as it turned out that his attainments in English were exactly of the same extent as hers in the Malay, there seemed to be an impassable gulf fixed between all communication of ideas, if either party had happened to possess any. In this dilemma, the girl, recollecting the reputed learning of her master (and, doubtless, giving me credit for a knowledge of all the languages of the earth, besides perhaps, a few of the lunar ones), came and gave me to understand that there was a sort of demon below whom she clearly imagined that my art could exorcise from the house. I did not immediately go down; but when I did, the group which presented itself, arranged as it was by accident, though not very elaborate, took hold of my fancy and my eye in a way that none of the statuesque attitudes exhibited in the ballets at the opera-house, though so ostentatiously complex, had ever done. In a cottage kitchen, but panelled on the wall with dark wood, that from age and rubbing resembled oak, and looking more like a rustic hall of entrance than a kitchen, stood the Malay, his turban and loose trousers of dingy white relieved upon the dark panelling; he had placed himself nearer to the girl than she seemed to relish, though her native spirit of mountain intrepidity contended with the feeling of simple awe which her countenance expressed, as she gazed upon the tiger-cat before her. And a more striking picture there could not be imagined, than the beautiful English face of the girl, and its exquisite fairness, together with her erect and independent attitude, contrasted with the sallow and bilious skin of the Malay, enamelled or veneered with mahogany by marine air, his small, fierce, restless eyes, thin lips, slavish gestures, and adorations. Half hidden by the ferocious-looking Malay, was a little child from a neighboring cottage, who had crept in after him, and was now in the act of reverting its head and gazing upwards at the turban and the fiery eyes beneath it, whilst with one hand he caught at the dress of the young woman for protection.

My knowledge of the Oriental tongues is not remarkably extensive, being, indeed, confined to two words, — the Arabic word for barley, and the Turkish for opium (madjoon), which I have learnt from Anastasius. And, as I had neither a Malay dictionary, nor even Adelung's *Mithridates*, which might have helped me to a few words, I addressed him in some lines from the Iliad; considering that, of such language as I possessed, the Greek, in point of longitude, came geographically nearest to an Oriental one. He worshipped me in a devout manner, and replied in what I suppose was Malay. In this way I saved my reputation with my neighbors; for the Malay had no means of betraying the secret. He lay down upon the floor for about an hour, and then pursued his journey. On his departure, I presented him with a piece of opium. To him, as an Orientalist, I concluded that opium must be familiar, and the expression of his face convinced me that it was. Nevertheless, I was struck with some little consternation when I saw him suddenly raise his hand to his mouth, and (in the school-boy phrase) bolt the whole, divided into three pieces, at one mouthful. The quantity was enough to kill three dragoons and their horses, and I felt some alarm for the poor creature; but what could be done? I had given him the opium in compassion for his solitary life, on recollecting that, if he had travelled on foot from London, it must be nearly three weeks since he could have exchanged a thought with any human being. I could not think of violating the laws of hospitality by having him seized and drenched with an emetic, and thus frightening him into a notion that we were going to sacrifice him to some English idol. No; there was clearly no help for it. He took his leave, and for some days I felt anxious; but, as I never heard of any Malay being found dead, I became convinced that he was used* to opium, and

* This, however, is not a necessary conclusion; the varieties of effect produced by opium on different constitutions are infinite. A London magistrate (Harriott's "Struggles through Life," vol. iii., p. 391, third edition) has recorded that on the first occasion of his trying laudanum for the gout, he took FORTY drops; the next night SIXTY, and on the fifth night EIGHTY, without any effect whatever; and this at an advanced age. I have an anecdote from a country surgeon, however, which sinks Mr. Harriott's case into a trifle; and, in my projected medical treatise on opium, which I will publish, provided the College of Surgeons will pay me for enlightening their benighted understandings upon this subject, I will relate it but it is far too good a story to be published gratis.

that I must have done him the service I designed, by giving him one night of respite from the pains of wandering.

This incident I have digressed to mention, because this Malay (partly from the picturesque exhibition he assisted to frame, partly from the anxiety I connected with his image for some days) fastened afterwards upon my dreams, and brought other Malays with him worse than himself, that ran "a-muck"* at me, and led me into a world of troubles. But, to quit this episode, and to return to my intercalary year of happiness. I have said already, that on a subject so important to us all as happiness, we should listen with pleasure to any man's experience or experiments, even though he were but a ploughboy, who cannot be supposed to have ploughed very deep in such an intractable soil as that of human pains and pleasures, or to have conducted his researches upon any very enlightened principles. But I, who have taken happiness, both in a solid and a liquid shape, both boiled and unboiled, both East India and Turkey,—who have conducted my experiments upon this interesting subject with a sort of galvanic battery,—and have, for the general benefit of the world, inoculated myself, as it were, with the poison of eight hundred drops of laudanum per day (just for the same reason as a French surgeon inoculated himself lately with a cancer,—an English one, twenty years ago, with plague,—and a third, I know not of what nation, with hydrophobia),—I, it will be admitted, must surely

* See the common accounts, in any Eastern traveller or voyager, of the frantic excesses committed by Malays who have taken opium, or are reduced to desperation by ill luck at gambling.

know what happiness is, if anybody does. And therefore I will here lay down an analysis of happiness and, as the most interesting mode of communicating it, I will give it, not didactically, but wrapt up and involved in a picture of one evening, as I spent every evening during the intercalary year when laudanum, though taken daily, was to me no more than the elixir of pleasure. This done, I shall quit the subject of happiness altogether, and pass to a very different one, — the *pains of opium.*

Let there be a cottage, standing in a valley, eighteen miles from any town; no spacious valley, but about two miles long by three quarters of a mile in average width, — the benefit of which provision is, that all the families resident within its circuit will compose, as it were, one larger household, personally familiar to your eye, and more or less interesting to your affections. Let the mountains be real mountains, between three and four thousand feet high, and the cottage a real cottage, not (as a witty author has it) "a cottage with a double coach-house;" let it be, in fact (for I must abide by the actual scene), a white cottage, embowered with flowering shrubs, so chosen as to unfold a succession of flowers upon the walls, and clustering around the windows, through all the months of spring, summer, and autumn; beginning, in fact, with May roses, and ending with jasmine. Let it, however, *not* be spring, nor summer, nor autumn; but winter, in its sternest shape. This is a most important point in the science of happiness. And I am surprised to see people overlook it, and think it matter of congratulation that winter is going, or, if coming, is not likely to be a severe one.

On the contrary, I put up a petition, annually, for as much snow, hail, frost, or storm of one kind or other, as the skies can possibly afford us. Surely everybody is aware of the divine pleasures which attend a winter fireside, — candles at four o'clock, warm hearth-rugs, tea, a fair tea-maker, shutters closed, curtains flowing in ample draperies on the floor, whilst the wind and rain are raging audibly without,

> And at the doors and windows seem to call
> As heaven and earth they would together mell;
> Yet the least entrance find they none at all;
> Whence sweeter grows our rest secure in massy hall.
>
> *Castle of Indolence.*

All these are items in the description of a winter evening which must surely be familiar to everybody born in a high latitude. And it is evident that most of these delicacies, like ice-cream, require a very low temperature of the atmosphere to produce them: they are fruits which cannot be ripened without weather stormy or inclement, in some way or other. I am not "*particular*," as people say, whether it be snow, or black frost, or wind so strong that (as Mr. —— says) "you may lean your back against it like a post." I can put up even with rain, provided that it rains cats and dogs; but something of the sort I must have, and if I have not, I think myself in a manner ill used: for why am I called on to pay so heavily for winter, in coals, and candles, and various privations that will occur even to gentlemen, if I am not to have the article good of its kind? No: a Canadian winter, for my money· or a Russian one, where every man is but a co-proprietor with the north wind in the fee-simple of his own ears. Indeed, so great an epicure am I in this matter, that I cannot relish a winter night fully, if it be much past St. Thomas' day, and have degenerated into disgusting tendencies to vernal appearances; — no. it must be divided by a thick wall of dark nights from all return of light and sunshine. From the latter weeks of October to Christmas-eve, therefore, is the period during which happiness is in season, which, in my judgment, enters the room with the tea-tray; for tea, though ridiculed by those who are naturally of coarse nerves, or are become so from wine-drinking, and are not susceptible of influence from so refined a stimulant, will always be the favorite beverage of the intellectual; and, for my part, I would have joined Dr. Johnson in a *bellum internecinum* against Jonas Hanway, or any other impious person who should presume to disparage it. But here, to save myself the trouble of too much verbal description, I will introduce a painter, and give him directions for the rest of the picture. Painters do not like white cottages, unless a good deal weather-stained; but, as the reader now understands that it is a winter night, his services will not be required except for the inside of the house.

Paint me, then, a room seventeen feet by twelve, and not more than seven and a half feet high. This, reader, is somewhat ambitiously styled, in my family, the drawing-room; but being contrived "a double debt to pay," it is also, and more justly, termed the library; for it happens that books are the only article of property in which I am richer than my neighbors. Of these I have about five thousand, collected gradually since my eighteenth year. Therefore, painter, put as many as you can into this room. Make it populous with books and, furthermore, paint me a good fire; and furniture plain and modest, befitting the unpretending cottage of a scholar. And near the fire paint me a tea-table; and (as it is clear that no creature can come to see one, such a stormy night) place only two cups and saucers on the tea-tray; and, if you know how to paint such a thing symbolically, or otherwise, paint me an eternal tea-pot, — eternal *à parte ante*, and *à parte post;* for I usually drink tea from eight o'clock at night to four in the morning. And, as it is very unpleasant to make tea, or to pour it out for one's self, paint me a lovely young woman, sitting at the table. Paint her arms like Aurora's, and her smiles like Hebe's; — but no, dear M., not even in jest let me insinuate that thy power to illuminate my cottage rests upon a tenure so perishable as mere personal beauty; or that the witchcraft of angelic smiles lies within the empire of any earthly pencil. Pass, then, my good painter, to something more within its power; and the next article brought forward should naturally be myself, — a picture of the Opium-eater, with his "little golden receptacle of the pernicious drug" lying beside him on the table. As to the opium, I have no objection to see a picture of *that*, though I would rather see the original; you may paint it, if you choose; but I apprize you that no "little" receptacle would, even in 1816, answer *my* purpose, who was at a distance from the "stately Pantheon," and all druggists (mortal or otherwise). No: you may as well paint the real receptacle, which was not of gold, but of glass, and as much like a wine-decanter as possible. Into this you may put a quart of ruby-colored laudanum; that, and a book of German metaphysics placed by its side, will sufficiently attest my being in the neighborhood; but as to myself, there I demur. I admit that, naturally, I ought to occupy the foreground of the picture; that being the hero of the piece, or (if you choose) the criminal at the bar, my body should be had into court. This seems reasonable; but why should I confess, on this point, to a painter? or, why confess at all? If the public (into whose private ear I am confidentially whispering my confessions, and not into any painter's) should chance to have framed some agreeable picture for itself of the Opium-eater's exterior, — should have ascribed to him, romantically, an elegant person, or a handsome face, why should I barbarously tear from it so pleasing a delusion, — pleasing both to the public and to me? No: paint me, if at all, according to your own fancy; and, as a painter's fancy should teem with beautiful creations, I cannot fail, in that way, to be a gainer. And now, reader, we have run through all the ten categories of my condition, as it stood about 1816—1817, up to the middle of which latter year I judge myself to have been a happy man; and the elements of that happiness I have endeavored to place before you, in the above sketch of the interior of a scholar's library, — in a cottage among the mountains, on a stormy winter evening.

But now farewell, a long farewell, to happiness, winter or summer! farewell to smiles and laughter! farewell to peace of mind! farewell to hope and to tranquil dreams, and to the blessed consolations of sleep! For more than three years and a half I am summoned away from these; I am now arrived at an Iliad of woes: for I have now to record

THE PAINS OF OPIUM.

———— as when some great painter dips
His pencil in the gloom of earthquake and eclipse.
Shelley's Revolt of Islam.

Reader, who have thus far accompanied me, I must request your attention to a brief explanatory note on three points:

1. For several reasons, I have not been able to compose the notes for this part of my narrative into any regular and connected shape. I give the notes disjointed as I find them, or have now drawn them up from memory. Some of them point to their own date; some I have dated; and some are undated. Whenever it could answer my purpose to transplant them from the natural or chronological order, I have not scrupled to do so. Sometimes I speak in the present, sometimes in the past tense. Few of the notes, perhaps, were written exactly at the period of time to which they relate; but this can little affect their accuracy, as the impressions were such that they can never fade from my mind. Much has been omitted. I could not, without effort, constrain myself to the task of either recalling, or constructing into a regular narrative, the

whole burden of horrors which lies upon my brain. This feeling, partly, I plead in excuse, and partly that I am now in London, and am a helpless sort of person who cannot even arrange his own papers without assistance; and I am separated from the hands which are wont to perform for me the offices of an amanuensis.

2. You will think, perhaps, that I am too confidential and communicative of my own private history. It may be so. But my way of writing is rather to think aloud, and follow my own humors, than much to consider who is listening to me; and, if I stop to consider what is proper to be said to this or that person, I shall soon come to doubt whether any part at all is proper. The fact is, I place myself at a distance of fifteen or twenty years ahead of this time, and suppose myself writing to those who will be interested about me hereafter; and wishing to have some record of a time, the entire history of which no one can know but myself, I do it as fully as I am able with the efforts I am now capable of making, because I know not whether I can ever find time to do it again.

3. It will occur to you often to ask, Why did I not release myself from the horrors of opium, by leaving it off, or diminishing it? To this I must answer briefly; it might be supposed that I yielded to the fascinations of opium too easily; it cannot be supposed that any man can be charmed by its terrors. The reader may be sure, therefore, that I made attempts innumerable to reduce the quantity. I add, that those who witnessed the agonies of those attempts, and not myself, were the first to beg me to desist. But could not I have reduced

at a drop a day, or, by adding water, have bisected or trisected a drop? A thousand drops bisected would thus have taken nearly six years to reduce; and that they would certainly not have answered. But this is a common mistake of those who know nothing of opium experimentally; I appeal to those who do, whether it is not always found that down to a certain point it can be reduced with ease, and even pleasure, but that, after that point, further reduction causes intense suffering. Yes, say many thoughtless persons, who know not what they are talking of, you will suffer a little low spirits and dejection, for a few days. I answer, no; there is nothing like low spirits; on the contrary, the mere animal spirits are uncommonly raised; the pulse is improved; the health is better. It is not there that the suffering lies. It has no resemblance to the sufferings caused by renouncing wine. It is a state of unutterable irritation of stomach (which surely is not much like dejection), accompanied by intense perspirations, and feelings such as I shall not attempt to describe without more space at my command.

I shall now enter "*in medias res,*" and shall anticipate, from a time when my opium pains might be said to be at their *acmè*, an account of their palsying effects on the intellectual faculties.

My studies have now been long interrupted. I cannot read to myself with any pleasure, hardly with a moment's endurance. Yet I read aloud sometimes for the pleasure of others; because reading is an accomplishment of mine, and, in the slang use of the word *accomplishment* as a superficial and ornamental attainment, almost the only one I possess; and formerly, if

I had any vanity at all connected with any endowment or attainment of mine, it was with this; for I had observed that no accomplishment was so rare. Players are the worst readers of all: —— reads vilely; and Mrs. ——, who is so celebrated, can read nothing well but dramatic compositions; Milton she cannot read sufferably. People in general either read poetry without any passion at all, or else overstep the modesty of nature, and read not like scholars. Of late, if I have felt moved by anything in books, it has been by the grand lamentations of Samson Agonistes, or the great harmonies of the Satanic speeches in Paradise Regained, when read aloud by myself. A young lady sometimes comes and drinks tea with us; at her request and M.'s, I now and then read W———'s poems to them. (W., by the by, is the only poet I ever met who could read his own verses; often, indeed, he reads admirably.)

For nearly two years I believe that I read no book but one; and I owe it to the author, in discharge of a great debt of gratitude, to mention what that was. The sublimer and more passionate poets I still read, as I have said, by snatches, and occasionally. But my proper vocation, as I well knew, was the exercise of the analytic understanding. Now, for the most part, analytic studies are continuous, and not to be pursued by fits and starts, or fragmentary efforts. Mathematics for instance, intellectual philosophy, &c., were all become insupportable to me; I shrunk from them with a sense of powerless and infantine feebleness that gave me an anguish the greater from remembering the time when I grappled with them to my own hourly delight; and for this further reason, because I had devoted the labor of my whole life, and had dedicated my intellect blossoms and fruits, to the slow and elaborate toil of constructing one single work, to which I had presumed to give the title of an unfinished work of Spinosa's, namely, *De Emendatione Humani Intellectûs*. This was now lying locked up as by frost, like any Spanish bridge or aqueduct, begun upon too great a scale for the resources of the architect; and, instead of surviving me as a monument of wishes at least, and aspirations, and a life of labor dedicated to the exaltation of human nature in that way in which God had best fitted me to promote so great an object, it was likely to stand a memorial to my children of hopes defeated, of baffled efforts, of materials uselessly accumulated, of foundations laid that were never to support a superstructure, of the grief and the ruin of the architect. In this state of imbecility, I had, for amusement, turned my attention to political economy; my understanding, which formerly had been as active and restless as a hyena, could not, I suppose (so long as I lived at all), sink into utter lethargy; and political economy offers this advantage to a person in my state, that though it is eminently an organic science (no part, that is to say, but what acts on the whole, as the whole again reäcts on each part), yet the several parts may be detached and contemplated singly. Great as was the prostration of my powers at this time, yet I could not forget my knowledge; and my understanding had been for too many years intimate with severe thinkers, with logic, and the great masters of knowledge, not to be aware of the utter feebleness of the main herd of modern economists. I had been led in 1811 to look into loads of books and pamphlets on many branches of economy; and, at my desire, M. sometimes read to me chapters from more recent works, or parts of parliamentary debates. I saw that these were generally the very dregs and rinsings of the human intellect; and that any man of sound head, and practised in wielding logic with scholastic adroitness, might take up the whole academy of modern economists, and throttle them between heaven and earth with his finger and thumb, or bray their fungous heads to powder with a lady's fan. At length, in 1819, a friend in Edinburgh sent me down Mr. Ricardo's book; and, recurring to my own prophetic anticipation of the advent of some legislator for this science, I said, before I had finished the first chapter, "Thou art the man!" Wonder and curiosity were emotions that had long been dead in me. Yet I wondered once more: I wondered at myself that I could once again be stimulated to the effort of reading; and much more I wondered at the book. Had this profound work been really written in England during the nineteenth century? Was it possible? I supposed thinking* had been extinct in England. Could it be that an Englishman, and he not in academic bowers, but oppressed by mercantile and senatorial cares, had accomplished what all the universities of Europe, and a century of thought, had failed even to advance by one

* The reader must remember what I here mean by *thinking;* because, else, this would be a very presumptuous expression. England, of late, has been rich to excess in fine thinkers, in the departments of creative and combining thought; but there is a sad dearth of masculine thinkers in any analytic path. A Scotchman of eminent name has lately told us, that he is obliged to quit even mathematics, for want of encouragement.

hair's breadth? All other writers had been crushed and overlaid by the enormous weights of facts and documents; Mr. Ricardo had deduced, *à priori*, from the understanding itself, laws which first gave a ray of light into the unwieldy chaos of materials, and had constructed what had been but a collection of tentative discussions into a science of regular proportions, now first standing on an eternal basis.

Thus did one simple work of a profound understanding avail to give me a pleasure and an activity which I had not known for years; — it roused me even to write, or, at least, to dictate what M. wrote for me. It seemed to me that some important truths had escaped even "the inevitable eye" of Mr. Ricardo; and, as these were, for the most part, of such a nature that I could express or illustrate them more briefly and elegantly by algebraic symbols than in the usual clumsy and[1] loitering diction of economists, the whole would not have filled a pocket-book; and being so brief, with M. for my amanuensis, even at this time, incapable as I was of all general exertion, I drew up my *Prolegomena to all Future Systems of Political Economy.* I hope it will not be found redolent of opium; though, indeed, to most people, the subject itself is a sufficient opiate.

This exertion, however, was but a temporary flash, as the sequel showed; for I designed to publish my work. Arrangements were made at a provincial press, about eighteen miles distant, for printing it. An additional compositor was retained for some days, on this account. The work was even twice advertised; and I was, in a manner, pledged to the fulfilment of my intention. But I had a preface to write; and a dedication, which I wished to make a splendid one, to Mr. Ricardo. I found myself quite unable to accomplish all this. The arrangements were countermanded, the compositor dismissed, and my "prolegomena" rested peacefully by the side of its elder and more dignified brother.

I have thus described and illustrated my intellectual torpor, in terms that apply, more or less, to every part of the four years during which I was under the Circean spells of opium. But for misery and suffering, I might, indeed, be said to have existed in a dormant state. I seldom could prevail on myself to write a letter; an answer of a few words, to any that I received, was the utmost that I could accomplish; and often *that* not until the letter had lain weeks, or even months, on my writing-table. Without the aid of M., all records of bills paid, or *to be* paid, must have perished; and my whole domestic economy, whatever became of Political Economy, must have gone into irretrievable confusion. I shall not afterwards allude to this part of the case; it is one, however, which the opium-eater will find, in the end, as oppressive and tormenting as any other, from the sense of incapacity and feebleness, from the direct embarrassments incident to the neglect or procrastination of each day's appropriate duties, and from the remorse which must often exasperate the stings of these evils to a reflective and conscientious mind. The opium-eater loses none of his moral sensibilities or aspirations; he wishes and longs as earnestly as ever to realize what he believes possible, and feels to be exacted by duty; but his intellectual apprehension what is possible infinitely outruns his power, not of execution only, but even of power to attempt. He lies under the weight of incubus and night-mare; he lies in sight of all that he would fain perform, just as a man forcibly confined to his bed by the mortal languor of a relaxing disease, who is compelled to witness injury or outrage offered to some object of his tenderest love: — he curses the spells which chain him down from motion; he would lay down his life if he might but get up and walk; but he is powerless as an infant, and cannot even attempt to rise.

I now pass to what is the main subject of these latter confessions, to the history and journal of what took place in my dreams; for these were the immediate and proximate cause of my acutest suffering.

The first notice I had of any important change going on in this part of my physical economy, was from the reäwaking of a state of eye generally incident to childhood, or exalted states of irritability. I know not whether my reader is aware that many children, perhaps most, have a power of painting, as it were, upon the darkness, all sorts of phantoms: in some that power is simply a mechanic affection of the eye; others have a voluntary or semi-voluntary power to dismiss or summon them; or, as a child once said to me, when I questioned him on this matter, "I can tell them to go, and they go; but sometimes they come when I don't tell them to come." Whereupon I told him that he had almost as unlimited a command over apparitions as a Roman centurion over his soldiers. In the middle of 1817, I think it was, that this faculty became positively distressing to me: at night, when I lay awake in bed, vast processions passed along in mournful pomp; friezes of never-ending stories, that to my feelings were as sad and solemn as if they were stories drawn from times before Œdipus or Priam, before Tyre, before Memphis. And, at the same time, a corresponding change took place in my dreams; a theatre seemed suddenly opened and lighted up within my brain, which presented, nightly, spectacles of more than earthly splendor. And the four following facts may be mentioned, as noticeable at this time:

I. That, as the creative state of the eye increased, a sympathy seemed to arise between the waking and the dreaming states of the brain in one point, — that whatsoever I happened to call up and to trace by a voluntary act upon the darkness was very apt to transfer itself to my dreams; so that I feared to exercise this faculty; for, as Midas turned all things to gold, that yet baffled his hopes and defrauded his human desires, so whatsoever things capable of being visually represented I did but think of in the darkness, immediately shaped themselves into phantoms of the eye; and, by a process apparently no less inevitable, when thus once traced in faint and visionary colors, like writings in sympathetic ink, they were drawn out, by the fierce chemistry of my dreams, into insufferable splendor that fretted my heart.

II. For this, and all other changes in my dreams, were accompanied by deep-seated anxiety and gloomy melancholy, such as are wholly incommunicable by words. I seemed every night to descend — not metaphorically, but literally to descend — into chasms and sunless abysses, depths below depths, from which it seemed hopeless that I could ever reäscend. Nor did I, by waking, feel that I *had* reäscended. This I do not dwell upon; because the state of gloom which attended these gorgeous spectacles, amounting at least to utter darkness, as of some suicidal despondency, cannot be approached by words.

III. The sense of space, and in the end the sense of time, were both powerfully affected. Buildings, landscapes, &c., were exhibited in proportions so vast as the bodily eye is not fitted to receive. Space swelled, and was amplified to an extent of unutterable infinity. This, however, did not disturb me so much as the vast expansion of time. I sometimes seemed to have lived for seventy or one hundred years in one night; nay, sometimes had feelings representative of a millennium, passed in that time, or, however, of a duration far beyond the limits of any human experience.

IV. The minutest incidents of childhood, or forgotten scenes of later years, were often revived. I could not be said to recollect them; for if I had been told of them when waking, I should not have been able to acknowledge them as parts of my past experience. But placed as they were before me, in dreams like intuitions, and clothed in all their evanescent circumstances and accompanying feelings, I *recognized* them instantaneously. I was once told by a near relative of mine, that having in her childhood fallen into a river, and being on the very verge of death but for the critical assistance which reached her, she saw in a moment her whole life, in its minutest incidents, arrayed before her simultaneously as in a mirror; and she had a faculty developed as suddenly for comprehending the whole and every part. This, from some opium experiences of mine, I can believe; I have, indeed, seen the same thing asserted twice in modern books, and accompanied by a remark which I am convinced is true, namely, that the dread book of account, which the Scriptures speak of, is, in fact, the mind itself of each individual. Of this, at least, I feel assured, that there is no such thing as *forgetting* possible to the mind; a thousand accidents may and will interpose a veil between our present consciousness and the secret inscriptions on the mind. Accidents of the same sort will also rend away this veil; but alike, whether veiled or unveiled, the inscription remains forever; just as the stars seem to withdraw before the common light of day, whereas, in fact, we all know that it is the light which is drawn over them as a veil; and that they are waiting to be revealed, when the obscuring daylight shall have withdrawn.

Having noticed these four facts as memorably distinguishing my dreams from those of health, I shall now cite a case illustrative of the first fact; and shall then cite any others that I remember, either in their chronological order, or any other that may give them more effect as pictures to the reader.

I had been in youth, and even since, for occasional amusement, a great reader of Livy, whom I confess that I prefer, both for style and matter, to any other of the Roman historians; and I had often felt as most solemn and appalling sounds, and most emphatically representative of the majesty of the Roman people, the two words so often occurring in Livy — *Consul Romanus;* especially when the consul is introduced in his military character. I mean to say, that the words king, sultan, regent, &c., or any other titles of those who embody in their own persons the collective majesty of a great people, had less power over my reverential feelings. I had, also, though no great reader of history, made myself minutely and critically familiar with one period of English history, namely, the period of the Parliamentary War, having been attracted by the moral grandeur of some who figured in that day, and by the many interesting memoirs which survive those unquiet times. Both these parts of my lighter reading, having furnished me often with matter of reflection, now furnish me with matter for my dreams. Often I used to see, after painting upon the blank darkness, a sort of rehearsal whilst waking, a crowd of ladies, and perhaps a festival and dances. And I heard it said, or I said to myself, "These are English ladies from the unhappy times of Charles I. These are the wives and daughters of those who met in peace, and sat at the same tables, and were allied by marriage or by blood; and yet, after a certain day in August, 1642, never smiled upon each other again, nor met but in the field of battle; and at Marston Moor, at Newbury, or at Naseby, cut asunder all ties of love by the cruel sabre, and washed away in blood the memory of ancient friendship." The ladies danced, and looked as lovely as the court of George IV. Yet I knew, even in my dream, that they had been in the grave for nearly two centuries. This pageant would suddenly dissolve; and, at a clapping of hands, would be heard the heart-quaking sound of *Consul Romanus;* and immediately came "sweeping by," in gorgeous paludaments, Paulus or Marius, girt around by a company of centurions, with the crimson tunic hoisted on a spear, and followed by the *alalagmos* of the Roman legions.

Many years ago, when I was looking over Piranesi's Antiquities of Rome, Mr. Coleridge, who was standing by, described to me a set of plates by that artist, called his *Dreams*, and which record the scenery of his own visions during the delirium of a fever. Some of them (I describe only from memory of Mr. Coleridge's account) represented vast Gothic halls; on the floor of which stood all sorts of engines and machinery, wheels, cables, pulleys, levers, catapults, &c., expressive of enormous power put forth, and resistance overcome. Creeping along the sides of the walls, you perceived a staircase; and upon it, groping his way upwards, was Piranesi himself. Follow the stairs a little further, and you perceive it to come to a sudden, abrupt termination, without any balustrade, and allowing no step onwards to him who had reached the extremity, except into the depths below. Whatever is to become of poor Piranesi, you suppose, at least, that his labors must in some way terminate here. But raise your eyes, and behold a second flight of stairs still higher; on which again Piranesi is perceived, by this time standing on the very brink of the abyss. Again elevate your eye, and a still more aërial flight of stairs is beheld; and again is poor Piranesi busy on his aspiring labors; and so on, until the unfinished stairs and Piranesi both are lost in the upper gloom of the hall. With the same power of endless growth and self-reproduction did my architecture proceed in dreams. In the early stage of my malady, the splendors of my dreams were indeed chiefly architectural; and I beheld such pomp of cities and palaces as was never yet beheld by the waking eye, unless in the clouds. From a great modern poet I cite the part of a passage which describes, as an appearance actually beheld in the clouds, what in many of its circumstances I saw frequently in sleep:

> The appearance, instantaneously disclosed,
> Was of a mighty city — boldly say
> A wilderness of building, sinking far
> And self-withdrawn into a wondrous depth,
> Far sinking into splendor — without end!
> Fabric it seemed of diamond, and of gold,
> With alabaster domes and silver spires,
> And blazing terrace upon terrace, high
> Uplifted; here, serene pavilions bright,
> In avenues disposed; there towers begirt
> With battlements that on their restless fronts
> Bore stars — illumination of all gems!
> By earthly nature had the effect been wrought
> Upon the dark materials of the storm
> Now pacified; on them, and on the coves,
> And mountain-steeps and summits, whereunto
> The vapors had receded — taking there
> Their station under a cerulean sky, &c. &c.

The sublime circumstance — "battlements that on their *restless* fronts bore stars" — might have been copied from my architectural dreams, for it often occurred. We hear it reported of Dryden, and of Fuseli in modern times, that they thought proper to eat raw meat for the sake of obtaining splendid dreams: how much better, for such a purpose, to have eaten opium, which yet I do not remember that any poet is recorded to have done, except the dramatist Shadwell; and in ancient days, Homer is, I think, rightly reputed to have known the virtues of opium.

To my architecture succeeded dreams of lakes, and silvery expanses of water: these haunted me so much, that I feared (though possibly it will appear ludicrous to a medical man) that some dropsical state or tendency of the brain might thus be making itself (to use a metaphysical word) *objective*, and the sentient organ *project* itself as its own object. For two months I suffered greatly in my head — a part of my bodily structure which had hitherto been so clear from all touch or taint of weakness (physically, I mean), that I used to say of it, as the last Lord Orford said of his stomach, that it seemed likely to survive the rest of my person. Till now I had never felt a headache even, or any the slightest pain, except rheumatic pains caused by my own folly. However, I got over this attack, though it must have been verging on something very dangerous.

The waters now changed their character, — from translucent lakes, shining like mirrors, they now became seas and oceans. And now came a tremendous change, which, unfolding itself slowly like a scroll, through many months, promised an abiding torment; and, in fact, it never left me until the winding up of my case. Hitherto the human face had often mixed in my dreams, but not despotically, nor with any special power of tormenting. But now that which I have called the tyranny of the human face, began to unfold itself. Perhaps some part of my London life might be answerable for this. Be that as it may, now it was that upon the rocking waters of the ocean the human face began to appear; the sea appeared paved with innumerable faces, upturned to the heavens; faces, imploring, wrathful, despairing, surged upwards by thousands, by myriads, by generations, by centuries: my agitation was infinite, my mind tossed, and surged with the ocean.

May, 1818.— The Malay had been a fearful enemy for months. I have been every night, through his means, transported into Asiatic scenes. I know not whether others share in my feelings on this point; but I have often thought that if I were compelled to forego England, and to live in China, and among Chinese manners and modes of life and scenery, I should go mad. The causes of my horror lie deep, and some of them must be common to others. Southern Asia, in general, is the seat of awful images and associations. As the cradle of the human race, it would alone have a dim and reverential feeling connected with it. But there are other reasons. No man can pretend that the wild, barbarous, and capricious superstitions of Africa, or of savage tribes elsewhere, affect him in the way that he is affected by the ancient, monumental, cruel, and elaborate religions of Indostan, &c. The mere antiquity of Asiatic things, of their institutions, histories, modes of faith, &c., is so impressive, that to me the vast age of the race and name overpowers the sense of youth in the individual. A young Chinese seems to me an antediluvian man renewed. Even Englishmen, though not bred in any knowledge of such institutions, cannot but shudder at the mystic sublimity of *castes* that have flowed apart, and refused to mix, through such immemorial tracts of time; nor can any man fail to be awed by the names of the Ganges, or the Euphrates. It contributes much to these feelings, that

Southern Asia is, and has been for thousands of years, the part of the earth most swarming with human life, the great *officina gentium*. Man is a weed in those regions. The vast empires, also, into which the enormous population of Asia has always been cast, give a further sublimity to the feelings associated with all oriental names or images. In China, over and above what it has in common with the rest of Southern Asia, I am terrified by the modes of life, by the manners, and the barrier of utter abhorrence, and want of sympathy, placed between us by feelings deeper than I can analyze. I could sooner live with lunatics, or brute animals. All this, and much more than I can say, or have time to say, the reader must enter into, before he can comprehend the unimaginable horror which these dreams of oriental imagery, and mythological tortures, impressed upon me. Under the connecting feeling of tropical heat and vertical sunlights, I brought together all creatures, birds, beasts, reptiles, all trees and plants, usages and appearances, that are found in all tropical regions, and assembled them together in China or Indostan. From kindred feelings, I soon brought Egypt and all her gods under the same law. I was stared at, hooted at, grinned at, chattered at, by monkeys, by paroquets, by cockatoos. I ran into pagodas, and was fixed, for centuries, at the summit, or in secret rooms: I was the idol; I was the priest; I was worshipped; I was sacrificed. I fled from the wrath of Brama through all the forests of Asia: Vishnu hated me; Seeva laid wait for me. I came suddenly upon Isis and Osiris: I had done a deed, they said, which the ibis and the crocodile trembled at. I was buried, for a thousand years, in stone coffins, with mummies and sphinxes, in narrow chambers at the heart of eternal pyramids. I was kissed, with cancerous kisses, by crocodiles; and laid, confounded with all unutterable slimy things, amongst reeds and Nilotic mud.

I thus give the reader some slight abstraction of my oriental dreams, which always filled me with such amazement at the monstrous scenery, that horror seemed absorbed, for a while, in sheer astonishment. Sooner or later came a reflux of feeling that swallowed up the astonishment, and left me, not so much in terror, as in hatred and abomination of what I saw. Over every form, and threat, and punishment, and dim sightless incarceration, brooded a sense of eternity and infinity that drove me into an oppression as of madness. Into these dreams only, it was, with one or two slight exceptions, that any circumstances of physical horror entered. All before had been moral and spiritual terrors. But here the main agents were ugly birds, or snakes, or crocodiles, especially the last. The cursed crocodile became to me the object of more horror than almost all the rest. I was compelled to live with him; and (as was always the case, almost, in my dreams) for centuries. I escaped sometimes, and found myself in Chinese houses with cane tables, &c. All the feet of the tables, sofas, &c., soon became instinct with life: the abominable head of the crocodile, and his leering eyes, looked out at me, multiplied into a thousand repetitions; and I stood loathing and fascinated. And so often did this hideous reptile haunt my dreams, that many times the very same dream was broken up in the very same way: I heard gentle voices speaking to me

(I hear everything when I am sleeping), and instantly I awoke: it was broad noon, and my children were standing, hand in hand, at my bedside; come to show me their colored shoes, or new frocks, or to let me see them dressed for going out. I protest that so awful was the transition from the damned crocodile, and the other unutterable monsters and abortions of my dreams, to the sight of innocent *human* natures and of infancy, that, in the mighty and sudden revulsion of mind, I wept, and could not forbear it, as I kissed their faces.

June, 1819.—I have had occasion to remark, at various periods of my life, that the deaths of those whom we love, and, indeed, the contemplation of death generally, is (*cæteris paribus*) more affecting in summer than in any other season of the year. And the reasons are these three, I think: first, that the visible heavens in summer appear far higher, more distant, and (if such a solecism may be excused) more infinite; the clouds by which chiefly the eye expounds the distance of the blue pavilion stretched over our heads are in summer more voluminous, massed, and accumulated in far grander and more towering piles: secondly, the light and the appearances of the declining and the setting sun are much more fitted to be types and characters of the infinite: and, thirdly (which is the main reason), the exuberant and riotous prodigality of life naturally forces the mind more powerfully upon the antagonist thought of death, and the wintry sterility of the grave. For it may be observed, generally, that wherever two thoughts stand related to each other by a law of antagonism, and exist, as it were, by mutual repulsion, they are apt to suggest each other. On these accounts it is that I find it impossible to banish the thought of death when I am walking alone in the endless days of summer; and any particular death, if not more affecting, at least haunts my mind more obstinately and besiegingly, in that season. Perhaps this cause, and a slight incident which I omit, might have been the immediate occasions of the following dream, to which, however, a predisposition must always have existed in my mind; but having been once roused, it never left me, and split into a thousand fantastic varieties, which often suddenly reünited, and composed again the original dream.

I thought that it was a Sunday morning in May; that it was Easter Sunday, and as yet very early in the morning. I was standing, as it seemed to me, at the door of my own cottage. Right before me lay the very scene which could really be commanded from that situation, but exalted, as was usual, and solemnized by the power of dreams. There were the same mountains, and the same lovely valley at their feet; but the mountains were raised to more than Alpine height, and there was interspace far larger between them of meadows and forest lawns; the hedges were rich with white roses; and no living creature was to be seen, excepting that in the green church-yard there were cattle tranquilly reposing upon the verdant graves, and particularly round about the grave of a child whom I had tenderly loved, just as I had really beheld them, a little before sunrise, in the same summer, when that child died. I gazed upon the well-known scene, and I said aloud (as I thought) to myself, "It yet wants much of sunrise; and it is Easter Sunday; and that is the day on which they celebrate the first fruits of resurrection. I will walk abroad; old griefs shall be forgotten to-day; for the air is cool and still, and the hills are high, and stretch away to heaven; and the forest glades are as quiet as the church-yard; and with the dew I can wash the fever from my forehead, and then I shall be unhappy no longer." And I turned, as if to open my garden gate; and immediately I saw upon the left a scene far different; but which yet the power of dreams had reconciled into harmony with the other. The scene was an oriental one; and there also it was Easter Sunday, and very early in the morning. And at a vast distance were visible, as a stain upon the horizon, the domes and cupolas of a great city — an image or faint abstraction, caught, perhaps, in childhood, from some picture of Jerusalem. And not a bow-shot from me, upon a stone, and shaded by Judean palms, there sat a woman; and I looked, and it was — Ann! She fixed her eyes upon me earnestly; and I said to her, at length, "So, then, I have found you, at last." I waited; but she answered me not a word. Her face was the same as when I saw it last, and yet, again, how different! Seventeen years ago, when the lamp-light fell upon her face, as for the last time I kissed her lips (lips, Ann, that to me were not polluted!), her eyes were streaming with tears; — her tears were now wiped away; she seemed more beautiful than she was at that time, but in all other points the same, and not older. Her looks were tranquil, but with unusual solemnity of expression, and I now gazed upon her with some awe; but suddenly her countenance grew dim, and, turning to the mountains, I perceived vapors rolling between us; in a moment, all had vanished; thick darkness came on; and in the twinkling of an eye I was far away from mountains, and by lamp-light in Oxford-street, walking again with Ann — just as we walked seventeen years before, when we were both children.

As a final specimen, I cite one of a different character, from 1820.

The dream commenced with a music which now I often heard in dreams — a music of preparation and of awakening suspense; a music like the opening of the Coronation Anthem, and which, like *that*, gave the feeling of a vast march, of infinite cavalcades filing off, and the tread of innumerable armies. The morning was come of a mighty day — a day of crisis and of final hope for human nature, then suffering some mysterious eclipse, and laboring in some dread extremity. Somewhere, I knew not where — somehow, I knew not how — by some beings, I knew not whom — a battle, a strife, an agony, was conducting, — was evolving like a great drama, or piece of music; with which my sympathy was the more insupportable from my confusion as to its place, its cause, its nature, and its possible issue. I, as is usual in dreams (where, of necessity, we make ourselves central to every movement), had the power, and yet had not the power, to decide it. I had the power, if I could raise myself, to will it; and yet again had not the power, for the weight of twenty Atlantics was upon me, or the oppression of inexpiable guilt. "Deeper than ever plummet sounded," I lay inactive. Then, like a chorus, the passion deepened. Some greater interest was at stake; some mightier cause than ever yet the sword had pleaded, or trumpet had proclaimed. Then came sudden alarms; hurryings to and fro; trepidations of innumerable fugitives. I knew not whether from the good cause or the bad; darkness and lights; tempest and human faces; and at last, with the sense that all was lost, female forms, and the features that were worth all the world to me, and but a moment allowed, — and clasped hands, and heart-breaking partings, and then — everlasting farewells! and, with a sigh, such as the caves of hell sighed when the incestuous mother uttered the abhorred name of death, the sound was reverberated — everlasting farewells! and again, and yet again reverberated — everlasting farewells!

And I awoke in struggles, and cried aloud — "I will sleep no more!"

But I am now called upon to wind up a narrative which has already extended to an unreasonable length. Within more spacious limits, the materials which I have used might have been better unfolded; and much which I have not used might have been added with effect. Perhaps, however, enough has been given. It now remains that I should say something of the way in which this conflict of horrors was finally brought to its crisis. The reader is already aware (from a passage near the beginning of the introduction to the first part) that the opium-eater has, in some way or other, "unwound, almost to its final links, the accursed chain which bound him." By what means? To have narrated this, according to the original intention, would have far exceeded the space which can now be allowed. It is fortunate, as such a cogent reason exists for abridging it, that I should, on a maturer view of the case, have been exceedingly unwilling to injure, by any such unaffecting details, the impression of the history itself, as an appeal to the prudence and the conscience of the yet unconfirmed opium-eater, or even (though a very inferior consideration) to injure its effect as a composition. The interest of the judicious reader will not attach itself chiefly to the subject of the fascinating spells, but to the fascinating power. Not the opium-eater, but the opium, is the true hero of the tale, and the legitimate centre on which the interest revolves. The object was to display the marvellous agency of opium, whether for pleasure or for pain; if that is done, the action of the piece has closed.

However, as some people, in spite of all laws to the contrary, will persist in asking what became of the opium-eater, and in what state he now is, I answer for him thus: The reader is aware that opium had long ceased to found its empire on spells of pleasure; it was solely by the tortures connected with the attempt to abjure it, that it kept its hold. Yet, as other tortures, no less, it may be thought, attended the non-abjuration of such a tyrant, a choice only of evils was left; and *that* might as well have been adopted, which, however terrific in itself, held out a prospect of final restoration to happiness. This appears true; but good logic gave the author no strength to act upon it. However, a crisis arrived for the author's life, and a crisis for other objects still dearer to him, and which will always be far dearer to him than his life, even now that it is again a happy one. I saw that I must die, if I continued the opium: I determined, therefore, if that should be required, to die in throwing it off. How much I was at that time taking, I cannot say; for the opium which I used had been purchased for me by a friend, who afterwards refused to let me pay him; so that I could not ascertain even what quantity I had used within a year. I apprehend, however, that I took it very irregularly, and that I varied from about fifty or sixty grains to one hundred and fifty a day. My first task was to reduce it to forty, to thirty, and, as fast as I could, to twelve grains.

I triumphed; but think not, reader, that therefore my sufferings were ended; nor think of me as of one sitting in a *dejected* state. Think of me as of one, even when four months had passed, still agitated, writhing, throbbing, palpitating, shattered; and much, perhaps, in the situation of him who has been racked, as I collect the torments of that state from the affecting account of them left by the most innocent sufferer* (of the time of James I.). Meantime, I derived no benefit from any medicine, except one prescribed to me by an Edinburgh surgeon of great eminence, namely, ammoniated tincture of valerian. Medical account, therefore, of my emancipation, I have not much to give; and even that little, as managed by a man so ignorant of medicine as myself, would probably tend only to mislead. At all events, it would be misplaced in this situation. The moral of the narrative is addressed to the opium-eater; and therefore, of necessity, limited in its application. If he is taught to fear and tremble, enough has been effected. But he may say, that the issue of my case is at least a proof that opium, after a seven-

* William Lithgow; his book (Travels, &c.) is ill and pedantically written; but the account of his own sufferings on the rack at Malaga is overpoweringly affecting.

teen years' use, and an eight years' abuse of its powers may still be renounced; and that he may chance tc bring to the task greater energy than I did, or that, with a stronger constitution than mine, he may obtain the same results with less. This may be true; I would not presume to measure the efforts of other men by my own. I heartily wish him more energy; I wish him the same success. Nevertheless, I had motives external to myself which he may unfortunately want; and these supplied me with conscientious supports, which mere personal interests might fail to supply to a mind debilitated by opium.

Jeremy Taylor conjectures that it may be as painful to be born as to die. I think it probable; and, during the whole period of diminishing the opium, I had the torments of a man passing out of one mode of existence into another. The issue was not death, but a sort of physical regeneration, and, I may add, that ever since, at intervals, I have had a restoration of more than youthful spirits, though under the pressure of difficulties, which, in a less happy state of mind, I should have called misfortunes.

One memorial of my former condition still remains; my dreams are not yet perfectly calm; the dread swell ana agitation of the storm have not wholly subsided; the legions that encamped in them are drawing off, but not all departed; my sleep is tumultuous, and like the gates of Paradise to our first parents when looking back from afar, it is still (in the tremendous line of Milton) —

With dreadful faces thronged and fiery arms.

APPENDIX.

APPENDIX.

The proprietors of this little work having determined on reprinting it, some explanation seems called for, to account for the non-appearance of a Third Part, promised in the London Magazine of December last; and the more so, because the proprietors, under whose guarantee that promise was issued, might otherwise be implicated in the blame — little or much — attached to its non-fulfilment. This blame, in mere justice, the author takes wholly upon himself. What may be the exact amount of the guilt which he thus appropriates, is a very dark question to his own judgment, and not much illuminated by any of the masters on casuistry whom he has consulted on the occasion. On the one hand, it seems generally agreed that a promise is binding in the *inverse* ratio of the numbers to whom it is made: for which reason it is that we see many persons break promises without scruple that are made to a whole nation, who keep their faith religiously in all private engagements, — breaches of promise towards the stronger party being committed at a man's own peril: on the other hand, the only parties interested in the promises of an author are his readers, and these it is a point of modesty in any author to believe as few as possible; or perhaps only one, in which case any promise imposes a sanctity of moral obligation which it is shocking to think of. Casuistry dismissed, however, — the author throws himself on the indulgent consideration of all who may conceive themselves aggrieved by his delay, in the following account of his own condition from the end of last year, when the engagement was made, up nearly to the present time. For any purpose of self-excuse, it might be sufficient to say, that intolerable bodily suffering had totally disabled him for almost any exertion of mind, more especially for such as demand and presuppose a pleasurable and a genial state of feeling; but, as a case that may by possibility contribute a trifle to the medical history of opium in a further stage of its action than can often have been brought under the notice of professional men, he has judged that it might be acceptable to some readers to have it described more at length. *Fiat experimentum in corpore vili* is a just rule where there is any reasonable presumption of benefit to arise on a large scale. What the benefit may be, will admit of a doubt; but there can be none as to the value of the body, for a more worthless body than his own, the author is free to confess, cannot be. (It is his pride to believe, that it is the very ideal of a base, crazy, despicable human system, that hardly ever could have been meant to be seaworthy for two days under the ordinary storms and wear-and-tear of life) and, indeed, if that were the creditable way of disposing of human bodies, he must own that he should almost be ashamed to bequeath his wretched structure to any respectable dog. But now to the case, which, for the sake of avoiding the constant recurrence of a cumbersome periphrasis, the author will take the liberty of giving in the first person.

Those who have read the Confessions will have closed them with the impression that I had wholly renounced the use of opium. This impression I meant to convey, and that for two reasons: first, because the very act of deliberately recording such a state of suffering necessarily presumes in the recorder a power of surveying his own case as a cool spectator, and a degree of spirits for adequately describing it, which it would be inconsistent to suppose in any person speaking from the station of an actual sufferer; secondly, because I, who had descended from so large a quantity as eight thousand drops to so small a one (comparatively speaking) as a quantity ranging between three hundred and one hundred and sixty drops, might well suppose that the victory was in effect achieved. In suffering my readers, therefore, to think of me as of a reformed opium-eater, I left no impression but what I shared myself, and, as may be seen, even this impression was left to be collected from the general tone of the conclusion, and not from any specific words, which are in no instance at variance with the literal truth. In no long time after that paper was written, I became sensible that the effort which remained would cost me far more energy than I had anticipated, and the necessity for making it was more apparent every month.

In particular, I became aware of an increasing callousness or defect of sensibility in the stomach: and this I imagined might imply a schirrous state of that organ either formed or forming. An eminent physician, to whose kindness I was, at that time, deeply indebted, informed me that such a termination of my case was not impossible, though likely to be forestalled by a different termination, in the event of my continuing the use of opium. Opium, therefore, I resolved wholly to abjure, as soon as I should find myself at liberty to bend my undivided attention and energy to this purpose. It was not, however, until the 24th of June last that any tolerable concurrence of facilities for such an attempt arrived. On that day I began my experiment, having previously settled in my own mind that I would not flinch, but would "stand up to the scratch," under any possible "punishment." I must premise, that about one hundred and seventy or one hundred and eighty drops had been my ordinary allowance for many months. Occasionally I had run up as high as five hundred, and once nearly to seven hundred. In repeated preludes to my final experiment I had also gone as low as one hundred drops, but had found it impossible to stand it beyond the fourth day, which, by the way, I have always found more difficult to get over than any of the preceding three. I went off under easy sail — one hundred and thirty drops a day for three days; on the fourth I plunged at once to eighty The misery which I now suffered "took the conceit" out of me, at once; and for about a month I continued off and on about this mark; then I sunk to sixty, and the next day to — none at all. This was the first day for nearly ten years that I had existed without opium. I persevered in my abstinence for ninety hours; that is, upwards of half a week. Then I took —— ask me not how much; say, ye severest, what would ye have done? Then I abstained again; then took about twenty-five drops; then abstained; and so on.

Meantime, the symptoms which attended my case for the first six weeks of the experiment were these: enormous irritability and excitement of the whole system; the stomach, in particular, restored to a full feeling of vitality and sensibility, but often in great pain; unceasing restlessness night and day; sleep — I scarcely knew what it was — three hours out of the twenty-four was the utmost I had, and that so agitated and shallow that I heard every sound that was near me; lower jaw constantly swelling; mouth ulcerated; and many other distressing symptoms that would be tedious to repeat, amongst which, however, I must mention one, because it had never failed to accompany any attempt to renounce opium, — namely, violent sternutation. This now became exceedingly troublesome; sometimes lasting for two hours at once, and recurring at least twice or three times a day. I was not much surprised at this, on recollecting what I had somewhere heard or read, that the membrane which lines the nostrils is a prolongation of that which lines the stomach; whence, I believe, are explained the inflammatory appearances about the nostrils of dram-drinkers. The sudden restoration of its original sensibility to the stomach expressed itself, I suppose, in this way. It is remarkable, also, that, during the whole period of years through which I had taken opium, I had never once caught cold (as the phrase is), nor even the slightest cough. But now a violent cold attacked me, and a cough soon after. In an unfinished fragment of a letter begun about this time to ——, I find these words: — "You ask me to write the —— ——. Do you know Beaumont and Fletcher's play of Thierry and Theodoret? There you will see my case as to sleep; nor is it much of an exaggeration in other features. I protest to you that I have a greater influx of thoughts in one hour at present than in a whole year under the reign of opium. It seems as though all the thoughts which had been frozen up for a decade of years by opium had now, according to the old fable, been thawed at once, such a multitude stream in upon me from all quarters. Yet such is my impatience and hideous irritability, that, for one which I detain and write down, fifty escape me. In spite of my weariness from suffering and want of sleep, I cannot stand still or sit for two minutes together. '*I nunc, et versus tecum meditare canoros.*' "

At this stage of my experiment I sent to a neighboring surgeon, requesting that he would come over to see me. In the evening he came, and after briefly stating the case to him, I asked this question: Whether he did not think that the opium might have acted as a stimulus to the digestive organs; and that the present state of suffering in the stomach, which manifestly was the cause of the inability to sleep, might arise from indigestion? His answer was, — No: on the contrary, he thought that the suffering was caused by digestion itself, which should naturally go on below the consciousness, but which, from the unnatural state of the stomach, vitiated by so long a use of opium, was become distinctly perceptible. This opinion was plausible, and the unintermitting nature of the suffering disposes me to think that it was true; for, if it had been any mere *irregular* affection of the stomach, it should naturally have intermitted occasionally, and constantly fluctuated as to degree. The intention of nature, as manifested in the healthy state, obviously is, to withdraw from our notice all the vital motions, such as the circulation of the blood, the expansion and contraction of the lungs, the peristaltic action of the stomach, &c.; and opium, it seems, is able in this, as in other instances, to counteract her purposes. By the advice of the surgeon, I tried *bitters*. For a short time these greatly mitigated the feelings under which I labored; but about the forty-second day of the experiment the symptoms already noticed began to retire, and new ones to arise of a different and far more tormenting class; under these, with but a few intervals of remission, I have since continued to suffer. But I dismiss them undescribed for two reasons: first, because the mind revolts from retracing circumstantially any sufferings from which it is removed by too short or by no interval. To do this with minuteness enough to make the review of any use, would be indeed "*infandum renovare dolorem*," and possibly without a sufficient motive: for, 2dly, I doubt whether this latter state be any way referable to opium, positively considered, or even negatively; that is, whether it is to be numbered amongst the last evils from the direct action of opium, or even amongst the earliest evils consequent upon a *want* of opium in a system long deranged by its use. Certainly one part of the symptoms might be ac counted for from the time of year (August); for though the summer was not a hot one, yet in any case the sum of all the heat *funded* (if one may say so) during the previous months, added to the existing heat of that month, naturally renders August in its better half the hottest part of the year; and it so happened that the excessive perspiration, which even at Christmas attends any great reduction in the daily quantum of opium, and which in July was so violent as to oblige me to use a bath five or six times a day, had about the setting in of the hottest season wholly retired, on which account any bad effect of the heat might be the more unmitigated. Another symptom, namely, what in my ignorance I call internal rheumatism (sometimes affecting the shoulders, &c., but more often appearing to be seated in the stomach), seemed again less probably attributable to the opium, or the want of opium, than to the dampness of the house* which I inhabit, which had about that time attained its maximum, July having been, as usual, a month of incessant rain in our most rainy part of England.

Under these reasons for doubting whether opium had any connection with the latter stage of my bodily

---

* In saying this, I meant no disrespect to the individual house, as the reader will understand when I tell him that, with the exception of one or two princely mansions, and some few inferior ones that have been coated with Roman cement, I am not acquainted with any house in this mountainous district which is wholly water-proof. The architecture of books, I flatter myself, is conducted on just principles in this country; but for any other architecture, it is in a barbarous state, and, what is worse, in a retrograde state.

wretchedness — (except, indeed, as an occasional cause, as having left the body weaker and more crazy, and thus predisposed to any mal-influence whatever), — I willingly spare my reader all description of it: let it perish to him; and would that I could as easily say, let it perish to my own remembrances, that any future hours of tranquillity may not be disturbed by too vivid an ideal of possible human misery!

So much for the sequel of my experiment; as to the former stage, in which properly lies the experiment and its application to other cases, I must request my reader not to forget the reasons for which I have recorded it. These were two. 1st, a belief that I might add some trifle to the history of opium as a medical agent; in this I am aware that I have not at all fulfilled my own intentions, in consequence of the torpor of mind, pain of body, and extreme disgust to the subject, which besieged me whilst writing that part of my paper; which part being immediately sent off to the press (distant about five degrees of latitude), cannot be corrected or improved. But from this account, rambling as it may be, it is evident that thus much of benefit may arise to the persons most interested in such a history of opium, — namely, to opium-eaters in general, — that it establishes, for their consolation and encouragement, the fact that opium may be renounced, and without greater sufferings than an ordinary resolution may support; and by a pretty rapid course* of descent.

* On which last notice I would remark that mine was *too* rapid, and the suffering therefore needlessly aggravated; or rather, perhaps, it was not sufficiently continuous and equably graduated. But, that the reader may judge for himself, and, above all, that

To communicate this result of my experiment, was my foremost purpose. 2dly, as a purpose collateral tc

---

the opium-eater, who is preparing to retire from business, may have every sort of information before him, I subjoin my diary.

FIRST WEEK.	Drops of Laud.
Mond. June 24	130
" 25	140
" 26	130
" 27	80
" 28	80
" 29	80
" 30	80

SECOND WEEK.	Drops of Lauc
Mond. July 1	80
" 2	80
" 3	90
" 4	100
" 5	80
" 6	80
" 7	80

THIRD WEEK.	Drops of Laud.
Mond. July 8	300
" 9	50
" 10	Hiatus in MS.
" 11	
" 12	
" 13	
" 14	76

FOURTH WEEK.	Drops of Laud.
Mond. July 15	76
" 16	73½
" 17	73½
" 18	70
" 19	240
" 20	80
" 21	350

FIFTH WEEK.	Drops of Laud.
Mond. July 22	60
" 23	none
" 24	none
" 25	none
" 26	200
" 27	none

What mean these abrupt relapses, the reader will ask, perhaps, to such numbers as 300, 350, &c.? The *impulse* to these relapses was mere infirmity of purpose; the *motive*, where any motive blended with this impulse, was either the principle of "*reculer pour mieux sauter*— (for under the torpor of a large dose, which lasted for a day or two, a less quantity satisfied the stomach, which, on awaking, found itself partly accustomed to this new ration), — or else it was this, I wished to explain how it had become impossible for me to compose a Third Part in time to accompany this republication: for during the very time of this experiment, the proof-sheets of this reprint were sent to me from London; and such was my inability to expand or to improve them, that I could not even bear to read them over with attention enough to notice the press errors, or to correct any verbal inaccuracies. These were my reasons for troubling my reader with any record, long or short, of experiments relating to so truly base a subject as my own body; and I am earnest with the reader, that he will not forget them, or so far misapprehend me as to believe it possible that I would condescend to so rascally a subject for its own sake, or, indeed, for any less object than that of general benefit to others. Such an animal as the self-observing valetudinarian, I know there is. I have met him myself occasionally, and I know that he is the worst imaginable *heautontimoroumenos;* aggravating and sustaining, by calling into distinct consciousness, every symptom that would else, perhaps, under a different direction given to the thoughts, become evanescent. But as to myself, so profound is my contempt for this undignified and selfish habit, that I could as little condescend to it as I could to spend my time in watching a poor servant-girl, to whom at this moment I hear some lad or other making love at the back of my house. Is it for a Transcendental philosopher to feel any curiosity

---

this principle — that of sufferings otherwise equal, those will be borne best which meet with a mood of anger; now, whenever I ascended to any large dose, I was furiously incensed on the following day, and could then have borne anything.

on such an occasion? Or can I, whose life is worth only eight and a half years' purchase, be supposed to have leisure for such trivial employments? However, to put this out of question, I shall say one thing which will, perhaps, shock some readers; but I am sure it ought not to do so, considering the motives on which I say it. No man, I suppose, employs much of his time on the phenomena of his own body without some regard for it; whereas the reader sees that, so far from looking upon mine with any complacency or regard, I hate it and make it the object of my bitter ridicule and contempt; and I should not be displeased to know that the last indignities which the law inflicts upon the bodies of the worst malefactors might hereafter fall upon it. And in testification of my sincerity in saying this, I shall make the following offer. Like other men, I have particular fancies about the place of my burial; having lived chiefly in a mountainous region, I rather cleave to the conceit that a grave in a green church-yard amongst the ancient and solitary hills will be a sublimer and more tranquil place of repose for a philosopher than any in the hideous Golgothas of London. Yet, if the gentlemen of Surgeons' Hall think that any benefit can redound to their science from inspecting the appearances in the body of an opium-eater, let them speak but a word, and I will take care that mine shall be legally secured to them — that is, as soon as I have done with it myself. Let them not hesitate to express their wishes upon any scruples of false delicacy and consideration for my feelings; I assure them that they will do me too much honor by "demonstrating" on such a crazy body as mine; and it will give me pleasure to anticipate this posthumous revenge and insult inflicted upon that which has caused me so much suffering in this life. Such bequests are not common; reversionary benefits contingent upon the death of the testator are indeed dangerous to announce in many cases. Of this we have a remarkable instance in the habits of a Roman prince, who used, upon any notification made to him by rich persons, that they had left him a handsome estate in their wills, to express his entire satisfaction at such arrangements, and his gracious acceptance of those royal legacies; but then, if the testators neglected to give him immediate possession of the property, — if they traitorously "persisted in living" (*si vivere perseverarent*, as Suetonius expresses it), he was highly provoked, and took his measures accordingly. In those times, and from one of the worst of the Cæsars, we might expect such conduct; but I am sure that, from English surgeons at this day, I need look for no expressions of impatience, or of any other feelings but such as are answerable to that pure love of science, and all its interests, which induces me to make such an offer.

Sept. 30*th*, 1822.

SUSPIRIA DE PROFUNDIS:

BEING A SEQUEL TO THE

CONFESSIONS OF AN ENGLISH OPIUM-EATER

SUSPIRIA DE PROFUNDIS:

BEING A SEQUEL TO THE

"CONFESSIONS OF AN ENGLISH OPIUM-EATER."

INTRODUCTORY NOTICE.

In 1821, as a contribution to a periodical work, — in 1822, as a separate volume, — appeared the "Confessions of an English Opium-Eater." The object of that work was to reveal something of the grandeur which belongs *potentially* to human dreams. Whatever may be the number of those in whom this faculty of dreaming splendidly can be supposed to lurk, there are not perhaps very many in whom it is developed. He whose talk is of oxen, will probably dream of oxen; and the condition of human life, which yokes so vast a majority to a daily experience incompatible with much elevation of thought, oftentimes neutralizes the tone of grandeur in the reproductive faculty of dreaming, even for those whose minds are populous with solemn imagery. Habitually to dream magnificently, a man must have a constitutional determination to reverie. This in the first place, and even this, where it exists strongly is too much liable to disturbance from the gathering agitation of our present English life. Already, in this year 1845, what by the procession through fifty years of mighty revolutions amongst the kingdoms of the earth, what by the continual development of vast physical agencies, — steam in all its applications, light getting under harness as a slave for man,* powers from heaven descending upon education and accelerations of the press, powers from hell (as it might seem, but these also celestial) coming round upon artillery and the forces of destruction, — the eye of the calmest observer is troubled; the brain is haunted as if by some jealousy of ghostly beings moving amongst us; and it becomes too evident that, unless this colossal pace of advance can be retarded (a thing not to be expected), or, which is happily more probable, can be met by counter forces of corresponding magnitude, forces in the direction of religion or profound philosophy, that shall radiate centrifugally against this storm of life so perilously centripetal towards the vortex of the merely human, left to itself, the natural tendency of so chaotic a tumult must be to evil; for some minds to lunacy, for others to a reägency of fleshly torpor. How much this fierce condition of eternal hurry upon an arena too exclusively human in its interests is likely to defeat the grandeur which is latent in all men, may be seen in the ordinary effect from living too constantly in varied company. The word *dissipation*, in one of its uses, expresses that effect; the action of thought and feeling is too much dissipated and squandered. To

* Daguerreotype, &c.

reconcentrate them into meditative habits, a necessity is felt by all observing persons for sometimes retiring from crowds. No man ever will unfold the capacities of his own intellect who does not at least checker his life with solitude. How much solitude, so much power. Or, if not true in that rigor of expression, to this formula undoubtedly it is that the wise rule of life must approximate.

Among the powers in man which suffer by this too intense life of the *social* instincts, none suffers more than the power of dreaming. Let no man think this a trifle. The machinery for dreaming planted in the human brain was not planted for nothing. That faculty, in alliance with the mystery of darkness, is the one great tube through which man communicates with the shadowy. And the dreaming organ, in connection with the heart, the eye and the ear, compose the magnificent apparatus which forces the infinite into the chambers of a human brain, and throws dark reflections from eternities below all life upon the mirrors of the sleeping mind.

But if this faculty suffers from the decay of solitude, which is becoming a visionary idea in England, on the other hand, it is certain that some merely physical agencies can and do assist the faculty of dreaming almost preternaturally. Amongst these is intense exercise; to some extent at least, and for some persons; but beyond all others is opium, which indeed seems to possess a *specific* power in that direction; not merely for exalting the colors of dream-scenery, but for deepening its shadows, and, above all, for strengthening the sense of its fearful *realities.*

The *Opium Confessions* were written with some slight secondary purpose of exposing this specific power of opium upon the faculty of dreaming, but much more with the purpose of displaying the faculty itself; and the outline of the work travelled in this course. Supposing a reader acquainted with the true object of the Confessions as here stated, namely, the revelation of dreaming to have put this question :

"But how came you to dream more splendidly than others?"

The answer would have been —

"Because (*præmissis præmittendis*) I took excessive quantities of opium."

Secondly, suppose him to say, "But how came you to take opium in this excess?"

The answer to *that* would be, "Because some early events in my life had left a weakness in one organ which required (or seemed to require) that stimulant."

Then, because the opium dreams could not always have been understood without a knowledge of these events, it became necessary to relate them. Now, these two questions and answers exhibit the *law* of the work; that is, the principle which determined its form, but precisely in the inverse or regressive order. The work itself opened with the narration of my early adventures. These, in the natural order of succession, led to the opium as a resource for healing their consequences; and the opium as naturally led to the dreams. But in the synthetic order of presenting the facts, what stood last in the succession of development stood first in the order of my purposes.

At the close of this little work, the reader was instructed to believe, and *truly* instructed, that I had mastered the tyranny of opium. The fact is, that *twice* I mastered it, and by efforts even more prodigious in the second of these cases than in the first. But one error I committed in both. I did not connect with the abstinence from opium, so trying to the fortitude under *any* circumstances, that enormity of excess which (as I have since learned) is the one sole resource for making it endurable. I overlooked, in those days, the one *sine quâ non* for making the triumph permanent. Twice I sank, twice I rose again. A third time I sank; partly from the cause mentioned (the oversight as to exercise), partly from other causes, on which it avails not now to trouble the reader. I could moralize, if I chose; and perhaps *he* will moralize, whether I choose it or not. But, in the mean time, neither of us is acquainted properly with the circumstances of the case: I, from natural bias of judgment, not altogether acquainted; and he (with his permission) not at all.

During this third prostration before the dark idol, and after some years, new and monstrous phenomena began slowly to arise. For a time, these were neglected as accidents, or palliated by such remedies as I knew of. But when I could no longer conceal from myself that these dreadful symptoms were moving forward forever, by a pace steadily, solemnly, and equably increasing, I endeavored, with some feeling of panic, for a third time to retrace my steps. But I had not reversed my motions for many weeks, before I became profoundly aware that this was impossible. Or, in the imagery of my dreams, which translated everything into their own language, I saw through vast avenues of gloom those towering gates of ingress which hitherto had always seemed to stand open, now at last barred against my retreat, and hung with funeral crape.

As applicable to this tremendous situation (the situation of one escaping by some refluent current from the maelstrom roaring for him in the distance, who finds suddenly that this current is but an eddy, wheeling round upon the same maelstrom), I have since remembered a striking incident in a modern novel. A lady abbess of a convent, herself suspected of Protestant leanings, and in that way already disarmed of all effectual power, finds one of her own nuns (whom she knows to be innocent) accused of an offence leading to the most terrific of punishments. The nun will be immured alive, if she is found guilty; and there is no chance that she will not, for the evidence against her is strong, unless something were made known that cannot be made known; and the judges are hostile. All follows in the order of the reader's fears. The witnesses depose; the evidence is without effectual contradiction: the conviction is declared; the judgment is delivered; nothing remains but to see execution done. At this crisis, the abbess, alarmed too late for effectual interposition, considers with herself that, according to the regular forms, there will be one single night open, during which the prisoner cannot be withdrawn from her own separate jurisdiction. This one night, therefore, she will use, at any hazard to herself, for the salvation of her friend. At midnight, when all is hushed in the convent, the lady traverses the passages which lead to the cells of prisoners. She bears a master-key under her professional habit. As this will open every door in every corridor, already, by anticipation, she feels the luxury of holding her emancipated friend within her arms. Suddenly she has reached the door; she descries a dusky object; she raises her lamp, and, ranged within the recess of the entrance, she beholds the funeral banner of the holy office, and the black robes of its inexorable officials.

I apprehend that, in a situation such as this, supposing it a real one, the lady abbess would not start, would not show any marks externally of consternation or horror. The case was beyond *that.* The sentiment which attends the sudden revelation that *all is lost* silently is gathered up into the heart; it is too deep for gestures or for words; and no part of it passes to the outside. Were the ruin conditional, or were it in any point doubtful, it would be natural to utter ejaculations, and to seek sympathy. But where the ruin is understood to be absolute, where sympathy cannot be consolation, and counsel cannot be hope, this is otherwise. The voice perishes; the gestures are frozen; and the spirit of man flies back upon its own centre. I, at least, upon seeing those awful gates closed and hung with draperies of woe, as for a death already past, spoke not, nor started, nor groaned. One profound sigh ascended from my heart, and I was silent for days.

It is the record of this third or final stage of opium, as one differing in something more than degree from the others, that I am now undertaking. But a scruple arises as to the true interpretation of these final symptoms. I have elsewhere explained, that it was no particular purpose of mine, and *why* it was no particular purpose, to warn other opium-eaters. Still, as some few persons may use the record in that way, it becomes a matter of interest to ascertain how far it is likely, that, even with the same excesses, other opium-eaters could fall into the same condition. I do not mean to lay a stress upon any supposed idiosyncrasy in myself. Possibly every man has an idiosyncrasy. In some things, undoubtedly, he has. For no man ever yet resembled another man so far, as not to differ from him in features innumerable of his inner nature. But what I point to are not peculiarities of temperament or of organization, so much as peculiar circumstances and incidents through which my own separate experience had revolved. Some of these were of a nature to alter the whole economy of my mind. Great convulsions, from whatever cause, — from conscience, from fear, from grief, from struggles of the will, — sometimes, in passing away themselves, do not carry off the changes which they have worked. *All* the agitations of this magnitude which a man may have threaded in his life, he neither ought to report, nor *could* report. But one which affected my childhood is a privileged exception. It is privileged as a proper communication for a stranger's ear; because, though relating to a man's proper self, it is a self so far removed from his present self as to wound no feelings of delicacy or just reserve. It is privileged, also as a proper subject for the sympathy of the narrator An adult sympathizes with himself in childhood because he *is* the same, and because (being the same) yet he is *not* the same. He acknowledges the deep, mysterious identity between himself, as adult and as infant, for the ground of his sympathy; and yet, with this general agreement, and necessity of agreement, he feels the differences between his two selves as the main quickeners of his sympathy. He pities the infirmities, as they arise to light in his young forerunner, which now, perhaps, he does not share; he looks indulgently upon the errors of the understanding, or limitations of view which now he has long survived; and sometimes, also, he honors in the infant that rectitude of will which, under *some* temptations, he may since have felt it so difficult to maintain.

The particular case to which I refer in my own childhood was one of intolerable grief; a trial, in fact, more severe than many people at *any* age are called upon to stand. The relation in which the case stands to my latter opium experiences is this: — Those vast clouds of gloomy grandeur which overhung my dreams at all stages of opium, but which grew into the darkest of miseries in the last, and that haunting of the human face, which latterly towered into a curse, — were they not partly derived from this childish experience? It is certain that, from the essential solitude in which my childhood was passed; from the depth of my sensibility; from the exaltation of this by the resistance of an intellect too prematurely developed; it resulted that the terrific grief which I passed through drove a shaft for me into the worlds of death and darkness which never again closed, and through which it might be said that I ascended and descended at will, according to the temper of my spirits. Some of the phenomena developed in my dream-scenery, undoubtedly, do but repeat the experiences of childhood; and others seem likely to have been growths and fructifications from seeds at that time sown.

The reasons, therefore, for prefixing some account of a "passage" in childhood to this record of a dreadful visitation from opium excess are, 1st, That, in coloring, it harmonizes with that record, and, therefore, is related to it at least in point of feeling; 2dly, That, possibly, it was in part the origin of some features in that record, and so far is related to it in logic; 3dly, That, the final assault of opium being of a nature to challenge the attention of medical men, it is important to clear away all doubts and scruples which can gather about the roots of such a malady. Was it opium, or was it opium in combination with something else, that raised these storms?

Some cynical reader will object, that for this last purpose it would have been sufficient to state the fact, without rehearsing *in extenso* the particulars of that case in childhood. But the reader of more kindness (for a surly reader is always a bad critic) will also have more discernment; and he will perceive that it is not for the mere facts that the case is reported, but because these facts move through a wilderness of natural thoughts or feelings: some in the child who suffers; some in the man who reports; but all so far interesting as they relate to solemn objects. Meantime, the objection of the sullen critic reminds me of a scene sometimes beheld at the English lakes. Figure to yourself an energetic tourist, who protests everywhere that he comes only to see the lakes. He has no business whatever; he is not searching for any recreant indorser of a bill, but simply in search of the picturesque. Yet this man adjures every landlord, "by the virtue of his oath," to tell him, and, as he hopes for peace in this world, to tell him truly, which is the *nearest* road to Keswick. Next, he applies to the postilions, — the Westmoreland postilions always fly down hills at full stretch without locking, — but, nevertheless, in the full career of their fiery race, our picturesque man lets down the glasses, pulls up four horses and two postilions, at the risk of six necks and twenty legs, adjuring them to reveal whether they are taking the *shortest* road. Finally, he descries my unworthy self upon the road; and, instantly stopping his flying equipage, he demands of me (as one whom he believes to be a scholar and a man of honor) whether there is not, in the possibility of things, a *shorter* cut to Keswick. Now, the answer which rises to the lips of landlord, two postilions, and myself, is this: "Most excellent stranger, as you come to the lakes simply to see their loveliness, might it not be as well to ask after the most beautiful road, rather than the shortest? Because, if abstract shortness, if τὸ brevity, is your object, then the shortest of all possible tours would seem, with submission, never to have left London." On the same principle, I tell my critic that the whole course of this narrative resembles, and was meant to resemble, a *caduceus* wreathed about with meandering ornaments, or the shaft of a tree's stem hung round and surmounted with some vagrant parasitical plant. The mere medical subject of the opium answers to the dry, withered pole, which shoots all the rings of the flowering plants, and seems to do so by some dexterity of its own; whereas, in fact, the plant and its tendrils have curled round the sullen cylinder by mere luxuriance of *theirs*. Just as in Cheapside, if you look right and left, the streets so narrow, that lead off at right angles, seem quarried and blasted out of some Babylonian brick-kiln; bored, not raised artificially by the builder's hand. But, if you inquire of the worthy men who live in that neighborhood, you will find it unanimously deposed — that not the streets were quarried out of the bricks, but, on the contrary (most ridiculous as it seems), that the bricks have supervened upon the streets.

The streets did not intrude amongst the bricks, but those cursed bricks came to imprison the streets. So, also, the ugly pole — hop-pole, vine-pole, espalier, no matter what — is there only for support. Not the flowers are for the pole, but the pole is for the flowers. Upon the same analogy, view me as one (in the words of a true and most impassioned poet *) "*viridantem floribus hastas*" — making verdant, and gay with the life of flowers, murderous spears and halberts — things that express death in their origin (being made from dead substances that once had lived in forests), things that express ruin in their use. The true object in my "Opium Confessions" is not the naked physiological theme, — on the contrary, *that* is the ugly pole, the murderous spear, the halbert, — but those wandering musical variations upon the theme, —

* Valerius Flaccus.

those parasitical thoughts, feelings, digressions, which climb up with bells and blossoms round about the arid stock; ramble away from it at times with perhaps too rank a luxuriance; but at the same time, by the eternal interest attached to the *subjects* of these digressions, no matter what were the execution, spread a glory over incidents that for themselves would be — less than nothing.

PART I.

THE AFFLICTION OF CHILDHOOD.

It is so painful to a lover of open-hearted sincerity that any indirect traits of vanity should even *seem* to creep into records of profound passion; and yet, on the other hand, it is so impossible, without an unnatural restraint upon the freedom of the narrative, to prevent oblique gleams reaching the reader from such circumstances of luxury or elegance as did really surround my childhood, that on all accounts I think it better to tell him, from the first, with the simplicity of truth, in what order of society my family moved at the time from which this preliminary narrative is dated. Otherwise it would happen that, merely by moving truly and faithfully through the circumstances of this early experience, I could hardly prevent the reader from receiving an impression as of some higher rank than did really belong to my family. My father was a merchant; not in the sense of Scotland, where it means a man who sells groceries in a cellar, but in the English sense, a sense severely exclusive — namely, he was a man engaged in *foreign* commerce, and no other; therefore, in *wholesale* commerce, and no other, — which last circumstance it is important to mention, because it brings him within the benefit of Cicero's condescending distinction* — as one to be despised, certainly, but not too intensely to be despised even by a Roman senator. He — this imperfectly despicable man — died at an early age, and very soon after the incidents here recorded, leaving to his family, then consisting of a wife and six children, an unburthened estate producing exactly £1600 a year. Naturally, therefore, at the date of my narrative, — if narrative it can be called, — he had an income still larger, from the addition of current commercial profits. Now, to any man who is acquainted with commercial life, but, above all, with such life in England, it will readily occur that in an opulent English family of that class, — opulent, though not rich in a mercantile estimate, — the domestic economy is likely to be upon a scale of liberality altogether unknown amongst the corresponding orders in foreign nations. Whether as to the establishment of servants, or as to the provision made for the comfort of all its members, such a household not uncommonly eclipses the scale of living even amongst the poorer classes of our nobility, though the most splendid in Europe — a fact which, since the period of my infancy, I have had many personal opportunities for verifying both in England and in Ireland. From this peculiar anomaly, affecting the domestic economy of merchants, there arises a disturbance upon the general scale of outward signs by which we measure the relations of rank. The equation, so to speak, between one order

*Cicero, in a well-known passage of his *Ethics*, speaks of trade as irredeemably base, if petty; but as not so absolutely felonious, if wholesale. He gives a *real* merchant (one who is such in the English sense) leave to think himself a shade above small beer.

of society and another, which usually travels in the natural line of their comparative expenditure, is here interrupted and defeated, so that one rank would be collected from the name of the occupation, and another rank much higher, from the splendor of the domestic *ménage.* I warn the reader, therefore (or, rather, my explanation has already warned him), that he is not to infer, from any casual gleam of luxury or elegance, a corresponding elevation of rank.

We, the children of the house, stood in fact upon the very happiest tier in the scaffolding of society for all good influences. The prayer of Agar — "Give me neither poverty nor riches" — was realized for us. That blessing had we, being neither too high nor too low: high enough we were to see models of good manners; obscure enough to be left in the sweetest of solitudes. Amply furnished with the nobler benefits of wealth, *extra* means of health, of intellectual culture, and of elegant enjoyment, on the other hand, we knew nothing of its social distinctions. Not depressed by the consciousness of privations too sordid, not tempted into restlessness by the consciousness of privileges too aspiring, we had no motives for shame, we had none for pride. Grateful also to this hour I am, that, amidst luxuries in all things else, we were trained to a Spartan simplicity of diet, — that we fared, in fact, very much less sumptuously than the servants. And if (after the model of the Emperor Marcus Aurelius) I should return thanks to Providence for all the separate blessings of my early situation, these four I would single out as chiefly worthy to be commemorated — that I lived in the country; that I lived in solitude, that my infant feelings were moulded by the gentlest of sisters, not by horrid pugilistic brothers; finally, that I and they were dutiful children, of a pure, holy, and magnificent church.

The earliest incidents in my life which affected me so deeply as to be rememberable at this day were two, and both before I could have completed my second year; namely, a remarkable dream of terrific grandeur about a favorite nurse, which is interesting for a reason to be noticed hereafter; and, secondly, the fact of having connected a profound sense of pathos with the reäppearance, very early in the spring, of some crocuses. This I mention as inexplicable, for such annual resurrections of plants and flowers affect us only as memorials, or suggestions of a higher change, and therefore in connection with the idea of death; but of death I could, at that time, have had no experience whatever.

This, however, I was speedily to acquire. My two eldest sisters — eldest of three *then* living, and also elder than myself — were summoned to an early death. The first who died was Jane, about a year older than myself. She was three and a half, I two and a half, *plus* or *minus* some trifle that I do not recollect. But death was then scarcely intelligible to me, and I could not so properly be said to suffer sorrow as a sad perplexity. There was another death in the house about the same time, namely, of a maternal grandmother; but as she had in a manner come to us for the express purpose of dying in her daughter's society, and from illness had lived perfectly secluded, our nursery party knew her but little, and were certainly more affected by the death (which I witnessed) of a favorite bird, namely, a kingfisher who had been injured by an accident. With my sister Jane's death (though otherwise, as I have said, less sorrowful than unintelligible) there was, however, connected an incident which made a most fearful impression upon myself, deepening my tendencies to thoughtfulness and abstraction beyond what would seem credible for my years. If there was one thing in this world from which, more than from any other, nature had forced me to revolt, it was brutality and violence. Now, a whisper arose in the family that a woman-servant, who by accident was drawn off from her proper duties to attend my sister Jane for a day or two, had on one occasion treated her harshly, if not brutally; and as this ill treatment happened within two days of her death, so that the occasion of it must have been some fretfulness in the poor child caused by her sufferings, naturally there was a sense of awe diffused through the family. I believe the story never reached my mother, and possibly it was exaggerated; but upon me the effect was terrific. I did not often see the person charged with this cruelty; but, when I did, my eyes sought the ground; nor could I have borne to look her in the face — not through anger; and as to vindictive thoughts, how could these lodge in a powerless infant? The feeling which fell upon me was a shuddering awe, as upon a first glimpse of the truth that I was in a world of evil and strife. Though born in a large town, I had passed the whole of my childhood, except for the few earliest weeks, in a rural seclusion. With three innocent little sisters for playmates, sleeping always amongst them, and shut up forever in a silent garden from all knowledge of poverty, or oppression, or outrage, I had not suspected until this moment the true complexion of the world in which myself and my sisters were living. Henceforward the character of my thoughts must have changed greatly; for so *representative* are some acts, that one single case of the class is sufficient to throw open before you the whole theatre of possibilities in that direction. I never heard that the woman, accused of this cruelty, took it at all to heart, even after the event which so immediately succeeded had reflected upon it a more painful emphasis. On the other hand, I knew of a case, and will pause to mention it, where a mere semblance and shadow of such cruelty, under similar circumstances, inflicted the grief of self-reproach through the remainder of life. A boy, interesting in his appearance, as also from his remarkable docility, was attacked, on a cold day of spring, by a complaint of the trachea — not precisely croup, but like it. He was three years old, and had been ill perhaps for four days; but at intervals had been in high spirits, and capable of playing. This sunshine, gleaming through dark clouds, had continued even on the fourth day; and from nine to eleven o'clock at night he had showed more animated pleasure than ever. An old servant, hearing of his illness, had called to see him; and her mode of talking with him had excited all the joyousness of his nature. About midnight, his mother, fancying that his feet felt cold, was muffling them up in flannels; and, as he seemed to resist her a little, she struck lightly on the sole of one foot as a mode of admonishing him to be quiet. He did not repeat his motion; and in less than a minute his mother had him in her arms with his face looking upwards. "What is the meaning," she exclaimed, in sudden affright, "of this strange repose settling upon his features?" She called loudly to a servant in another room; but before the servant could reach her, the child had drawn two inspirations, deep, yet gentle — and had died in his mother's arms! Upon this, the poor afflicted lady made the discovery that those struggles, which she had supposed to be expressions of resistance to herself, were the struggles of departing life. It followed, or seemed to follow, that with these final struggles had blended an expression, on *her* part, of displeasure. Doubtless the child had not distinctly perceived it; but the mother could never look back to that incident without self-reproach. And seven years after, when her own death happened, no progress had been made in reconciling her thoughts to that which only the depth of love could have viewed as an offence.

So passed away from earth one out of those sisters that made up my nursery playmates; and so did my acquaintance (if such it could be called) commence with mortality. Yet, in fact, I knew little more of mortality than that Jane had disappeared. She had gone away; but, perhaps, she would come back. Happy interval of heaven-born ignorance! Gracious immunity of infancy from sorrow disproportioned to its strength! I was sad for Jane's absence. But still in my heart I trusted that she would come again. Summer and winter came again — crocuses and roses; why not little Jane?

Thus easily was healed, then, the first wound in my infant heart. Not so the second. For thou, dear, noble Elizabeth, around whose ample brow, as often as thy sweet countenance rises upon the darkness, I fancy a *tiara* of light or a gleaming *aureola* in token of thy premature intellectual grandeur, — thou whose head, for its superb developments, was the astonishment of science,* — thou next, but after an interval of happy years, thou also wert summoned away from our nursery; and the night which, for me, gathered upon that event, ran after my steps far into life; and perhaps at this day I resemble little for good or for ill that which else I should have been. Pillar of fire that didst go before me to guide and to quicken, — pillar of darkness, when thy countenance was turned away to God,

* "*The astonishment of science.*" — Her medical attendants were Dr. Percival, a well-known literary physician, who had been a correspondent of Condorcet, D'Alembert, &c., and Mr. Charles White, a very distinguished surgeon. It was he who pronounced her head to be the finest in its structure and development of any that he had ever seen, — an assertion which, to my own knowledge, he repeated in after years, and with enthusiasm. That he had some acquaintance with the subject may be presumed from this, that he wrote and published a work on the human skull, supported by many measurements which he had made of heads selected from all varieties of the human species. Meantime, as I would be loath that any trait of what might seem vanity should creep into this record, I will candidly admit that she died of hydrocephalus; and it has been often supposed that the premature expansion of the intellect in cases of that class is altogether morbid, — forced on, in fact, by the mere stimulation of the disease. I would, however, suggest, as a possibility, the very inverse order of relation between the disease and the intellectual manifestations. Not the disease may always have caused the preternatural growth of the intellect; but, on the contrary, this growth coming on spontaneously, and outrunning the capacities of the physical structure, may have caused the disease.

that didst too truly shed the shadow of death over my young heart, — in what scales should I weigh thee? Was the blessing greater from thy heavenly presence, or the blight which followed thy departure? Can a man weigh off and value the glories of dawn against the darkness of hurricane? Or, if he could, how is it that, when a memorable love has been followed by a memorable bereavement, even suppose that God would replace the sufferer in a point of time anterior to the entire experience, and offer to cancel the woe, but so that the sweet face which had caused the woe should also be obliterated, vehemently would every man shrink from the exchange! In the *Paradise Lost*, this strong instinct of man, to prefer the heavenly, mixed and polluted with the earthly, to a level experience offering neither one nor the other, is divinely commemorated. What words of pathos are in that speech of Adam's — "If God should make another Eve," &c.; that is, if God should replace him in his primitive state, and should condescend to bring again a second Eve, one that would listen to no temptation, still that original partner of his earliest solitude —

"Creature in whom excelled
Whatever can to sight or thought be formed,
Holy, divine, good, amiable, or sweet" —

even now, when she appeared in league with an eternity of woe, and ministering to his ruin, could not be displaced for him by any better or happier Eve. "Loss of thee!" he exclaims, in this anguish of trial —

"Loss of thee
Would never from my heart; no, no, I feel
The link of nature draw me; flesh of flesh,

Bone of my bone thou art; and from thy state
Mine never shall be parted, bliss or woe." *

But what was it that drew my heart, by gravitation so strong, to my sister? Could a child, little above six years of age, place any special value upon her intellectual forwardness? Serene and capacious as her mind appeared to me upon after review, was *that* a charm for stealing away the heart of an infant? O, no! I think of it *now* with interest, because it lends, in a stranger's ear, some justification to the excess of my fondness. But then it was lost upon me; or, if not lost, was but dimly perceived. Hadst thou been an idiot, my sister, not the less I must have loved thee, having that capacious heart overflowing, even as mine overflowed, with tenderness, and stung, even as mine was stung, by the necessity of being loved. This it was which crowned thee with beauty —

"Love, the holy sense,
Best gift of God, in thee was most intense."

---

* Amongst the oversights in the *Paradise Lost*, some of which have not yet been perceived, it is certainly *one* — that, by placing n such overpowering light of pathos the sublime sacrifice of Adam to his love for his frail companion, he has too much lowered the guilt of his disobedience to God. All that Milton can say afterwards does not, and cannot, obscure the beauty of that action; reviewing it calmly, we condemn, but taking the impassioned station of Adam at the moment of temptation, we approve in our hearts. This was certainly an oversight; but it was one very difficult to redress. I remember, amongst the many exquisite thoughts of John Paul (Richter), one which strikes me as particularly touching, upon this subject. He suggests, not as any grave theological comment, but as the wandering fancy of a poetic heart, that, had Adam conquered the anguish of separation as a pure sacrifice of obedience to God, his reward would have been the pardon and reconciliation of Eve, together with her restoration to innocence.

That lamp lighted in Paradise was kindled for me which shone so steadily in thee; and never but to thee only, never again since thy departure, *durst* I utter the feelings which possessed me. For I was the shyest of children; and a natural sense of personal dignity held me back at all stages of life, from exposing the least ray of feelings which I was not encouraged *wholly* to reveal.

It would be painful, and it is needless, to pursue the course of that sickness which carried off my leader and companion. She (according to my recollection at this moment) was just as much above eight years as I above six. And perhaps this natural precedency of authority in judgment, and the tender humility with which she declined to assert it, had been amongst the fascinations of her presence. It was upon a Sunday evening, or so people fancied, that the spark of fatal fire fell upon that train of predispositions to a brain complaint which had hitherto slumbered within her. She had been permitted to drink tea at the house of a laboring man, the father of an old female servant. The sun had set when she returned in the company of this servant through meadows reeking with exhalations after a fervent day. From that time she sickened. Happily, a child in such circumstances feels no anxieties. Looking upon medical men as people whose natural commission it is to heal diseases, since it is their natural function to profess it, knowing them only as *ex officio* privileged to make war upon pain and sickness, I never had a misgiving about the result. I grieved, indeed, that my sister should lie in bed, I grieved still more sometimes to hear her moan. But all this appeared to me no more than a night of trouble, on which the dawn would soon arise. O! moment of darkness and delirium, when a nurse awakened me from that delusion, and launched God's thunderbolt at my heart in the assurance that my sister *must* die. Rightly it is said of utter, utter misery, that it "cannot be *remembered*."* Itself, as a remarkable thing, is swallowed up in its own chaos. Mere anarchy and confusion of mind fell upon me. Deaf and blind I was, as I reeled under the revelation. I wish not to recall the circumstances of that time, when *my* agony was at its height, and hers in another sense was approaching. Enough to say, that all was soon over; and the morning of that day had at last arrived which looked down upon her innocent face, sleeping the sleep from which there is no awaking, and upon me sorrowing the sorrow for which there is no consolation.

On the day after my sister's death, whilst the sweet temple of her brain was yet unviolated by human scrutiny, I formed my own scheme for seeing her once more. Not for the world would I have made this known, nor have suffered a witness to accompany me. I had never heard of feelings that take the name of "sentimental," nor dreamed of such a possibility. But grief even in a child hates the light, and shrinks from human eyes. The house was large; there were two staircases; and by one of these I knew that about noon, when all would be quiet, I could steal up into her chamber. I imagine that it was exactly high noon

---

* "I stood in unimaginable trance
And agony, which cannot be remembered."
Speech of Alhadra, in Coleridge's Remorse.

when I reached the chamber door; it was locked but the key was not taken away. Entering, I closed the door so softly, that, although it opened upon a hall which ascended through all the stories, no echo ran along the silent walls. Then turning round, I sought my sister's face. But the bed had been moved, and the back was now turned. Nothing met my eyes but one large window wide open, through which the sun of midsummer at noonday was showering down torrents of splendor. The weather was dry, the sky was cloudless, the blue depths seemed the express types of infinity; and it was not possible for eye to behold or for heart to conceive any symbols more pathetic of life and the glory of life. "The gay will laugh when thou art gone" etc. Bry

Let me pause for one instant in approaching a remembrance so affecting and revolutionary for my own mind, and one which (if any earthly remembrance) will survive for me in the hour of death, — to remind some readers, and to inform others, that in the original *Opium Confessions* I endeavored to explain the reason* why death, *cæteris paribus*, is more profoundly affecting in summer than in other parts of the year; so far, at least, as it is liable to any modification at all from accidents of scenery or season. The reason, as I there suggested, lies in the antagonism between the tropical redundancy of life in summer and the dark sterilities of the grave. The summer we see, the grave we haunt with our thoughts; the glory is around us, the darkness is within us. And the two coming into collision, each exalts the other into stronger relief.

* Some readers will question the *fact*, and seek no reason. Bu did they ever suffer grief at *any* season of the year?

But in my case there was even a subtler reason why the summer had this intense power of vivifying the spectacle or the thoughts of death. And, recollecting it, often I have been struck with the important truth, that far more of our deepest thoughts and feelings pass to us through perplexed combinations of *concrete* objects, pass to us as *involutes* (if I may coin that word) in compound experiences incapable of being disentangled, than ever reach us *directly*, and in their own abstract shapes. It had happened that amongst our nursery collection of books was the Bible illustrated with many pictures. And in long dark evenings, as my three sisters with myself sate by the firelight round the *guard* of our nursery, no book was so much in request amongst us. It ruled us and swayed us as mysteriously as music. One young nurse, whom we all loved, before any candle was lighted, would often strain her eye to read it for us; and, sometimes, according to her simple powers, would endeavor to explain what we found obscure. We, the children, were all constitutionally touched with pensiveness; the fitful gloom and sudden lambencies of the room by firelight suited our evening state of feelings; and they suited, also, the divine revelations of power and mysterious beauty which awed us. Above all, the story of a just man — man and yet *not* man, real above all things, and yet shadowy above all things, who had suffered the passion of death in Palestine — slept upon our minds like early dawn upon the waters The nurse knew and explained to us the chief differences in oriental climates; and all these differences (as it happens) express themselves in the great varieties of summer. The cloudless sunlights of Syria — those seemed to argue everlasting summer; the disciples plucking the ears of corn — that *must* be summer; but, above all, the very name of Palm Sunday (a festival in the English church) troubled me like an anthem. "Sunday!" what was *that?* That was the day of peace which masked another peace deeper than the heart of man can comprehend. "Palms!" what were they? *That* was an equivocal word; palms, in the sense of trophies, expressed the pomps of life; palms, as a product of nature, expressed the pomps of summer. Yet still even this explanation does not suffice; it was not merely by the peace and by the summer, by the deep sound of rest below all rest, and of ascending glory, that I had been haunted. It was also because Jerusalem stood near to those deep images both in time and in place. The great event of Jerusalem was at hand when Palm Sunday came; and the scene of that Sunday was near in place to Jerusalem. Yet what then was Jerusalem? Did I fancy it to be the *omphalos* (navel) of the earth? That pretension had once been made for Jerusalem, and once for Delphi; and both pretensions had become ridiculous, as the figure of the planet became known. Yes; but if not of the earth, for earth's tenant, Jerusalem was the *omphalos* of mortality. Yet how? there, on the contrary, it was, as we infants understood, that mortality had been trampled under foot. True; but, for that very reason, there it was that mortality had opened its very gloomiest crater. There it was, indeed that the human had risen on wings from the grave but, for that reason, there also it was that the divine had been swallowed up by the abyss; the lesser star could not rise, before the greater would submit to eclipse. Summer, therefore, had connected itself with death, not merely as a mode of antagonism, but also through intricate relations to scriptural scenery and events.

Out of this digression, which was almost necessary for the purpose of showing how inextricably my feelings and images of death were entangled with those of summer, I return to the bed-chamber of my sister. From the gorgeous sunlight I turned round to the corpse. There lay the sweet childish figure; there the angel face; and, as people usually fancy, it was said in the house that no features had suffered any change. Had they not? The forehead, indeed, — the serene and noble forehead,—*that* might be the same; but the frozen eyelids, the darkness that seemed to steal from beneath them, the marble lips, the stiffening hands, laid palm to palm, as if repeating the supplications of closing anguish, — could these be mistaken for life? Had it been so, wherefore did I not spring to those heavenly lips with tears and never-ending kisses? But so it was *not*. I stood checked for a moment; awe, not fear, fell upon me; and, whilst I stood, a solemn wind began to blow, — the most mournful that ear ever heard. Mournful! that is saying nothing. It was a wind that had swept the fields of mortality for a hundred centuries. Many times since, upon a summer day, when the sun is about the hottest, I have remarked the same wind arising and uttering the same hollow, solemn, Memnonian, but saintly swell: it is in this world the one sole *audible* symbol of eternity. And three times in my life I have happened to hear the same sound in the same circumstances, namely, when standing between an open window and a dead body on a summer day.

Instantly, when my ear caught this vast Æolian intonation, when my eye filled with the golden fulness of life, the pomps and glory of the heavens outside, and turning when it settled upon the frost which overspread my sister's face, instantly a trance fell upon me. A vault seemed to open in the zenith of the far blue sky, a shaft which ran up forever. I, in spirit, rose as if on billows that also ran up the shaft forever; and the billows seemed to pursue the throne of God; but *that* also ran before us and fled away continually. The flight and the pursuit seemed to go on for ever and ever. Frost, gathering frost, some Sarsar wind of death, seemed to repel me; I slept — for how long I cannot say: slowly I recovered my self-possession, and found myself standing, as before, close to my sister's bed.

O* flight of the solitary child to the solitary God — flight from the ruined corpse to the throne that could not be ruined! — how rich wert thou in truth for after years! Rapture of grief that, being too mighty for a child to sustain, foundest a happy oblivion in a heaven-born dream, and within that sleep didst conceal a dream, whose meaning, in after years, when slowly I deciphered, suddenly there flashed upon me new light; and even by the grief of a child, as I will show you, reader, hereafter, were confounded the falsehoods of philosophers.†

---

* Φυγη μονου προς μονον. — *Plotinus.*

† The thoughts referred to will be given in final notes; as at this point they seemed too much to interrupt the course of the narrative.

In the *Opium Confessions* I touched a little upon the extraordinary power connected with opium (after long use) of amplifying the dimensions of time. Space, also, it amplifies by degrees that are sometimes terrific. But time it is upon which the exalting and multiplying power of opium chiefly spends its operation. Time becomes infinitely elastic, stretching out to such immeasurable and vanishing termini, that it seems ridiculous to compute the sense of it, on waking, by expressions commensurate to human life. As in starry fields one computes by diameters of the earth's orbit, or of Jupiter's, so, in valuing the *virtual* time lived during some dreams, the measurement by generations is ridiculous — by millenia is ridiculous; by æons, I should say, if æons were more determinate, would be also ridiculous. On this single occasion, however, in my life, the very inverse phenomenon occurred. But why speak of it in connection with opium? Could a child of six years old have been under that influence? No, but simply because it so exactly reversed the operation of opium. Instead of a short interval expanding into a vast one, upon this occasion a long one had contracted into a minute. I have reason to believe that a *very* long one had elapsed during this wandering or suspension of my perfect mind. When I returned to myself, there was a foot (or I fancied so) on the stairs. I was alarmed; for I believed that, if anybody should detect me, means would be taken to prevent my coming again. Hastily, therefore, I kissed the lips that I should kiss no more, and slunk like a guilty thing with stealthy steps from the room. Thus perished the vision, loveliest amongst all the shows which earth has revealed to me; thus mutilated was the parting which should have lasted forever; thus tainted with fear was the farewell sacred to love and grief, to perfect love and perfect grief.

O, Ahasuerus, everlasting Jew!* fable or not a fable, thou when first starting on thy endless pilgrimage of woe, — thou when first flying through the gates of Jerusalem, and vainly yearning to leave the pursuing curse behind thee,— couldst not more certainly have read thy doom of sorrow in the misgivings of thy troubled brain than I when passing forever from my sister's room. The worm was at my heart; and, confining myself to that state of life, I may say, the worm that could not die. For if, when standing upon the threshold of manhood, I had ceased to feel its perpetual gnawings, *that* was because a vast expansion of intellect, it was because new hopes, new necessities, and the frenzy of youthful blood, had translated me into a new creature. Man is doubtless *one* by some subtle *nexus* that we cannot perceive, extending from the new-born infant to the superannuated dotard: but as regards many affections and passions incident to his nature at different stages, he is *not* one; the unity of man in this respect is coëxtensive only with the particular stage to which the passion belongs. Some passions, as that of sexual love, are celestial by one half of their origin, animal and earthly by the other half. These will not survive their own appropriate stage. But love, which is *altogether* holy, like that between two children, will

* "Everlasting Jew!" — *der ewige Jude* — which is the common German expression for *The Wandering Jew*, and sublimer even than our own.

revisit undoubtedly by glimpses the silence and the darkness of old age: and I repeat my belief — that, unless bodily torment should forbid it, that final experience in my sister's bed-room, or some other in which her innocence was concerned, will rise again for me, to illuminate the hour of death.

On the day following this which I have recorded, came a body of medical men to examine the brain, and the particular nature of the complaint, for in some of its symptoms it had shown perplexing anomalies. Such is the sanctity of death, and especially of death alighting on an innocent child, that even gossiping people do not gossip on such a subject. Consequently, I knew nothing of the purpose which drew together these surgeons, nor suspected anything of the cruel changes which might have been wrought in my sister's head. Long after this, I saw a similar case; I surveyed the corpse (it was that of a beautiful boy, eighteen years old, who had died of the same complaint) one hour *after* the surgeons had laid the skull in ruins; but the dishonors of this scrutiny were hidden by bandages, and had not disturbed the repose of the countenance. So it might have been here; but, if it were *not* so, then I was happy in being spared the shock, from having that marble image of peace, icy and rigid as it was, unsettled by disfiguring images. Some hours after the strangers had withdrawn, I crept again to the room; but the door was now locked, the key was taken away — and I was shut out forever.

Then came the funeral. I, as a point of decorum, was carried thither. I was put into a carriage with some gentlemen whom I did not know. They were kind to me; but naturally they talked of things disconnected with the occasion, and their conversation was a torment. At the church, I was told to hold a white handkerchief to my eyes. Empty hypocrisy! What need had *he* of masques or mockeries, whose heart died within him at every word that was uttered? During that part of the service which passed within the church, I made an effort to attend; but I sank back continually into my own solitary darkness, and I heard little consciously, except some fugitive strains from the sublime chapter of St. Paul, which in England is always read at burials. And here I notice a profound error of our present illustrious laureate. When I heard those dreadful words, — for dreadful they were to me, — "It is sown in corruption, it is raised in incorruption; it is sown in dishonor, it is raised in glory;" such was the recoil of my feelings, that I could even have shrieked out a protesting — "O, no, no!" if I had not been restrained by the publicity of the occasion. In after years, reflecting upon this revolt of my feelings, which, being the voice of nature in a child, must be as true as any mere *opinion* of a child might probably be false, I saw, at once, the unsoundness of a passage in *The Excursion.* The book is not here, but the substance I remember perfectly. Mr. Wordsworth argues, that if it were not for the unsteady faith which people fix upon the beatific condition after death of those whom they deplore, nobody could be found so selfish as even secretly to wish for the restoration to earth of a beloved object. A mother, for instance, could never dream of yearning for her child and secretly calling it back by her silent aspirations from the arms of God, if she were but reconciled to the belief that really it *was* in those arms. But this I utterly deny. To take my own case, when I heard those dreadful words of St. Paul applied to my sister, namely, that she should be raised a spiritual body, nobody can suppose that selfishness, or any other feeling than that of agonizing love, caused the rebellion of my heart against them. I knew already that she was to come again in beauty and power. I did not now learn this for the first time. And that thought, doubtless, made my sorrow sublimer; but also it made it deeper. For here lay the sting of it, namely, in the fatal words — "We shall be *changed*." How was the unity of my interest in her to be preserved, if she were to be altered, and no longer to reflect in her sweet countenance the traces that were sculptured on my heart? Let a magician ask any woman whether she will permit him to improve her child, to raise it even from deformity to perfect beauty, if that must be done at the cost of its identity, and there is no loving mother but would reject his proposal with horror. Or, to take a case that has actually happened, if a mother were robbed of her child, at two years old, by gypsies, and the same child were restored to her at twenty, a fine young man, but divided by a sleep as it were of death from all remembrances that could restore the broken links of their once tender connection, — would she not feel her grief unhealed, and her heart defrauded? Undoubtedly she would. All of us ask not of God for a better thing than that we have lost; we ask for the same, even with its faults and its frailties. It is true that the sorrowing person will also be changed eventually, but that must be by death. And a prospect so remote as that, and so alien from our present nature, cannot console us in an affliction which is not remote, but present — which is not spiritual, but human.

Lastly came the magnificent service which the English Church performs at the side of the grave. There is exposed once again, and for the last time, the coffin. All eyes survey the record of name, of sex, of age, and the day of departure from earth, — records how useless! and dropped into darkness as if messages addressed to worms. Almost at the very last comes the symbolic ritual, tearing and shattering the heart with volleying discharges, peal after peal, from the final artillery of woe. The coffin is lowered into its home; it has disappeared from the eye. The sacristan stands ready, with his shovel of earth and stones. The priest's voice is heard once more, — *earth to earth*, and the dread rattle ascends from the lid of the coffin; *ashes to ashes*, and again the killing sound is heard; *dust to dust*, and the farewell volley announces that the grave — the coffin — the face are sealed up for ever and ever.

O, grief! thou art classed amongst the depressing passions. And true it is, that thou humblest to the dust, but also thou exaltest to the clouds. Thou shakest as with ague, but also thou steadiest like frost. Thou sickenest the heart, but also thou healest its infirmities. Among the very foremost of mine was morbid sensibility to shame. And, ten years afterwards, I used to reproach myself with this infirmity, by supposing the case, that, if it were thrown upon me to seek aid for a perishing fellow-creature, and that I could obtain that aid only by facing a vast company of critical or sneering faces, I might, perhaps, shrink basely from the duty It is true, that no such case had ever actually occurred, so that it was a mere romance of casuistry to tax myself with cowardice so shocking. But, to feel a doubt, was to feel condemnation; and the crime which *might* have been was in my eyes the crime which *had* been. Now, however, all was changed; and for anything which regarded my sister's memory, in one hour I received a new heart. Once in Westmoreland I saw a case resembling it. I saw a ewe suddenly put off and abjure her own nature, in a service of love, — yes, slough it as completely as ever serpent sloughed his skin. Her lamb had fallen into a deep trench, from which all escape was hopeless, without the aid of man. And to a man she advanced boldly, bleating clamorously, until he followed her and rescued her beloved. Not less was the change in myself. Fifty thousand sneering faces would not have troubled me in any office of tenderness to my sister's memory. Ten legions would not have repelled me from seeking her, if there was a chance that she could be found. Mockery! it was lost upon me. Laugh at me, as one or two people did! I valued not their laughter. And when I was told insultingly to cease "my girlish tears," that word "*girlish*" had no sting for me, except as a verbal echo to the one eternal thought of my heart, — that a girl was the sweetest thing I, in my short life, had known, — that a girl it was who had crowned the earth with beauty, and had opened to my thirst fountains of pure celestial love, from which, in this world, I was to drink no more.

Interesting it is to observe how certainly all deep feelings agree in this, that they seek for solitude, and are nursed by solitude. Deep grief, deep love, how naturally do these ally themselves with religious feeling; and all three — love, grief, religion — are haunters of solitary places. Love, grief, the passion of reverie, or the mystery of devotion, — what were these, without solitude? All day long, when it was not impossible for me to do so, I sought the most silent and sequestered nooks in the grounds about the house, or in the neighboring fields. The awful stillness occasionally of summer noons, when no winds were abroad, the appealing silence of gray or misty afternoons, — these were fascinations as of witchcraft. Into the woods or the desert air I gazed, as if some comfort lay hid in *them*. I wearied the heavens with my inquest of beseeching looks. I tormented the blue depths with obstinate scrutiny, sweeping them with my eyes, and searching them forever after one angelic face that might, perhaps, have permission to reveal itself for a moment. The faculty of shaping images in the distance out of slight elements, and grouping them after the yearnings of the heart, aided by a slight defect in my eyes, grew upon me at this time. And I recall at the present moment one instance of that sort, which may show how merely shadows, or a gleam of brightness, or nothing at all, could furnish a sufficient basis for this creative faculty. On Sunday mornings I was always taken to church: it was a church on the old and natural model of England, having aisles, galleries, organs, all things ancient and venerable, and the proportions majestic. Here, whilst the congregation knelt through the long litany, as often as we came to that passage, so beautiful amongst many that are so, where God is supplicated on behalf of "all sick persons and young children," and that he would "show his pity upon all prisoners and captives," — I wept in secret, and raising my streaming eyes to the windows of the galleries, saw, on days when the sun was shining, a spectacle as affecting as ever prophet can have beheld. The sides of the windows were rich with storied glass; through the deep purples and crimsons streamed the golden light; emblazonries of heavenly illumination mingling with the earthly emblazonries of what is grandest in man. There were the apostles that had trampled upon earth, and the glories of earth, out of celestial love to man. There were the martyrs that had borne witness to the truth through flames, through torments, and through armies of fierce insulting faces. There were the saints who, under intolerable pangs, had glorified God by meek submission to his will. And all the time, whilst this tumult of sublime memorials held on as the deep chords from an accompaniment in the bass, I saw through the wide central field of the window, where the glass was uncolored, white fleecy clouds sailing over the azure depths of the sky; were it but a fragment or a hint of such a cloud, immediately under the flash of my sorrow-haunted eye, it grew and shaped itself into visions of beds with white lawny curtains; and in the beds lay sick children, dying children, that were tossing in anguish, and weeping clamorously for death. God, for some mysterious reason, could not suddenly release them from their pain; but he suffered the beds, as it seemed, to rise slowly through the clouds; slowly the beds ascended into the chambers of the air; slowly, also, his arms descended from the heavens, that he and his young children, whom in Judea, once and forever, he had blessed, though they *must* pass slowly through the dreadful chasm of separation, might yet meet the sooner. These visions were self-sustained. These visions needed not that any sound should speak to me, or music mould my feelings. The hint from the litany, the fragment from the clouds, — those and the storied windows were sufficient. But not the less the blare of the tumultuous organ wrought its own separate creations. And oftentimes in anthems, when the mighty instrument threw its vast columns of sound, fierce yet melodious, over the voices of the choir, — when it rose high in arches, as might seem, surmounting and overriding the strife of the vocal parts, and gathering by strong coërcion the total storm into unity, — sometimes I seemed to walk triumphantly upon those clouds which so recently I had looked up to as mementos of prostrate sorrow, and even as ministers of sorrow in its creations; yes, sometimes under the transfigurations of music I felt* of grief itself as a fiery chariot for mounting victoriously above the causes of grief.

* "*I felt*" — The reader must not forget, in reading this and other passages, that, though a child's feelings are spoken of, it is not the child who speaks. *I* decipher what the child only felt in cipher. And so far is this distinction or this explanation from pointing to anything metaphysical or doubtful, that a man must be

a point so often to the feelings, the ideas, or the ceremonies of religion, because there never yet was profound grief nor profound philosophy which did not inosculate at many points with profound religion. But I request the reader to understand, that of all things I was not, and could not have been, a child trained to *talk* of religion, least of all to talk of it controversially or polemically. Dreadful is the picture, which in books we sometimes find, of children discussing the doctrines of Christianity, and even teaching their seniors the boundaries and distinctions between doctrine and doctrine. And it has often struck me with amazement, that the two things which God made most beautiful among his works, namely, infancy and pure religion, should, by the folly of man (in yoking them together on erroneous principles), neutralize each other's beauty, or even form a combination positively hateful. The religion becomes nonsense, and the child becomes a hypocrite. The religion is transfigured into cant, and the innocent child into a dissembling liar.*

grossly unobservant who is not aware of what I am here noticing, not as a peculiarity of this child or that, but as a necessity of all children. Whatsoever in a man's mind blossoms and expands to his own consciousness in mature life, must have preëxisted in germ during his infancy. I, for instance, did not, as a child, *consciously* read in my own deep feelings these ideas. No, not at all; nor was it possible for a child to do so. I, the child, had the feelings; I, the man, decipher them. In the child lay the handwriting mysterious to *him;* in me, the interpretation and the comment.

* I except, however, one case, — the case of a child dying of an organic disorder, so, therefore, as to die slowly, and aware of its own condition. Because such a child is solemnized, and sometimes, in a partial sense, inspired, — inspired by the depth of its sufferings, and by the awfulness of its prospect. Such a child, having put off the earthly mind in many things, may naturally have put off the

God, be assured, takes care for the religion of children, wheresoever his Christianity exists. Wheresoever there is a national church established, to which a child sees his friends resorting, — wheresoever he beholds all whom he honors periodically prostrate before those illimitable heavens which fill to overflowing his young adoring heart, — wheresoever he sees the sleep of death falling at intervals upon men and women whom he knows, depth as confounding to the plummet of his mind as those heavens ascend beyond his power to pursue, — *there* take you no thought for the religion of a child, any more than for the lilies how they shall be arrayed, or for the ravens how they shall feed their young.

God speaks to children, also, in dreams, and by the oracles that lurk in darkness. But in solitude, above all things, when made vocal by the truths and services of a national church, God holds "communion undisturbed" with children. Solitude, though silent as light, is, like light, the mightiest of agencies; for solitude is essential to man. All men come into this world *alone;* all leave it *alone.* Even a little child has a dread, whispering consciousness, that if he should be summoned to travel into God's presence, no gentle nurse will be allowed to lead him by the hand, nor mother to carry him in her arms, nor little sister to share his trepidations. King and priest, warrior and maiden,

childish mind in all things. I thereby, speaking for myself only, acknowledge to have read with emotion a record of a little girl, who, knowing herself for months to be amongst the elect of death, became anxious, even to sickness of heart, for what she called the *conversion* of her father. Her filial duty and reverence had been swallowed up in filial love.

philosopher and child, all must walk those mighty galleries alone. The solitude, therefore, which in this world appals or fascinates a child's heart, is but the echo of a far deeper solitude through which already he has passed, and of another solitude, deeper still, through which he *has* to pass: reflex of one solitude — prefiguration of another.

O, burthen of solitude, that cleavest to man through every stage of his being! in his birth, which *has* been, — in his life, which *is*, — in his death, which *shall* be, — mighty and essential solitude! that wast, and art, and art to be; — thou broodest, like the spirit of God moving upon the surface of the deeps, over every heart that sleeps in the nurseries of Christendom. Like the vast laboratory of the air, which, seeming to be nothing, or less than the shadow of a shade, hides within itself the principles of all things, solitude for the child is the Agrippa's mirror of the unseen universe. Deep is the solitude in life of millions upon millions, who, with hearts welling forth love, have none to love them. Deep is the solitude of those who, with secret griefs, have none to pity them. Deep is the solitude of those who, fighting with doubts or darkness, have none to counsel them. But deeper than the deepest of these solitudes is that which broods over childhood, bringing before it, at intervals, the final solitude which watches for it, and is waiting for it within the gates of death. Reader, I tell you a truth, and hereafter I will convince you of this truth, that for a Grecian child solitude was nothing, but for a Christian child it has become the power of God and the mystery of God. O, mighty and essential solitude, that wast, and art, and art to be! thou kindling under the torch of Christian revelations, art now transfigured forever, and hast passed from a blank negation into a secret hieroglyphic from God, shadowing in the hearts of infancy the very dimmest of his truths!

"*But you forget her*," says the cynic; "*you happened one day to forget this sister of yours.*" Why not? To cite the beautiful words of Wallenstein, —

> "What pang
> Is permanent with man? From the highest,
> As from the vilest thing of every day,
> He learns to wean himself. For the strong hours
> Conquer him." *

Yes, *there* lies the fountain of human oblivions. It is Time, the great conqueror, it is the "strong hours" whose batteries storm every passion of men. For, in the fine expression of Schiller, "*Was verschmerzte nicht der mensch?*" What sorrow is in man that will not finally fret itself to sleep? Conquering, at last, gates of brass, or pyramids of granite, why should it be a marvel to us, or a triumph to Time, that he is able to conquer a frail human heart?

However, for this once, my cynic must submit to be told that he is wrong. Doubtless, it is presumption in me to suggest that his sneers can ever go awry, any more than the shafts of Apollo. But still, however impossible such a thing is, in this one case it happens that they *have*. And when it happens that they do not, I will tell you, reader, why, in my opinion, it is; and you will see that it warrants no exultation in the

* *Death of Wallenstein*, Act v. Scene 1 (Coleridge's Translation), relating to his remembrances of the younger Piccolomini.

cynic. Repeatedly I have heard a mother reproaching herself when the birth-day revolved of the little daughter whom so suddenly she had lost, with her own insensibility, that could so soon need a remembrancer of the day. But, besides that the majority of people in this world (as being people called to labor) have no time left for cherishing grief by solitude and meditation, always it is proper to ask whether the memory of the lost person were chiefly dependent upon a visual image. No death is usually half so affecting as the death of a young child from two to five years old.

But yet, for the same reason which makes the grief more exquisite, generally for such a loss it is likely to be more perishable. Wherever the image, visually or audibly, of the lost person, is more essential to the life of the grief, there the grief will be more transitory.

Faces begin soon (in Shakspeare's fine expression) to "dislimn;" features fluctuate; combinations of feature unsettle. Even the expression becomes a mere idea that you can describe to another, but not an image that you can reproduce for yourself. Therefore it is that the faces of infants, though they are divine as flowers in a savanna of Texas, or as the carolling of birds in a forest, are, like flowers in Texas, and the carolling of birds in a forest, soon overtaken by the pursuing darkness that swallows up all things human. All glories of flesh vanish; and this, the glory of infantine beauty seen in the mirror of the memory, soonest of all. But when the departed persons worked upon yourself by powers that were intellectual and moral, — powers *in* the flesh, though not *of* the flesh, — the memorials in your own heart become more steadfast, if less affecting at the first. Now, in my sister were combined for me both graces, — the graces of childhood, and the graces of expanding thought. Besides that, as regards merely the *personal* image, always the smooth rotundity of baby features must vanish sooner, as being less individual than the features in a child of eight, touched with a pensive tenderness, and exalted into a characteristic expression by a premature intellect.

Rarely do things perish from my memory that are worth remembering. Rubbish dies instantly. Hence it happens that passages in Latin or English poets, which I never could have read but once (and *that* thirty years ago), often begin to blossom anew when I am lying awake, unable to sleep. I become a distinguished compositor in the darkness: and, with my aërial composing-stick, sometimes I "set up" half a page of verses, that would be found tolerably correct if collated with the volume that I never had in my hand but once. I mention this in no spirit of boasting. Far from it: for, on the contrary, among my mortifications have been compliments to my memory, when, in fact, any compliment that I had merited was due to the higher faculty of an electric aptitude for seizing analogies, and by means of those aërial pontoons passing over like lightning from one topic to another. Still it is a fact that this pertinacious life of memory for things that simply touch the ear, without touching the consciousness, does, in fact, beset me. Said but once, said but softly, not marked at all, words revive before me in darkness and solitude; and they arrange themselves gradually into sentences, but through an effort sometimes of a distressing kind, to which I am in a manner forced to become a party. This being so, it was no great instance of that power, that three separate passages in the funeral service, all of which but one had escaped my notice at the time, and even that one as to the part I am going to mention, but all of which must have struck on my ear, restored themselves perfectly when I was lying awake in bed; and though struck by their beauty, I was also incensed by what seemed to me the harsh sentiment expressed in two of these passages. I will cite all the three in an abbreviated form, both for my immediate purpose, and for the indirect purpose of giving to those unacquainted with the English funeral service some specimens of its beauty.

The first passage was this: "Forasmuch as it hath pleased Almighty God, of his great mercy, to take unto himself the soul of our dear sister here departed, we therefore commit her body to the ground, earth to earth, ashes to ashes, dust to dust, in sure and certain hope of the resurrection to eternal life." * * *

I pause to remark that a sublime effect arises at this point through a sudden rapturous interpolation from the Apocalypse, which, according to the rubric, "shall be said or sung;" but always let it be sung, and by the full choir:

"I heard a voice from heaven saying unto me, Write from henceforth blessed are the dead which die in the Lord; even so saith the Spirit; for they rest from their labors."

The second passage, almost immediately succeeding to this awful burst of heavenly trumpets, and the [illegible] which more particularly offended me, though otherwise even then, in my seventh year, I could not but be touched by its beauty, was this:—"Almighty God, with whom do live the spirits of them that depart hence in the Lord, and with whom the souls of the faithful, after they are delivered from the burden of the flesh, are in joy and felicity; we give thee hearty thanks that it hath pleased thee to deliver this our sister out of the miseries of this sinful world; beseeching thee, that it may please thee of thy gracious goodness shortly to accomplish the number of thine elect, and to hasten thy kingdom." * * * *

In what world was I living when a man (calling himself a man of God) could stand up publicly and give God "hearty thanks" that he had taken away my sister? But, young child, understand—taken her away from the miseries of this sinful world. O yes! I hear what you say; I understand *that;* but that makes no difference at all. She being gone, this world doubtless (as you say) is a world of unhappiness. But for me *ubi Cæsar, ibi Roma*—where my sister was, there was paradise; no matter whether in heaven above, or on the earth beneath. And he had taken her away, cruel priest! of his "*great* mercy!" I did not presume, child though I was, to think rebelliously against *that.* The reason was not any hypocritical or canting submission where my heart yielded none, but because already my deep musing intellect had perceived a mystery and a labyrinth in the economies of this world. God, I saw, moved not as *we* moved—walked not as *we* walked—thought not as *we* think Still I saw no mercy to myself, a poor, frail, dependen creature, torn away so suddenly from the prop on which altogether it depended. O yes! perhaps there was; and many years after I came to suspect it. Nevertheless it was a benignity that pointed far ahead; such as by a child could not have been perceived, because then the great arch had not come round; could not have been recognized, if it *had* come round; could not have been valued, if it had even been dimly recognized.

Finally, as the closing prayer in the whole service, stood this, which I acknowledged then, and now acknowledge, as equally beautiful and consolatory; for in this was no harsh peremptory challenge to the infirmities of human grief, as to a thing not meriting notice in a religious rite. On the contrary, there was a gracious condescension from the great apostle to grief, as to a passion that he might perhaps himself have participated. "O, merciful God! the Father of our Lord Jesus Christ, who is the resurrection and the life, in whom whosoever believeth shall live, though he die; who also taught us by his holy apostle St. Paul not to be sorry, as men without hope, for them that sleep in *him;* we meekly beseech thee, oh Father! to raise us from the death of sin unto the life of righteousness; that, when we shall depart this life, we may rest in *him* as our hope is — that this our sister doth."

Ah, *that* was beautiful, — that was heavenly! We might be sorry, we had leave to be sorry; only not without hope. And we were by hope to rest in *Him*, as this our sister doth. And howsoever a man may think that he is without hope, I, that have read the writing upon these great abysses of grief, and viewed their shadows under the correction of mightier shadows from deeper abysses since then, abysses of aboriginal fear and eldest darkness, in which yet I believe that all hope had not absolutely died, know that he is in a natural error. If, for a moment, I and so many others, wallowing in the dust of affliction, could yet rise up suddenly like the dry corpse * which stood upright in the glory of life when touched by the bones of the prophet; if in those vast choral anthems, heard by my childish ear, the voice of God wrapt itself as in a cloud of music, saying — "Child, that sorrowest, I command thee to rise up and ascend for a season into my heaven of heavens," — then it was plain that despair, that the anguish of darkness, was not *essential* to such sorrow, but might come and go even as light comes and goes upon our troubled earth.

Yes! the light may come and go; grief may wax and wane; grief may sink; and grief again may rise, as in impassioned minds oftentimes it does, even to the heaven of heavens; but there is a necessity that, if too much left to itself in solitude, finally it will descend into a depth from which there is no reäscent; into a disease which seems no disease; into a languishing which, from its very sweetness, perplexes the mind, and is fancied to be very health. Witchcraft has seized upon you, — nympholepsy has struck you. Now you rave no more. You acquiesce; nay, you are passion-

---

* "*Like the dry corpse which stood upright.*" — See the *Second* Book of Kings, chapter xiii. v. 20 and 21. Thirty years ago this impressive incident was made the subject of a large altar-piece by Mr. Allston, an interesting American artist, then resident in London.

ately delighted in your condition. Sweet becomes the grave, because you also hope immediately to travel thither: luxurious is the separation, because only perhaps for a few weeks shall it exist for you; and it will then prove but the brief summer night that had retarded a little, by a refinement of rapture, the heavenly dawn of reünion. Inevitable sometimes it is in solitude — that this should happen with minds morbidly meditative; that, when we stretch out our arms in darkness, vainly striving to draw back the sweet faces that have vanished, slowly arises a new stratagem of grief, and we say, — "Be it that they no more come back to us, yet what hinders but we should go to *them?*"

Perilous is that crisis for the young. In its effect perfectly the same as the ignoble witchcraft of the poor African *Obeah*,* this sublimer witchcraft of grief will, if left to follow its own natural course, terminate in the same catastrophe of death. Poetry, which neglects no phenomena that are interesting to the heart of man, has sometimes touched a little

"On the sublime attractions of the grave."

---

* "*African Obeah.*" — Thirty years ago it would not have been necessary to say one word of the Obi or Obeah magic; because at that time several distinguished writers (Miss Edgeworth, for instance, in her Belinda) had made use of this superstition in fictions, and because the remarkable history of Three-fingered Jack, a story brought upon the stage, had made the superstition notorious as a fact. Now, however, so long after the case has probably passed out of the public mind, it may be proper to mention, that when an Obeah man — that is, a professor of this dark collusion with human fears and human credulity — had once woven his dreadful net of ghostly terrors, and had thrown it over his selected victim, vainly did that victim flutter, struggle, languish in the meshes; unless the spells were reversed, he generally perished; and without a wound, except from his own too domineering fancy.

But you think that these attractions, existing at times for the adult, could not exist for the child. Understand that you are wrong. Understand that these attractions *do* exist for the child; and perhaps as much more strongly than they *can* exist for the adult, by the whole difference between the concentration of a childish love, and the inevitable distraction upon multiplied objects of any love that can affect any adult. There is a German superstition (well known by a popular translation) of the Erl-king's Daughter, who fixes her love upon some child, and seeks to wile him away into her own shadowy kingdom in forests.

> "Who is it that rides through the forest so fast?"

It is a knight, who carries his child before him on the saddle. The Erl-king's Daughter rides on his right hand, and still whispers temptations to the infant audible only to *him*.

> "If thou wilt, dear baby, with me go away,
> We will see a fine show, we will play a fine play."

The consent of the baby is essential to her success. And finally she *does* succeed. Other charms, other temptations, would have been requisite for me. My intellect was too advanced for those fascinations. But could the Erl-king's Daughter have revealed herself to me, and promised to lead me where my sister was, she might have wiled me by the hand into the dimmest forests upon earth. Languishing was my condition at that time. Still I languished for things "which" (a voice from heaven seemed to answer through my own heart) "*can*not be granted;" and which, when again

I languished, again the voice repeated, "*can*not be granted."

Well it was for me that, at this crisis, I was summoned to put on the harness of life by commencing my classical studies under one of my guardians, a clergyman of the English Church, and (so far as regarded Latin) a most accomplished scholar.

At the very commencement of my new studies there happened an incident which afflicted me much for a short time, and left behind a gloomy impression, that suffering and wretchedness were diffused amongst all creatures that breathe. A person had given me a kitten. There are three animals which seem, beyond all others, to reflect the beauty of human infancy in two of its elements — namely, joy and guileless innocence, though less in its third element of simplicity, because *that* requires language for its full expression: these three animals are the kitten, the lamb, and the fawn. Other creatures may be as happy, but they do not show it so much. Great was the love which poor silly I had for this little kitten; but, as I left home at ten in the morning, and did not return till near five in the afternoon, I was obliged, with some anxiety, to throw it for those seven hours upon its own discretion, as infirm a basis for reasonable hope as could be imagined. I did not wish the kitten, indeed, at all less foolish than it was, except just when I was leaving home, and then its exceeding folly gave me a pang. Just about that time, it happened that we had received, as a present from Leicestershire, a fine young Newfoundland dog, who was under a cloud of disgrace for crimes of his youthful blood committed in that county. One day he had taken too great a liberty with a pretty little cousin of mine, Emma H——, about four years old. He had, in fact, bitten off her cheek, which, remaining attached by a shred, was, through the energy of a governess, replaced, and subsequently healed without a scar. His name being *Turk*, he was immediately pronounced by the best Greek scholar of that neighborhood, ἐπωνυμος, (that is, named significantly, or reporting his nature in his name). But as Miss Emma confessed to having been engaged in taking away a bone from him, on which subject no dog can be taught to understand a joke, it did not strike our own authorities that he was to be considered in a state of reprobation; and as our gardens (near to a great town) were, on account chiefly of melons, constantly robbed, it was held that a moderate degree of fierceness was rather a favorable trait in his character. My poor kitten, it was supposed, had been engaged in the same playful trespass upon Turk's property as my Leicestershire cousin, and Turk laid her dead on the spot. It is impossible to describe my grief when the case was made known to me at five o'clock in the evening, by a man's holding out the little creature dead: she that I had left so full of glorious life —life which even in a kitten is infinite,—was now stretched in motionless repose. I remember that there was a large coal-stack in the yard. I dropped my Latin books, sat down upon a huge block of coal, and burst into a passion of tears. The man, struck with my tumultuous grief, hurried into the house; and from the lower regions deployed instantly the women of the laundry and the kitchen. No one subject is so absolutely sacred, and enjoys so *classical* a sanctity among servant-girls, as 1. Grief; and 2. Love which is unfortunate. All the young women took me up in their arms and kissed me; and, last of all, an elderly woman, who was the cook, not only kissed me, but wept so audibly, from some suggestion doubtless of grief personal to herself, that I threw my arms about her neck and kissed *her* also. It is probable, as I now suppose, that some account of my grief for my sister had reached them. Else I was never allowed to visit *their* region of the house. But, however *that* might be, afterwards it struck me, that if I had met with so much sympathy, or with any sympathy at all, from the servant chiefly connected with myself in the desolating grief I had suffered, possibly I should not have been so profoundly shaken.

But did I in the mean time feel anger towards Turk? Not the least. And the reason was this: — My guardian, who taught me Latin, was in the habit of coming over and dining at my mother's table whenever he pleased. On these occasions, he, who like myself pitied *dependent* animals, went invariably into the yard of the offices, taking me with him, and unchained the dogs. There were two, — *Grim*, a mastiff, and *Turk*, our young friend. My guardian was a bold, athletic man, and delighted in dogs. He told me, which also my own heart told me, that these poor dogs languished out their lives under this confinement. The moment that I and my guardian (*ego et rex meus*) appeared in sight of the two kennels, it is impossible to express the joy of the dogs. Turk was usually restless; Grim slept away his life in surliness. But at the sight of us, — of my little insignificant self and my six-foot guardian, — both dogs yelled with delight. We unfastened their chains with our own hands, they licking our hands; and as to myself, licking my miserable little face; and at one bound they reëntered upon their natural heritage of joy. Always we took them through the fields, where they molested nothing, and closed with giving them a cold bath in the brook which bounded my father's property. What despair must have possessed our dogs when they were taken back to their hateful prisons! and I, for my part, not enduring to see their misery, slunk away when the rechaining commenced. It was in vain to tell me that all people, who had property out of doors to protect, chained up dogs in the same way. *This* only proved the extent of the oppression; for a monstrous oppression it *did* seem, that creatures, boiling with life and the desires of life, should be thus detained in captivity until they were set free by death. That liberation visited poor *Grim* and *Turk* sooner than any of us expected, for they were both poisoned, within the year that followed, by a party of burglars. At the end of that year, I was reading the Æneid; and it struck me, who remembered the howling recusancy of *Turk*, as a peculiarly fine circumstance, introduced amongst the horrors of Tartarus, that sudden gleam of powerful animals, full of life and conscious rights, rebelling against chains: —

> "Iræque leonum
> Vincla recusantum." *

* What follows, I think (for book I have none of any kind where this paper is proceeding), namely: *et serâ sub nocte rudentum*, is

Virgil had doubtless picked up that gem in his visits at feeding-time to the *caveæ* of the Roman amphitheatre. But the rights of brute creatures to a merciful forbearance on the part of man could not enter into the feeblest conceptions of one belonging to a nation that (although too noble to be *wantonly* cruel) yet in the same amphitheatre manifested so little regard even to human rights. Under Christianity the condition of the brute has improved, and will improve much more. There is ample room. For, I am sorry to say, that the commonest vice of Christian children, too often surveyed with careless eyes by mothers that in their *human* relations are full of kindness, is cruelty to the inferior creatures thrown upon their mercy. For my own part, what had formed the ground-work of my happiness (since joyous was my nature, though overspread with a cloud of sadness) had been from the first a heart overflowing with love. And I had drunk in too profoundly the spirit of Christianity from our many nursery readings, not to read also in its divine words the justification of my own tendencies. That which I desired was the thing which I ought to desire; the mercy that I loved was the mercy that God had blessed. From the Sermon on the Mount resounded forever in my ears — "Blessed are the merciful!" I needed not to add — "For they shall obtain mercy." By lips so holy, and when standing in the atmosphere of truths so divine, simply to have been blessed — *that* was a sufficient ratification; every truth so revealed, and so hallowed by

probably a mistake of Virgil's; the lions did not roar because night was approaching, but because night brought with it their principal meal, and consequently the impatience of hunger.

position, starts into sudden life, and becomes to itself its own authentication, needing no proof to convince, — needing no promise to allure.

It may well be supposed, therefore, that having so early awakened within me what may be philosophically called the *transcendental* justice of Christianity, I blamed not *Turk* for yielding to the coërcion of his nature. He had killed the object of my love. But, besides that he was under the constraint of a primary appetite, Turk was himself the victim of a killing oppression. He was doomed to a fretful existence so long as he should exist at all. Nothing could reconcile this to my benignity, which at that time rested upon two pillars, — upon the deep, deep heart which God had given to me at my birth, and upon exquisite health. Up to the age of two, and almost through that entire space of twenty-four months, I had suffered from ague; but when *that* left me, all germs and traces of ill health fled away forever, except only such (and those how curable!) as I inherited from my school-boy distresses in London, or had created by means of opium Even the long ague was not without ministrations of favor to my prevailing temper; and, on the whole, no subject for pity, since naturally it won for me the sweet caresses of female tenderness, both young and old. I was a little petted; but you see by this time, reader, that I must have been too much of a philosopher, even in the year one *ab urbe conditâ* of my frail earthly tenement, to abuse such indulgence. It also won for me a ride on horseback whenever the weather permitted. I was placed on a pillow, in front of a cankered old man, upon a large white horse, not so young as I was, but still showing traces of blood. And even the old man, who was both the oldest and the worst of the three, talked with gentleness to myself, reserving his surliness for all the rest of the world.

These things pressed with a gracious power of incubation upon my predispositions; and in my overflowing love I did things fitted to make the reader laugh, and sometimes fitted to bring myself into perplexity. One instance from a thousand may illustrate the combination of both effects. At four years old, I had repeatedly seen the housemaid raising her long broom, and pursuing (generally destroying) a vagrant spider. The holiness of all life, in my eyes, forced me to devise plots for saving the poor doomed wretch; and thinking intercession likely to prove useless, my policy was, to draw off the housemaid on pretence of showing her a picture, until the spider, already *en route*, should have had time to escape. Very soon, however, the shrewd housemaid, marking the coincidence of these picture exhibitions with the agonies of fugitive spiders, detected my stratagem; so that, if the reader will pardon an expression borrowed from the street, henceforwards the picture was "no go." However, as she approved of my motive, she told me of the many murders that the spider had committed, and next (which was worse) of the many that he certainly *would* commit, if reprieved. This staggered me. I could have gladly forgiven the past; but it *did* seem a false mercy to spare one spider in order to scatter death amongst fifty flies. I thought timidly, for a moment, of suggesting that people sometimes repented, and that *he* might repent; but I checked myself, on considering that I had never read any account, and that she might laugh at the idea, of a penitent spider. To desist was a necessity, in these circumstances. But the difficulty which the housemaid had suggested did not depart, it troubled my musing mind to perceive that the welfare of one creature might stand upon the ruin of another; and the case of the spider remained thenceforwards even more perplexing to my understanding than it was painful to my heart.

The reader is likely to differ from me upon the question, moved by recurring to such experiences of childhood, whether much value attaches to the perceptions and intellectual glimpses of a child. Children, like men, range through a gamut that is infinite, of temperaments and characters, ascending from the very dust below our feet to highest heaven. I have seen children that were sensual, brutal, devilish. But, thanks be to the *vis medicatrix* of human nature, and to the goodness of God, these are as rare exhibitions as all other monsters. People thought, when seeing such odious travesties and burlesques upon lovely human infancy, that perhaps the little wretches might be *kilcrops.** Yet, possibly (it has since occurred to me), even these children of the fiend, as they seemed, might have one chord in their horrible natures that answered to the call of some sublime purpose. There is a mimic instance of this kind, often found amongst ourselves in natures that are not really "horrible," but

* "*Kilcrops.*" — See, amongst Southey's early poems, one upon this superstition. Southey argues *contra;* but, for my part, I should have been more disposed to hold a brief on the other side

which *seem* such to persons viewing them from a station not sufficiently central: — Always there are mischievous boys in a neighborhood, — boys who tie canisters to the tails of cats belonging to ladies, — a thing which *greatly* I disapprove; and who rob orchards, — a thing which *slightly* I disapprove; and, behold! the next day, on meeting the injured ladies, they say to me, "O, my dear friend, never pretend to argue for him! This boy, we shall all see, will come to be hanged." Well, *that* seems a disagreeable prospect for all parties; so I change the subject; and, lo! five years later, there is an English frigate fighting with a frigate of heavier metal (no matter of what nation). The noble captain has manœuvred as only *his* countrymen can manœuvre; he has delivered his broadsides as only the proud islanders can deliver them. Suddenly he sees the opening for a *coup-de-main;* through his speaking-trumpet he shouts, "*Where are my boarders?*" And instantly rise upon the deck, with the gayety of boyhood, in white shirt-sleeves bound with black ribands, fifty men, the *élite* of the crew; and, behold! at the very head of them, cutlass in hand, is our friend, the tier of canisters to the tails of ladies' cats, — a thing which *greatly* I disapprove, and also the robber of orchards, — a thing which *slightly* I disapprove. But here is a man that will not suffer you either greatly or slightly to disapprove him. Fire celestial burns in his eye; his nation — his glorious nation — is in his mind; himself he regards no more than the life of a cat, or the ruin of a canister. On the deck of the enemy he throws himself with rapture; and if *he* is amongst the killed, — if he, for an object so gloriously unselfish, lays down with joy his life and glittering youth, — mark this, that, perhaps, he will not be the least in heaven.

But coming back to the case of childhood, I maintain steadfastly that into all the *elementary* feelings of man children look with more searching gaze than adults. My opinion is, that where circumstances favor, where the heart is deep, where humility and tenderness exist in strength, where the situation is favorable as to solitude and as to genial feelings, children have a specific power of contemplating the truth, which departs as they enter the world. It is clear to me, that children, upon elementary paths which require no knowledge of the world to unravel, tread more firmly than men; have a more pathetic sense of the beauty which lies in justice; and, according to the immortal ode of our great laureate [ode "On the Intimations of Immortality in Childhood"], a far closer communion with God. I, if you observe, do not much intermeddle with religion, properly so called. My path lies on the interspace between religion and philosophy, that connects them both. Yet here, for once, I shall trespass on grounds not properly mine, and desire you to observe in St. Matthew, chapter xxi., and verse 15, *who* were those that, crying in the temple, made the first public recognition of Christianity. Then, if you say, "O, but children echo what they hear, and are no independent authorities." I must request you to extend your reading into verse 16, where you will find that the testimony of these children, as bearing an *original* value, was ratified by the highest testimony; and the recognition of these children did itself receive a heavenly recognition And this could *not* have been, unless there were children in Jerusalem who saw into truth with a far sharper eye than Sanhedrims and Rabbis.

It is impossible, with respect to any memorable grief, that it can be adequately exhibited so as to indicate the enormity of the convulsion which really it caused, without viewing it under a variety of aspects,—a thing which is here almost necessary for the effect of proportion to what follows: 1st, for instance, in its immediate pressure, so stunning and confounding; 2dly, in its oscillations, as in its earlier agitations, frantic with tumults, that borrow the wings of the winds; or in its diseased impulses of sick languishing desire, through which sorrow transforms itself to a sunny angel, that beckons us to a sweet repose. These phases of revolving affection I have already sketched. And I shall also sketch a third, that is, where the affliction, seemingly hushing itself to sleep, suddenly soars upwards again upon combining with *another* mode of sorrow, namely, anxiety without definite limits, and the trouble of a reproaching conscience. As sometimes,* upon the English lakes, water-fowl that have careered in the air until the eye is wearied with the eternal wheelings of their inimitable flight — Grecian simplicities of motion, amidst a labyrinthine infinity of curves that would baffle the geometry of Apollonius — seek the water at last, as if with some settled purpose (you imagine) of reposing. Ah, how little have you understood the

* In this place I derive my feeling partly from a lovely sketch of the appearance, in verse, by Mr. Wordsworth; partly from my own experience of the case; and, not having the poems here I know not how to proportion my acknowledgments.

omnipotence of that life which they inherit! *They* want no rest: they laugh at resting; all is "make believe," as when an infant hides its laughing face behind its mother's shawl. For a moment it is still. Is it meaning to rest? Will its impatient heart endure to lurk there for long? Ask, rather, if a cataract will stop from fatigue. Will a sunbeam sleep on its travels? or the Atlantic rest from its labors? As little can the infant, as little can the water-fowl of the lakes, suspend their play, except as a variety of play, or rest unless when nature compels them. Suddenly starts off the infant, suddenly ascend the birds, to new evolutions as incalculable as the caprices of a kaleidoscope; and the glory of their motions, from the mixed immortalities of beauty and inexhaustible variety, becomes at least pathetic to survey. So also, and with such life of variation, do the *primary* convulsions of nature — such, perhaps, as only *primary** formations in the human system can experience — come round again and again by reverberating shocks.

* "And so, then," the cynic objects, "you rank your own mind (and you tell us so frankly) amongst the primary formations?" As I love to annoy him, it would give me pleasure to reply — "Perhaps I do." But as I never answer more questions than are necessary, I confine myself to saying, that this is not a necessary construction of the words. Some minds stand nearer to the type of the original nature in man, are truer than others to the great magnet in our dark planet. Minds that are impassioned on a more colossal scale than ordinary, deeper in their vibrations, and more extensive in the scale of their vibrations, whether, in other parts of their intellectual system, they had or had not a corresponding compass, will tremble to greater depths from a fearful convulsion, and will come round by a longer curve of undulations.

The new intercourse with my guardian, and the changes of scene which naturally it led to, were of use in weaning my mind from the mere disease which threatened it in case I had been left any longer to my total solitude. But out of these changes grew an incident which restored my grief, though in a more troubled shape, and now for the first time associated with something like remorse and deadly anxiety. I can safely say that this was my earliest trespass, and perhaps a venial one, all things considered. Nobody ever discovered it; and but for my own frankness it would not be known to this day. But *that* I could not know; and for years, — that is, from seven or earlier up to ten, — such was my simplicity, that I lived in constant terror. This, though it revived my grief, did me probably great service; because it was no longer a state of languishing desire tending to torpor, but of feverish irritation and gnawing care, that kept alive the activity of my understanding. The case was this: — It happened that I had now, and commencing with my first introduction to Latin studies, a large weekly allowance of pocket-money, — too large for my age, but safely intrusted to myself, who never spent or desired to spend one fraction of it upon anything but books. But all proved too little for my colossal schemes. Had the Vatican, the Bodleian, and the *Bibliothèque du Roi*, been all emptied into one collection for my private gratification, little progress would have been made towards content in this particular craving. Very soon I had run ahead of my allowance, and was about three guineas deep in debt. There I paused; for deep anxiety now began to oppress me as to the course in which this mysterious (and indeed guilty) current of debt would finally flow. For the present it was frozen up; but I had some reason for thinking that Christmas thawed all debts whatsoever, and set them in motion towards innumerable pockets. Now *my* debt would be thawed with all the rest; and in what direction would it flow? There was no river that would carry it off to sea; to somebody's pocket it would beyond a doubt make its way; and who *was* that somebody? This question haunted me forever. Christmas had come, Christmas had gone, and I heard nothing of the three guineas. But I was not easier for *that*. Far rather I *would* have heard of it; for this indefinite approach of a loitering catastrophe gnawed and fretted my feelings. No Grecian audience ever waited with more shuddering horror for the anagnorisis* of the Œdipus, than I for the explosion of my debt. Had I been less ignorant, I should have proposed to mortgage my weekly allowance for the debt, or to form a sinking fund for redeeming it; for the *weekly* sum was nearly five per cent. on the entire debt. But I had a mysterious awe of ever alluding to it. This arose from my want of some confidential friend; whilst my grief pointed continually to the remembrance, that *so* it had not always been. But was not the bookseller to blame in suffering a child scarcely seven years old to contract such a debt? Not in the least. He was both a rich man,

---

* That is (as on account of English readers is added), the recognition of his true identity, which, in one moment, and by a horrid flash of revelation, connects him with acts incestuous, murderous, parricidal in the past, and with a mysterious fatality of woe lurking in the future.

who could not possibly care for my trifling custom, and notoriously an honorable man. Indeed, the money which I myself spent every week in books would reasonably have caused him to presume that so small a sum as three guineas might well be authorized by my family. He stood, however, on plainer ground; for my guardian, who was very indolent (as people chose to call it), — that is, like his little melancholy ward, spent all his time in reading, — often enough would send me to the bookseller's with a written order for books. This was to prevent my forgetting. But when he found that such a thing as "forgetting," in the case of a book, was wholly out of the question for me, the trouble of writing was dismissed. And thus I had become factor-general, on the part of my guardian, both for *his* books, and for such as were wanted on my own account, in the natural course of my education. My private "little account" had therefore in fact flowed homewards at Christmas, not (as I anticipated) in the shape of an independent current, but as a little tributary rill, that was lost in the waters of some more important river. This I now know, but could not then have known with any certainty. So far, however, the affair would gradually have sunk out of my anxieties, as time wore on. But there was another item in the case, which, from the excess of my ignorance, preyed upon my spirits far more keenly; and this, keeping itself alive, kept also the other incident alive. With respect to the debt, I was not so ignorant as to think it of much danger by the mere amount, — my own allowance furnished a scale for preventing *that* mistake; — it was the principle, — the having presumed to contract debts on my own account, — that I feared to have exposed. But this other case was a ground for anxiety, even as regarded the amount; not really, but under the jesting representation made to me, which I (as ever before and after) swallowed in perfect faith. Amongst the books which I had bought, all English, was a history of Great Britain, commencing, of course, with Brutus and a thousand years of impossibilities; these fables being generously thrown in as a little gratuitous *extra* to the mass of truths which were to follow. This was to be completed in sixty or eighty parts, I believe. But there was another work left more indefinite as to its ultimate extent, and which, from its nature, seemed to imply a far higher range. It was a general history of navigation, supported by a vast body of voyages. Now, when I considered with myself what a huge thing the sea was, and that so many thousands of captains, commodores, admirals, were eternally running up and down it, and scoring lines upon its face so rankly, that in some of the main "streets" and "squares" (as one might call them), their tracts would blend into one undistinguishable blot, I began to fear that such a work tended to infinity. What was little England to the universal sea? And yet *that* went perhaps to fourscore parts. Not enduring the uncertainty that now besieged my tranquillity, I resolved to know the worst; and, on a day ever memorable to me, I went down to the bookseller's. He was a mild, elderly man, and to myself had always shown a kind, indulgent manner. Partly, perhaps, he had been struck by my extreme gravity; and partly, during the many conversations I had with him, on occasion of my guardian's orders for books, with my laughable simplicity. But there was another reason which had early won for me his paternal regard. For the first three or four months I had found Latin something of a drudgery; and the incident which forever knocked away the "shores," at that time preventing my launch upon the general bosom of Latin literature, was this: — One day, the bookseller took down a Beza's *Latin Testament;* and, opening it, asked me to translate for him the chapter which he pointed to. I was struck by perceiving that it was the great chapter of St. Paul on the grave and resurrection. I had never seen a Latin version; yet, from the simplicity of the scriptural style in *any* translation (though Beza's is far from good), I could not well have failed in construing. But, as it happened to be this particular chapter, which in English I had read again and again with so passionate a sense of its grandeur, I read it off with a fluency and effect like some great opera singer uttering a rapturous *bravura.* My kind old friend expressed himself gratified, making me a present of the book as a mark of his approbation. And it is remarkable, that from this moment, when the deep memory of the English words had forced me into seeing the precise correspondence of the two concurrent streams, — Latin and English, — never again did any difficulty arise to check the velocity of my progress in this particular language. At less than eleven years of age, when as yet I was a very indifferent Grecian, I had become a brilliant master of Latinity, as my alcaics and choriambics remain to testify; and the whole occasion of a change so memorable to a boy, was this casual summons to translate a composition with which my heart was filled. Ever after this, ne showed me a caressing kindness, and so condescend ingly, that, generally, he would leave any people, for a moment, with whom he was engaged, to come and speak to me. On this fatal day, however, — for such it proved to me, — he could not do this. He saw me, indeed, and nodded, but could not leave a party of elderly strangers. This accident threw me unavoidably upon one of his young people. Now, this was a market day, and there was a press of country people present, whom I did not wish to hear my question. Never did a human creature, with his heart palpitating at Delphi for the solution of some killing mystery, stand before the priestess of the oracle, with lips that moved more sadly than mine, when now advancing to a smiling young man at a desk. His answer was to decide, though I could not exactly know *that*, whether, for the next two years, I was to have an hour of peace. He was a handsome, good-natured young man, but full of fun and frolic; and I dare say was amused with what must have seemed to *him* the absurd anxiety of my features. I described the work to him, and he understood me at once. How many volumes did he think it would extend to? There was a whimsical expression, perhaps, of drollery about his eyes, but which, unhappily, under my preconceptions, I translated into scorn, as he replied, "How many volumes? O! really, I can 't say; may-be a matter of 15,000, be the same more or less." "*More?*" I said, in horror, altogether neglecting the contingency of "less." "Why," he said, "we can't settle these things to a nicety. But, considering the subject" [ay, *that* was the very thing which I myself considered], "I should say there might be some trifle over, as suppose 400 or 500 volumes, be the same more or less." What, then, — here there might be supplements to supplements, — the work might positively *never* end! On one pretence or another, if an author or publisher might add 500 volumes, he might add another round 15,000. Indeed, it strikes one even now, that by the time all the one-legged commodores and yellow admirals of that generation had exhausted their long yarns, another generation would have grown another crop of the same gallant spinners. I asked no more, but slunk out of the shop, and never again entered it with cheerfulness, or propounded any frank questions, as heretofore. For I was now seriously afraid of pointing attention to myself as one that, by having purchased some numbers, and obtained others on credit, had silently contracted an engagement to take all the rest, though they should stretch to the crack of doom. Certainly I had never heard of a work that extended to 15,000 volumes; but still there was no natural impossibility that it should; and, if in any case, in none so reasonably as one upon the inexhaustible sea. Besides, any slight mistake as to the letter of the number could not affect the horror of the final prospect. I saw by the imprint, and I heard, that this work emanated from London, a vast centre of mystery to me, and the more so, as a thing unseen at any time by my eyes, and nearly two hundred miles distant. I felt the fatal truth, that here was a ghostly cobweb radiating into all the provinces from the mighty metropolis. I secretly had trodden upon the outer circumference, — had damaged or deranged the fine threads or links, —

concealment or reparation there could be none. Slowly perhaps, but surely, the vibration would travel back to London. The ancient spider that sat there at the centre would rush along the net-work through all longitudes and latitudes, until he found the responsible caitiff, author of so much mischief. Even with less ignorance than mine, there *was* something to appal a child's imagination in the vast systematic machinery by which any elaborate work could disperse itself, could levy money, could put questions and get answers,— all in profound silence, nay, even in darkness, searching every nook of every town and of every hamlet in so populous a kingdom. I had some dim terrors, also, connected with the Stationers' Company. I had often observed them in popular works threatening unknown men with unknown chastisements, for offences equally unknown; nay, to myself, absolutely inconceivable. Could I be the mysterious criminal so long pointed out, as it were, in prophecy? I figured the stationers, doubtless all powerful men, pulling at one rope, and my unhappy self hanging at the other end. But an image, which seems now even more ludicrous than the rest, at that time, was the one most connected with the revival of my grief. It occurred to my subtlety, that the Stationers' Company, or any other company, could not possibly demand the money until they had delivered the volumes. And, as no man could say that I had ever positively refused to receive them, they would have no pretence for not accomplishing this delivery in a civil manner. Unless I should turn out to be no customer at all, at present it was clear that I had a right to be considered a most excellent customer; one, in fact who had given an order for fifteen thousand volumes. Then rose up before me this great opera-house "scena" of the delivery. There would be a ring at the front door. A wagoner in the front, with a bland voice, would ask for "a young gentleman who had given an order to *their* house." Looking out, I should perceive a procession of carts and wagons, all advancing in measured movements; each in turn would present its rear, deliver its cargo of volumes, by shooting them, like a load of coals, on the lawn, and wheel off to the rear, by way of clearing the road for its successors. Then the impossibility of even asking the servants to cover with sheets, or counterpanes, or table-cloths, such a mountainous, such a "star-y-pointing" record of my past offences, lying in so conspicuous a situation! Men would not know my guilt merely, they would see it. But the reason why this form of the consequences, so much more than any other, stuck by my imagination was, that it connected itself with one of the Arabian Nights which had particularly interested myself and my sister. It was that tale, where a young porter, having his ropes about his person, had stumbled into the special "preserve" of some old magician. He finds a beautiful lady imprisoned, to whom (and not without prospects of success) he recommends himself as a suitor more in harmony with her own years than a withered magician. At this crisis, the magician returns. The young man bolts, and for that day successfully; but unluckily he leaves his ropes behind. Next morning he hears the magician, too honest by half, inquiring at the front door, with much expression of condolence, for the unfortunate young man who had lost his ropes in his own zenana. Upon this story I used to amuse my sister by ventriloquizing to the magician, from the lips of the trembling young man,— "O, Mr. Magician, these ropes cannot be mine! They are far too good; and one would n't like, you know, tc rob some other poor young man. If you please, Mr Magician, I never had money enough to buy so beautiful a set of ropes." But argument is thrown away upon a magician, and off he sets on his travels with the young porter, not forgetting to take the ropes along with him.

Here now was the case, that had once seemed so impressive to me in a mere fiction from a far distant age and land, literally reproduced in myself. For, what did it matter whether a magician dunned one with old ropes for his engine of torture, or Stationers' Hall with fifteen thousand volumes (in the rear of which there might also be ropes)? Should *I* have ventriloquized, would my sister have laughed, had either of us but guessed the possibility that I myself, and within one twelve months, and, alas! standing alone in the world as regarded *confidential* counsel, should repeat within my own inner experience the shadowy panic of the young Bagdat intruder upon the privacy of magicians? It appeared, then, that I had been reading a legend concerning myself in the *Arabian Nights.* I had been contemplated in types a thousand years before, on the banks of the Tigris. It was horror and grief that prompted that thought.

O, heavens! that the misery of a child should by possibility become the laughter of adults!—that even I, the sufferer, should be capable of amusing myself, as if it had been a jest, with what for three years had constituted the secret affliction of my life, and its eternal trepidation — like the ticking of a death-watch to patients lying awake in the plague! I durst ask no counsel; there was no one to ask. Possibly my sister could have given me none in a case which neither of us should have understood, and where to seek for information from others would have been at once to betray the whole reason for seeking it. But, if no advice, she would have given me her pity, and the expression of her endless love; and, with the relief of sympathy, that heals for a season all distresses, she would have given me that exquisite luxury — the knowledge that, having parted with my secret, yet also I had *not* parted with it, since it was in the power only of one that could much less betray me than I could betray myself. At this time, — that is, about the year when I suffered most, — I was reading Cæsar. O, laurelled scholar, sunbright intellect, "foremost man of all this world," how often did I make out of thy immortal volume a pillow to support my wearied brow, as at evening, on my homeward road, I used to turn into some silent field, where I might give way unobserved to the reveries which besieged me! I wondered, and found no end of wondering, at the revolution that one short year had made in my happiness. I wondered that such billows *could* overtake me. At the beginning of that year, how radiantly happy! At the end, how insupportably alone!

"Into what depth thou seest,
From what height fallen."

Forever I searched the abysses with some wandering

thoughts unintelligible to myself. Forever I dallied with some obscure notion, how my sister's love might be made in some dim way available for delivering me from misery; or else how the misery I had suffered and was suffering might be made, in some way equally dim, the ransom for winning back her love.

* * * * * * * *

Here pause, reader! Imagine yourself seated in some cloud-scaling swing, oscillating under the impulse of lunatic hands; for the strength of lunacy may belong to human dreams, the fearful caprice of lunacy, and the malice of lunacy, whilst the *victim* of those dreams may be all the more certainly removed from lunacy; even as a bridge gathers cohesion and strength from the increasing resistance into which it is forced by increasing pressure. Seated in such a swing, fast as you reach the lowest point of depression, may you rely on racing up to a starry altitude of corresponding ascent. Ups and downs you will see, heights and depths, in our fiery course together, such as will sometimes tempt you to look shyly and suspiciously at me, your guide, and the ruler of the oscillations. Here, at the point where I have called a halt, the reader has reached the lowest depths in my nursery afflictions. From that point, according to the principles of *art* which govern the movement of these Confessions, I had meant to launch him upwards through the whole arch of ascending visions which seemed requisite to balance the sweep downwards, so recently described in his course. But accidents of the press have made it impossible to accomplish this purpose in the present month's journal. There is reason to regret that the advantages of position, which were essential to the full effect of passages planned for the equipoise and mutual resistance, have thus been lost. Meantime, upon the principle of the mariner, who rigs a *jury*-mast in default of his regular spars, I find my resource in a sort of "jury" peroration, not sufficient in the way of a balance by its *proportions*, but sufficient to indicate the *quality* of the balance which I had contemplated. He who has *really* read the preceding parts of these present Confessions will be aware that a stricter scrutiny of the past, such as was natural after the whole economy of the dreaming faculty had been convulsed beyond all precedents on record, led me to the conviction that not one agency, but two agencies, had coöperated to the tremendous result. The nursery experience had been the ally and the natural coëfficient of the opium. For that reason it was that the nursery experience has been narrated. Logically it bears the very same relation to the convulsions of the dreaming faculty as the opium. The idealizing tendency existed in the dream-theatre of my childhood; but the preternatural strength of its action and coloring was first developed after the confluence of the *two* causes. The reader must suppose me at Oxford; twelve years and a half are gone by; I am in the glory of youthful happiness: but I have now first tampered with opium; and now first the agitations of my childhood reöpened in strength, now first they swept in upon the brain with power, and the grandeur of recovered life, under the separate and the concurring inspirations of opium.

Once again, after twelve years' interval, the nursery

of my childhood expanded before me: my sister was moaning in bed; I was beginning to be restless with fears not intelligible to myself. Once again the nurse, but now dilated to colossal proportions, stood as upon some Grecian stage with her uplifted hand, and, like the superb Medea standing alone with her children in the nursery at Corinth,* smote me senseless to the ground. Again I was in the chamber with my sister's corpse, again the pomps of life rose up in silence, the glory of summer, the frost of death. Dream formed itself mysteriously within dream; within these Oxford dreams remoulded itself continually the trance in my sister's chamber, — the blue heavens, the everlasting vault, the soaring billows, the throne steeped in the thought (but not the sight) of "Him that sate thereon;" the flight, the pursuit, the irrecoverable steps of my return to earth. Once more the funeral procession gathered; the priest in his white surplice stood waiting with a book in his hand by the side of an open grave, the sacristan with his shovel; the coffin sank; the *dust to dust* descended. Again I was in the church on a heavenly Sunday morning. The golden sunlight of God slept amongst the heads of his apostles, his martyrs, his saints; the fragment from the litany, the fragment from the clouds, awoke again the lawny beds that went up to scale the heavens — awoke again the shadowy arms that moved downward to meet them. Once again arose the swell of the anthem, the burst of the Hallelujah chorus, the storm, the trampling movement of the choral passion, the agita-

* Euripides.

tion of my own trembling sympathy, the tumult of the choir, the wrath of the organ. Once more I, that wallowed, became he that rose up to the clouds. And now in Oxford all was bound up into unity; the first state and the last were melted into each other as in some sunny glorifying haze. For high above my own station hovered a gleaming host of heavenly beings surrounding the pillows of the dying children. And such beings sympathize equally with sorrow that grovels and with sorrow that soars. Such beings pity alike the children that are languishing in death, and the children that live only to languish in tears.

THE PALIMPSEST.

You know perhaps, masculine reader, better than I can tell you, what is a *Palimpsest*. Possibly, you have one in your own library. But yet, for the sake of others who may *not* know, or may have forgotten, suffer me to explain it here, lest any female reader, who honors these papers with her notice, should tax me with explaining it once too seldom; which would be worse to bear than a simultaneous complaint from twelve proud men, that I had explained it three times too often. You therefore, fair reader, understand, that for *your* accommodation exclusively, I explain the meaning of this word. It is Greek; and our sex enjoys the office and privilege of standing counsel to yours, in all questions of Greek.* We are, under favor, perpetual and hereditary dragomans to you. So that if, by accident you know the meaning of a Greek word, yet by courtesy to us, your counsel learned in that matter, you will always seem *not* to know it.

A palimpsest, then, is a membrane or roll cleansed of its manuscript by reiterated successions.

What was the reason that the Greeks and the Romans had not the advantage of printed books? The answer will be, from ninety-nine persons in a hundred, — Because the mystery of printing was not then discovered. But this is altogether a mistake. The secret of printing must have been discovered many thousands of times before it was used, or *could* be used. The inventive powers of man are divine; and also his stupidity is divine, as Cowper so playfully illustrates in the slow development of the *sofa* through successive generations of immortal dulness. It took centuries of blockheads to raise a joint stool into a chair; and it required something like a miracle of genius, in the estimate of elder generations, to reveal the possibility of lengthening a chair into a *chaise-longue*, or a sofa. Yes, these were inventions that cost mighty throes of intellectual power. But still, as respects printing, and admirable as is the stupidity of man, it was really not quite equal to the task of evading an object which stared him in the face with so broad a gaze. It did not require an Athenian intellect to read the main secret of printing in many scores of processes which the ordinary uses of life were *daily* repeating. To say nothing of analogous artifices amongst various mechanic artisans, all that is essential in printing must have been known to every nation that struck coins and medals. Not therefore, any want of a printing art, — that is, of an art for multiplying impressions, — but the want of a cheap material for *receiving* such impressions, was the obstacle to an introduction of printed books, even as early as Pisistratus. The ancients *did* apply printing to records of silver and gold; to marble, and many other substances cheaper than gold and silver, they did *not*, since each monument required a *separate* effort of inscription. Simply this defect it was of a cheap material for receiving impresses, which froze in its very fountains the early resources of printing.

Some twenty years ago, this view of the case was luminously expounded by Dr. Whately, the present Archbishop of Dublin, and with the merit, I believe, of having first suggested it. Since then, this theory has received indirect confirmation. Now, out of that original scarcity affecting all materials proper for durable books, which continued up to times comparatively modern, grew the opening for palimpsests. Naturally, when once a roll of parchment or of vellum had done its office, by propagating through a series of generations what once had possessed an interest for *them*, but which, under changes of opinion or of taste, had faded to their feelings or had become obsolete for their undertakings, the whole *membrana* or vellum skin, the two-fold product of human skill, costly material, and costly freight of thought, which it carried, drooped in value concurrently — supposing that each were inalienably associated to the other. Once it had been the impress of a human mind which stamped its value upon the vellum; the vellum, though costly, had contributed but a secondary element of value to the total result.

At length, however, this relation between the vehicle and its freight has gradually been undermined. The vellum, from having been the setting of the jewel, has risen at length to be the jewel itself; and the burden of thought, from having given the chief value to the vellum, has now become the chief obstacle to its value; nay, has totally extinguished its value, unless it can be dissociated from the connection. Yet, if this unlinking *can* be effected, then, fast as the inscription upon the membrane is sinking into rubbish, the membrane itself is reviving in its separate importance; and, from bearing a ministerial value, the vellum has come at last to absorb the whole value.

Hence the importance for our ancestors that the separation *should* be effected. Hence it arose in the middle ages, as a considerable object for chemistry, to discharge the writing from the roll, and thus to make it available for a new succession of thoughts. The soil, if cleansed from what once had been hot-house plants, but now were held to be weeds, would be ready to receive a fresh and more appropriate crop. In tha object the monkish chemist succeeded; but after a fashion which seems almost incredible, — incredible not as regards the extent of their success, but as regards the delicacy of restraints under which it moved, — so equally adjusted was their success to the immediate interests of that period, and to the reversionary objects of our own. They did the thing; but not so radically as to prevent us, their posterity, from *un*doing it. They expelled the writing sufficiently to leave a field for the new manuscript, and yet not sufficiently to make the traces of the elder manuscript irrecoverable for us.

Could magic, could Hermes Trismegistus, have done more? What would you think, fair reader, of a problem such as this, — to write a book which should be sense for your own generation, nonsense for the next, should revive into sense for the next after that, but again become nonsense for the fourth; and so on by alternate successions, sinking into night or blazing into day, like the Sicilian river Arethusa, and the English river Mole; or like the undulating motions of a flattened stone which children cause to skim the breast of a river, now diving below the water, now grazing its surface, sinking heavily into darkness, rising buoyantly into light, through a long vista of alternations? Such a problem, you say, is impossible. But really it is a problem not harder apparently than — to bid a generation kill, but so that a subsequent generation may call back into life; bury, but so that posterity may command to rise again. Yet *that* was what the rude chemistry of past ages effected when coming into combination with the reäction from the more refined chemistry of our own. Had *they* been better chemists, had *we* been worse, the mixed result, namely, that, dying for *them*, the flower should revive for *us*, could not have been effected. They did the thing proposed to them: they did it effectually, for they founded upon it all that was wanted: and yet ineffectually, since we unravelled their work; effacing all above which they had superscribed; restoring all below which they had effaced.

Here, for instance, is a parchment which contained some Grecian tragedy, the Agamemnon of Æschylus, or the Phœnissæ of Euripides. This had possessed a value almost inappreciable in the eyes of accomplished scholars, continually growing rarer through generations But four centuries are gone by since the destruction of the Western Empire. Christianity, with towering grandeurs of another class, has founded a different empire; and some bigoted, yet perhaps holy monk, has washed away (as he persuades himself) the heathen's tragedy, replacing it with a monastic legend; which legend is disfigured with fables in its incidents, and yet in a higher sense is true, because interwoven with Christian morals, and with the sublimest of Christian revelations. Three, four, five centuries more, find man still devout as ever; but the language has become obsolete, and even for Christian devotion a new era has arisen, throwing it into the channel of crusading zeal or of chivalrous enthusiasm. The *membrana* is wanted now for a knightly romance — for "my Cid," or Cœur de Lion; for Sir Tristrem, or Lybæus Disconus. In this way, by means of the imperfect chemistry known to the mediæval period, the same roll has served as a conservatory for three separate generations of flowers and fruits, all perfectly different, and yet all specially adapted to the wants of the successive possessors. The Greek tragedy, the monkish legend, the knightly romance, each has ruled its own period. One harvest after another has been gathered into the garners of man through ages far apart. And the same hydraulic machinery has distributed, through the same marble fountains, water, milk, or wine, according to the habits and training of the generations that came to quench their thirst.

Such were the achievements of rude monastic chemistry. But the more elaborate chemistry of our own days has reversed all these motions of our simple ancestors, which results in every stage that to *them* would have realized the most fantastic amongst the promises of thaumaturgy. Insolent vaunt of Paracelsus, that he would restore the original rose or violet out of the ashes settling from its combustion — *that* is now rivalled in this modern achievement. The traces of each successive handwriting, regularly effaced, as had been imagined, have, in the inverse order, been regularly called back: the footsteps of the game pursued, wolf or stag, in each several chase, have been unlinked, and hunted back through all their doubles; and, as the chorus of the Athenian stage unwove through the antistrophe every step that had been mystically woven through the strophe, so, by our modern conjurations of science, secrets of ages remote from each other have been exorcised* from the accumulated shadows of centuries. Chemistry, a witch as potent as the Erictho of Lucanto (*Pharsalia*, lib. vi. or vii.), has extorted by her torments, from the dust and ashes of forgotten centuries, the secrets of a life extinct for the general eye, but still glowing in the embers. Even the fable of the Phœnix, that secular bird, who propagated his solitary existence, and his solitary births, along the line of centuries, through eternal relays of funeral mists, is but a type of what we have done with Palimpsests. We have backed

* Some readers may be apt to suppose, from all English experience, that the word *exorcise* means ptoperly banishment to the shades. Not so. Citation *from* the shades, or sometimes the torturing coërcion of mystic adjurations, is more truly the primar sense.

upon each phœnix in the long *regressus*, and forced him to expose his ancestral phœnix, sleeping in the ashes below his own ashes. Our good old forefathers would have been aghast at our sorceries; and, if they speculated on the propriety of burning Dr. Faustus. *us* they would have burned by acclamation. Trial there would have been none; and they could not otherwise have satisfied their horror of the brazen profligacy marking our modern magic, than by ploughing up the houses of all who had been parties to it, and sowing the ground with salt.

Fancy not, reader, that this tumult of images, illustrative or allusive, moves under any impulse or purpose of mirth. It is but the coruscation of a restless understanding, often made ten times more so by irritation of the nerves, such as you will first learn to comprehend (its *how* and its *why*) some stage or two ahead. The image, the memorial, the record, which for me is derived from a palimpsest, as to one great fact in our human being, and which immediately I will show you, is but too repellent of laughter; or, even if laughter *had* been possible, it would have been such laughter as oftentimes is thrown off from the fields of ocean,* laughter that hides, or that seems to

---

* "*Laughter from the fields of ocean.*" — Many readers will recall, though, at the moment of writing, my own thoughts did *not* recall, the well-known passage in the Prometheus —

—— *ποντιων τε κυματων*
Ανηριθμον γελασηα.

"O multitudinous laughter of the ocean billows!" It is not clear whether Æschylus contemplated the laughter as addressing the ear or the eye.

evade mustering tumult; foam-bells that weave garlands of phosphoric radiance for one moment round the eddies of gleaming abysses; mimicries of earth-born flowers that for the eye raise phantoms of gayety, as oftentimes for the ear they raise the echoes of fugitive laughter, mixing with the ravings and choir-voices of an angry sea.

What else than a natural and mighty palimpsest is the human brain? Such a palimpsest is my brain; such a palimpsest, oh reader! is yours. Everlasting layers of ideas, images, feelings, have fallen upon your brain softly as light. Each succession has seemed to bury all that went before. And yet, in reality, not one has been extinguished. And if, in the vellum palimpsest, lying amongst the other *diplomata* of human archives or libraries, there is anything fantastic or which moves to laughter, as oftentimes there is in the grotesque collisions of those successive themes, having no natural connection, which by pure accident have consecutively occupied the roll, yet, in our own heaven-created palimpsest, the deep memorial palimpsest of the brain, there are not and cannot be such incoherencies. The fleeting accidents of a man's life, and its external shows, may indeed be irrelate and incongruous; but the organizing principles which fuse into harmony, and gather about fixed predetermined centres, whatever heterogeneous elements life may have accumulated from without, will not permit the grandeur of human unity greatly to be violated, or its ultimate repose to be troubled, in the retrospect from dying moments, or from other great convulsions.

Such a convulsion is the struggle of gradual suffo

cation, as in drowning; and, in the original Opium Confessions, I mentioned a case of that nature communicated to me by a lady from her own childish experience. The lady is still living, though now of unusually great age; and I may mention that amongst her faults never was numbered any levity of principle, or carelessness of the most scrupulous veracity; but, on the contrary, such faults as arise from austerity, too harsh, perhaps, and gloomy indulgent neither to others nor herself. And, at the time of relating this incident, when already very old, she had become religious to asceticism. According to my present belief, she had completed her ninth year, when, playing by the side of a solitary brook, she fell into one of its deepest pools. Eventually, but after what lapse of time nobody ever knew, she was saved from death by a farmer, who, riding in some distant lane, had seen her rise to the surface; but not until she had descended within the abyss of death, and looked into its secrets, as far, perhaps, as ever human eye *can* have looked that had permission to return. At a certain stage of this descent, a blow seemed to strike her, phosphoric radiance sprang forth from her eyeballs; and immediately a mighty theatre expanded within her brain. In a moment, in the twinkling of an eye, every act, every design of her past life, lived again, arraying themselves not as a succession, but as parts of a coëxistence. Such a light fell upon the whole path of her life backwards into the shades of infancy, as the light, perhaps, which wrapt the destined Apostle on his road to Damascus. Yet that light blinded for a season; but hers poured celestial vision upon the brain, so that her consciousness became omnipresent at one moment to every feature in the infinite review.

This anecdote was treated sceptically at the time by some critics. But, besides that it has since been confirmed by other experience essentially the same, reported by other parties in the same circumstances, who had never heard of each other, the true point for astonishment is not the *simultaneity* of arrangement under which the past events of life, though in fact successive, had formed their dread line of revelation. This was but a secondary phenomenon; the deeper lay in the resurrection itself, and the possibility of resurrection, for what had so long slept in the dust. A pall, deep as oblivion, had been thrown by life over every trace of these experiences; and yet suddenly, at a silent command, at the signal of a blazing rocket sent up from the brain, the pall draws up, and the whole depths of the theatre are exposed. Here was the greater mystery: now this mystery is liable to no doubt; for it is repeated, and ten thousand times repeated, by opium, for those who are its martyrs.

Yes, reader, countless are the mysterious hand-writings of grief or joy which have inscribed themselves successively upon the palimpsest of your brain; and, like the annual leaves of aboriginal forests, or the undissolving snows on the Himalaya, or light falling upon light, the endless strata have covered up each other in forgetfulness. But by the hour of death, but by fever, but by the searchings of opium, all these can revive in strength. They are not dead, but sleeping In the illustration imagined by myself, from the case of some individual palimpsest, the Grecian tragedy had seemed to be displaced, but was *not* displaced, by the monkish legend; and the monkish legend had seemed to be displaced, but was *not* displaced, by the knightly romance. In some potent convulsion of the system, all wheels back into its earliest elementary stage. The bewildering romance, light tarnished with darkness, the semi-fabulous legend, truth celestial mixed with human falsehoods, these fade even of themselves, as life advances. The romance has perished that the young man adored; the legend has gone that deluded the boy; but the deep, deep tragedies of infancy, as when the child's hands were unlinked forever from his mother's neck, or his lips forever from his sister's kisses, these remain lurking below all, and these lurk to the last. Alchemy there is none of passion or disease that can scorch away these immortal impresses; and the dream which closed the preceding section, together with the succeeding dreams of this (which may be viewed as in the nature of choruses winding up the overture contained in Part I.), are but illustrations of this truth, such as every man probably will meet experimentally who passes through similar convulsions of dreaming or delirium from any similar or equal disturbance in his nature.*

* This, it may be said, requires a corresponding duration of experience but, as an argument for this mysterious power lurking in our nature, I may remind the reader of one phenomenon open to the notice of everybody, namely, the tendency of very aged persons to throw back and concentrate the light of their memory upon scenes of early childhood, as to which they recall many traces that had faded even to *themselves* in middle life, whilst they often forget altogether the whole intermediate stages of their experience. This shows that naturally, and without violent agencies, the human brain is by tendency a palimpsest.

LEVANA AND OUR LADIES OF SORROW.

Oftentimes at Oxford I saw Levana in my dreams. I knew her by her Roman symbols. Who is Levana? Reader, that do not pretend to have leisure for very much scholarship, you will not be angry with me for telling you. Levana was the Roman goddess that performed for the new-born infant the earliest office of ennobling kindness, — typical, by its mode, of that grandeur which belongs to man everywhere, and of that benignity in powers invisible which even in Pagan worlds sometimes descends to sustain it. At the very moment of birth, just as the infant tasted for the first time the atmosphere of our troubled planet, it was laid on the ground. *That* might bear different interpretations. But immediately, lest so grand a creature should grovel there for more than one instant, either the paternal hand, as proxy for the goddess Levana, or some near kinsman, as proxy for the father, raised it upright, bade it look erect as the king of all this world, and presented its forehead to the stars, saying, perhaps, in his heart, "Behold what is greater than yourselves!" This symbolic act represented the function of Levana. And that mysterious lady, who never revealed her face (except to me in dreams), but always acted by delegation, had her name from the Latin verb (as still it is the Italian verb) *levare*, to raise aloft.

This is the explanation of Levana. And hence it has arisen that some people have understood by Levana the tutelary power that controls the education of the nursery. She, that would not suffer at his birth even a prefigurative or mimic degradation for her awful ward, far less could be supposed to suffer the real degradation attaching to the non-development of his powers. She therefore watches over human education. Now, the word *edŭco*, with the penultimate short, was derived (by a process often exemplified in the crystallization of languages) from the word *edūco*, with the penultimate long. Whatsoever *educes*, or develops, *educates*. By the education of Levana, therefore, is meant, — not the poor machinery that moves by spelling-books and grammars, but by that mighty system of central forces hidden in the deep bosom of human life, which by passion, by strife, by temptation, by the energies of resistance, works forever upon children, — resting not day or night, any more than the mighty wheel of day and night themselves, whose moments, like restless spokes, are glimmering* forever as they revolve.

If, then, *these* are the ministries by which Levana works, how profoundly must she reverence the agencies of grief! But you, reader! think, — that children

* "*Glimmering*." — As I have never allowed myself to covet any man's ox nor his ass, nor anything that is his, still less would it become a philosopher to covet other people's images, or metaphors. Here, therefore, I restore to Mr. Wordsworth this fine image of the revolving wheel, and the glimmering spokes, as applied by him to the flying successions of day and night. I borrowed it for one moment in order to point my own sentence; which being done, the reader is witness that I now pay it back instantly by a note made for that sole purpose. On the same principle I often borrow their seals from young ladies, when closing my letters. Because there is sure to be some tender sentiment upon them about "memory," or "hope," or "roses, or "reünion;" and my correspondent must be a sad brute who is not touched by the eloquenc of the seal, even if his taste is so bad that he remains deaf to mine.

generally are not liable to grief such as mine. There are two senses in the word *generally*, — the sense of Euclid, where it means *universally* (or in the whole extent of the *genus*), and a foolish sense of this world, where it means *usually*. Now, I am far from saying that children universally are capable of grief like mine. But there are more than you ever heard of who die of grief in this island of ours. I will tell you a common case. The rules of Eton require that a boy on the *foundation* should be there twelve years: he is superannuated at eighteen, consequently he must come at six. Children torn away from mothers and sisters at that age not unfrequently die. I speak of what I know. The complaint is not entered by the registrar as grief; but *that* it is. Grief of that sort, and at that age, has killed more than ever have been counted amongst its martyrs.

Therefore it is that Levana often communes with the powers that shake man's heart: therefore it is that she dotes upon grief. "These ladies," said I softly to myself, on seeing the ministers with whom Levana was conversing, "these are the Sorrows; and they are three in number, as the *Graces* are three, who dress man's life with beauty: the *Parcæ* are three, who weave the dark arras of man's life in their mysterious loom always with colors sad in part, sometimes angry with tragic crimson and black; the *Furies* are three, who visit with retributions called from the other side of the grave offences that walk upon this; and at once even the *Muses* were but three, who fit the harp, the trumpet, or the lute, to the great burdens of man's impassioned creations. These are the Sorrows, all three of whom I know." The last words I say *now;* but in Oxford I said, "one of whom I know, and the others too surely I *shall* know." For already, in my fervent youth, I saw (dimly relieved upon the dark back-ground of my dreams) the imperfect lineaments of the awful sisters. These sisters — by what name shall we call them?

If I say simply, "The Sorrows," there will be a chance of mistaking the term; it might be understood of individual sorrow, — separate cases of sorrow, — whereas I want a term expressing the mighty abstractions that incarnate themselves in all individual sufferings of man's heart; and I wish to have these abstractions presented as impersonations, that is, as clothed with human attributes of life, and with functions pointing to flesh. Let us call them, therefore, *Our Ladies of Sorrow.* I know them thoroughly, and have walked in all their kingdoms. Three sisters they are, of one mysterious household; and their paths are wide apart; but of their dominion there is no end. Them I saw often conversing with Levana, and sometimes about myself. Do they talk, then? O, no! Mighty phantoms like these disdain the infirmities of language. They may utter voices through the organs of man when they dwell in human hearts, but amongst themselves is no voice nor sound; eternal silence reigns in *their* kingdoms. *They* spoke not, as they talked with Levana; *they* whispered not; *they* sang not; though oftentimes methought they *might* have sung: for I upon earth had heard their mysteries oftentimes deciphered by harp and timbrel, by dulcimer and organ. Like God, whose servants they are, they utter their pleasure not by sounds that perish, or by words that go astray, but by signs in heaven, by changes on earth, by pulses in secret rivers, heraldries painted on darkness, and hieroglyphics written on the tablets of the brain. *They* wheeled in mazes; *I* spelled the steps. *They* telegraphed from afar; *I* read the signals. *They* conspired together; and on the mirrors of darkness *my* eye traced the plots. *Theirs* were the symbols; *mine* are the words.

What is it the sisters are? What is it that they do? Let me describe their form, and their presence; if form it were that still fluctuated in its outline; or presence it were that forever advanced to the front, or forever receded amongst shades.

The eldest of the three is named *Mater Lachrymarum*, Our Lady of Tears. She it is that night and day raves and moans, calling for vanished faces. She stood in Rama, where a voice was heard of lamentation, — Rachel weeping for her children, and refused to be comforted. She it was that stood in Bethlehem on the night when Herod's sword swept its nurseries of Innocents, and the little feet were stiffened forever, which, heard at times as they tottered along floors overhead, woke pulses of love in household hearts that were not unmarked in heaven.

Her eyes are sweet and subtile, wild and sleepy, by turns; oftentimes rising to the clouds, oftentimes challenging the heavens. She wears a diadem round her head. And I knew by childish memories that she could go abroad upon the winds, when she heard that sobbing of litanies, or the thundering of organs, and when she beheld the mustering of summer clouds. This sister, the elder, it is that carries keys more than papal at her

16

girdle, which open every cottage and every palace. She, to my knowledge, sate all last summer by the bedside of the blind beggar, him that so often and so gladly I talked with, whose pious daughter, eight years old with the sunny countenance, resisted the temptations of play and village mirth to travel all day long on dusty roads with her afflicted father. For this did God send her a great reward. In the spring-time of the year, and whilst yet her own spring was budding, he recalled her to himself. But her blind father mourns forever over *her;* still he dreams at midnight that the little guiding hand is locked within his own; and still he wakens to a darkness that is *now* within a second and a deeper darkness. This *Mater Lachrymarum* also has been sitting all this winter of 1844–5 within the bedchamber of the Czar, bringing before his eyes a daughter (not less pious) that vanished to God not less suddenly, and left behind her a darkness not less profound. By the power of her keys it is that Our Lady of Tears glides a ghostly intruder into the chambers of sleepless men, sleepless women, sleepless children, from Ganges to the Nile, from Nile to Mississippi. And her, because she is the first-born of her house, and has the widest empire, let us honor with the title of "Madonna."

The second sister is called *Mater Suspiriorum,* Our Lady of Sighs. She never scales the clouds, nor walks abroad upon the winds. She wears no diadem. And her eyes, if they were ever seen, would be neither sweet nor subtile; no man could read their story; they would be found filled with perishing dreams, and with wrecks of forgotten delirium. But she raises not her eyes; her head, on which sits a dilapidated turban, droops forever, forever fastens on the dust. She weeps not. She groans not. But she sighs inaudibly at intervals. Her sister Madonna is oftentimes stormy and frantic, raging in the highest against heaven, and demanding back her darlings. But Our Lady of Sighs never clamors, never defies, dreams not of rebellious aspirations. She is humble to abjectness. Hers is the meekness that belongs to the hopeless. Murmur she may, but it is in her sleep. Whisper she may, but it is to herself in the twilight. Mutter she does at times, but it is in solitary places that are desolate as she is desolate, in ruined cities, and when the sun has gone down to his rest. This sister is the visiter of the Pariah, of the Jew, of the bondsman to the oar in the Mediterranean galleys; of the English criminal in Norfolk Island, blotted out from the books of remembrance in sweet far-off England; of the baffled penitent reverting his eyes forever upon a solitary grave, which to him seems the altar overthrown of some past and bloody sacrifice, on which altar no oblations can now be availing, whether towards pardon that he might implore, or towards reparation that he might attempt. Every slave that at noonday looks up to the tropical sun with timid reproach, as he points with one hand to the earth, our general mother, but for *him* a step-mother,—as he points with the other hand to the Bible, our general teacher, but against *him* sealed and sequestered;* — every

* This, the reader will be aware, applies chiefly to the cotton and tobacco States of North America; but not to them only: on which account I have not scrupled to figure the sun, which looks down upon slavery, as *tropical;* no matter if strictly within the tropics or simply so near to them as to produce a similar climate.

woman sitting in darkness, without love to shelter her head, or hope to illumine her solitude, because the heaven-born instincts kindling in her nature germs of holy affections, which God implanted in her womanly bosom, having been stifled by social necessities, now burn sullenly to waste, like sepulchral lamps amongst the ancients; every nun defrauded of her unreturning May-time by wicked kinsman, whom God will judge; every captive in every dungeon; all that are betrayed, and all that are rejected; outcasts by traditionary law, and children of *hereditary* disgrace, — all these walk with Our Lady of Sighs. She also carries a key; but she needs it little. For her kingdom is chiefly amongst the tents of Shem, and the houseless vagrant of every clime. Yet in the very highest ranks of man she finds chapels of her own; and even in glorious England there are some that, to the world, carry their heads as proudly as the reindeer, who yet secretly have received her mark upon their foreheads.

But the third sister, who is also the youngest ——! Hush! whisper whilst we talk of *her!* Her kingdom is not large, or else no flesh should live; but within that kingdom all power is hers. Her head, turreted like that of Cybèle, rises almost beyond the reach of sight. She droops not; and her eyes rising so high *might* be hidden by distance. But, being what they are, they cannot be hidden; through the treble veil of crape which she wears, the fierce light of a blazing misery, that rests not for matins or for vespers, for noon of day or noon of night, for ebbing or for flowing tide, may be read from the very ground. She is the defier of God. She also is the mother of lunacies, and the suggestress of suicides. Deep lie the roots of her power; but narrow is the nation that she rules. For she can approach only those in whom a profound nature has been upheaved by central convulsions; in whom the heart trembles and the brain rocks under conspiracies of tempest from without and tempest from within. Madonna moves with uncertain steps, fast or slow, but still with tragic grace. Our Lady of Sighs creeps timidly and stealthily. But this youngest sister moves with incalculable motions, bounding, and with a tiger's leaps. She carries no key; for, though coming rarely amongst men, she storms all doors at which she is permitted to enter at all. And *her* name is *Mater Tenebrarum*, — Our Lady of Darkness.

These were the *Semnai Theai*, or Sublime Goddesses,* these were the *Eumenides*, or Gracious Ladies (so called by antiquity in shuddering propitiation) of my Oxford dreams. Madonna spoke. She spoke by her mysterious hand. Touching my head, she beckoned to Our Lady of Sighs; and *what* she spoke, translated out of the signs which (except in dreams) no man reads, was this:

"Lo! here is he, whom in childhood I dedicated to my altars. This is he that once I made my darling. Him I led astray, him I beguiled, and from heaven I stole away his young heart to mine. Through me did he become idolatrous; and through me it was, by lan-

---

* "*Sublime Goddesses.*" — The word σεμνος is usually rendered *venerable* in dictionaries; not a very flattering epithet for females. But by weighing a number of passages in which the word is used pointedly, I am disposed to think that it comes nearest to our idea of the *sublime*, as near as a Greek word *could* come.

guishing desires, that he worshipped the worm, and prayed to the wormy grave. Holy was the grave to him; lovely was its darkness; saintly its corruption. Him, this young idolator, I have seasoned for thee dear gentle Sister of Sighs! Do thou take him now to *thy* heart, and season him for our dreadful sister. And thou," — turning to the *Mater Tenebrarum*, she said, — "wicked sister, that temptest and hatest, do thou take him from *her*. See that thy sceptre lie heavy on his head. Suffer not woman and her tenderness to sit near him in his darkness. Banish the frailties of hope, wither the relenting of love, scorch the fountains of tears, curse him as only thou canst curse. So shall he be accomplished in the furnace, so shall he see the things that ought *not* to be seen, sights that are abominable, and secrets that are unutterable. So shall he read elder truths, sad truths, grand truths, fearful truths. So shall he rise again *before* he dies. And so shall our commission be accomplished which from God we had, — to plague his heart until we had unfolded the capacities of his spirit." *

---

* The reader, who wishes at all to understand the course of these Confessions, ought not to pass over this dream-legend. There is no great wonder that a vision, which occupied my waking thoughts in those years, should reäppear in my dreams. It was, in fact, a legend recurring in sleep, most of which I had myself silently written or sculptured in my daylight reveries. But its importance to the present Confessions is this, that it rehearses or prefigures their course. This FIRST part belongs to Madonna. The THIRD belongs to the "Mater Suspiriorum," and will be entitled *The Pariah Worlds*. The FOURTH, which terminates the work, belongs to the "Mater Tenebrarum," and will be entitled *The Kingdom of Darkness*. As to the SECOND, it is an interpolation requisite to the effect of the others, and will be explained in its proper place.

THE APPARITION OF THE BROCKEN.

Ascend with me on this dazzling Whitsunday the Brocken of North Germany. The dawn opened in cloudless beauty; it is a dawn of bridal June; but, as the hours advanced, her youngest sister April, that sometimes cares little for racing across both frontiers of May, frets the bridal lady's sunny temper with sallies of wheeling and careering showers, flying and pursuing, opening and closing, hiding and restoring. On such a morning, and reaching the summits of the forest mountain about sunrise, we shall have one chance the more for seeing the famous Spectre of the Brocken.* Who and what is he? He is a solitary

* "*Spectre of the Brocken.*" — This very striking phenomenon has been continually described by writers, both German and English, for the last fifty years. Many readers, however, will not have met with these descriptions; and on *their* account I add a few words in explanation, referring them for the best scientific comment on the case to Sir David Brewster's "Natural Magic." The spectre takes the shape of a human figure, or, if the visiters are more than one, then the spectres multiply; they arrange themselves on the blue ground of the sky, or the dark ground of any clouds that may be in the right quarter, or perhaps they are strongly relieved against a curtain of rock, at a distance of some miles, and always exhibiting gigantic proportions. At first, from the distance and the colossal size, every spectator supposes the appearance to be quite independent of himself. But very soon he is surprised to observe his own motions and gestures mimicked; and wakens to the conviction that the phantom is but a dilated reflection of himself. This Titan amongst the apparitions of earth is exceedingly capricious vanishing abruptly for reasons best known to himself, and more coy in coming forward than the Lady Echo of Ovid. One reason why he is seen so seldom must be ascribed to the concurrence of conditions under which only the phenomenon can be manifested; the sun must

apparition, in the sense of loving solitude; else he is not always solitary in his personal manifestations, but, on proper occasions, has been known to unmask a strength quite sufficient to alarm those who had been insulting him.

Now, in order to test the nature of this mysterious apparition, we will try two or three experiments upon him. What we fear, and with some reason, is, that as he lived so many ages with foul Pagan sorcerers, and witnessed so many centuries of dark idolatries, his heart may have been corrupted; and that even now his faith may be wavering or impure. We will try.

Make the sign of the cross, and observe whether he repeats it (as on Whitsunday* he surely ought to do).

be near to the horizon (which of itself implies a time of day inconvenient to a person starting from a station as distant as Elbingerode); the spectator must have his back to the sun; and the air must contain some vapor, but *partially* distributed. Coleridge ascended the Brocken on the Whitsunday of 1799, with a party of English students from Goettingen, but failed to see the phantom; afterwards in England (and under the three same conditions) he saw a much rarer phenomenon, which he described in the following eight lines. I give them from a correct copy (the apostrophe in the beginning must be understood as addressed to an ideal conception):

"And art thou nothing? Such thou art as when
The woodman winding westward up the glen
At wintry dawn, when o'er the sheep-track's maze
The viewless snow-mist weaves a glistening haze,
Sees full before him, gliding without tread,
An image with a glory round its head;
This shade he worships for its golden hues,
And *makes* (not knowing) that which he pursues."

* "*On Whitsunday.*" — It is singular, and perhaps owing to the temperature and weather likely to prevail in that early part of summer, that more appearances of the spectre have been witnessed on Whitsunday than on any other day.

Look! he *does* repeat it; but the driving showers perplex the images, and *that*, perhaps, it is which gives him the air of one who acts reluctantly or evasively. Now, again, the sun shines more brightly, and the showers have swept off like squadrons of cavalry to the rear. We will try him again.

Pluck an anemone, one of these many anemones which once was called the sorcerer's flower,* and bore a part, perhaps, in this horrid ritual of fear; carry it to that stone which mimics the outline of a heathen altar, and once was called the sorcerer's altar;* then bending your knee, and raising your right hand to God, say, — "Father, which art in heaven, this lovely anemone, that once glorified the worship of fear, has travelled back into thy fold; this altar, which once reeked with bloody rites to Cortho, has long been rebaptized into thy holy service. The darkness is gone; the cruelty is gone which the darkness bred; the moans have passed away which the victims uttered; the cloud has vanished which once sate continually upon their graves, cloud of protestation that ascended forever to thy throne from the tears of the defenceless, and the anger of the just. And lo! I thy servant, with this dark phantom, whom for one hour on this thy festival of Pentecost I make *my* servant, render thee united worship in this thy recovered temple."

* "*The sorcerer's flower*," and "*the sorcerer's altar.*" — These are names still clinging to the anemone of the Brocken, and to an altar-shaped fragment of granite near one of the summits; and it is not doubted that they both connect themselves, through links of ancient tradition, with the gloomy realities of Paganism, when the whole Hartz and the Brocken formed for a very long time the last asylum to a ferocious but perishing idolatry.

Look now! the apparition plucks an anemone, and places it on an altar; he also bends his knee, he also raises his right hand to God. Dumb he is; but sometimes the dumb serve God acceptably. Yet still it occurs to you, that perhaps on this high festival of the Christian church he may be overruled by supernatural influence into confession of his homage, having so often been made to bow and bend his knee at murderous rites. In a service of religion he may be timid. Let us try him, therefore, with an earthly passion, where he will have no bias either from favor or from fear.

If, then, once in childhood you suffered an affection that was ineffable, — if once, when powerless to face such an enemy, you were summoned to fight with the tiger that couches within the separations of the grave, — in that case, after the example of Judæa (on the Roman coins), — sitting under her palm-tree to weep, but sitting with her head veiled, — do you also veil your head. Many years are passed away since then; and you were a little ignorant thing at that time, hardly above six years old; or perhaps (if you durst tell all the truth), not quite so much. But your heart was deeper than the Danube; and, as was your love, so was your grief. Many years are gone since that darkness settled on your head; many summers, many winters; yet still its shadows wheel round upon you at intervals, like these April showers upon this glory of bridal June. Therefore now, on this dovelike morning of Pentecost, do you veil your head like Judæa in memory of that transcendent woe, and in testimony that, indeed, it surpassed all utterance of words. Immediately you see that the apparition of the Brocken veils *his* head, after the model of Judæa weeping under her palm-tree, as if he also had a human heart, and that *he* also, in childhood, having suffered an affliction which was ineffable, wished by these mute symbols to breathe a sigh towards heaven in memory of that affliction, and by way of record, though many a year after, that it was indeed unutterable by words.

This trial is decisive. You are now satisfied that the apparition is but a reflex of yourself; and, in uttering your secret feelings to *him*, you make this phantom the dark symbolic mirror for reflection to the daylight what else must be hidden forever.

Such a relation does the Dark Interpreter, whom immediately the reader will learn to know as an intruder into my dreams, bear to my own mind. He is originally a mere reflex of my inner nature. But as the apparition of the Brocken sometimes is disturbed by storms or by driving showers, so as to dissemble his real origin, in like manner the Interpreter sometimes swerves out of my orbit, and mixes a little with alien natures. I do not always know him in these cases as my own parhelion. What he says, generally, is but that which *I* have said in daylight, and in meditation deep enough to sculpture itself on my heart. But sometimes, as his face alters, his words alter; and they do not always seem such as I have used, or *could* use. No man can account for all things that occur in dreams. Generally I believe this,—that he is a faithful representative of myself; but he also is at times subject to the action of the good *Phantasus*, who rules in dreams.

Hailstone choruses* besides, and storms, enter my dreams. Hailstones and fire that run along the ground, sleet and blinding hurricanes, revelations of glory insufferable pursued by volleying darkness, — these are powers able to disturb any features that originally were but shadow, and so send drifting the anchors of any vessel that rides upon deeps so treacherous as those of dreams. Understand, however, the Interpreter to bear generally the office of a tragic chorus at Athens. The Greek chorus is perhaps not quite understood by critics, any more than the Dark Interpreter by myself. But the leading function of both must be supposed this — not to tell you anything absolutely new, — *that* was done by the actors in the drama; but to recall you to your own lurking thoughts, — hidden for the moment or imperfectly developed, — and to place before you, in immediate connection with groups vanishing too quickly for any effort of meditation on your own part, such commentaries, prophetic or looking back, pointing the moral or deciphering the mystery, justifying Providence, or mitigating the fierceness of anguish, as would or might have occurred to your own meditative heart, had only time been allowed for its motions.

The Interpreter is anchored and stationary in my dreams; but great storms and driving mists cause him to fluctuate uncertainly, or even to retire altogether, like his gloomy counterpart, the shy phantom of the Brocken, — and to assume new features or strange

---

* "*Hailstone choruses.*" — I need not tell any lover of Handel that his oratorio of "Israel in Egypt" contains a chorus familiarly known by this name. The words are: "And he gave them hail stones for rain; fire, mingled with hail, ran along upon the ground."

features, as in dreams always there is a power not contented with reproduction, but which absolutely creates or transforms. This dark being the reader will see again in a further stage of my opium experience; and I warn him that he will not always be found sitting inside my dreams, but at times outside, and in open daylight.

FINALE TO PART I. — SAVANNAH-LA-MAR.

God smote Savannah-la-mar, and in one night, by earthquake, removed her, with all her towers standing and population sleeping, from the steadfast foundations of the shore to the coral floors of ocean. And God said, — "Pompeii did I bury and conceal from men through seventeen centuries: this city I will bury, but not conceal. She shall be a monument to men of my mysterious anger, set in azure light through generations to come; for I will enshrine her in a crystal dome of my tropic seas." This city, therefore, like a mighty galleon with all her apparel mounted, streamers flying, and tackling perfect, seems floating along the noiseless depths of ocean; and oftentimes in glassy calms, through the translucid atmosphere of water that now stretches like an air-woven awning above the silent encampment, mariners from every clime look down into her courts and terraces, count her gates, and number the spires of her churches. She is one ample cemetery, and *has* been for many a year; but in the mighty calms that brood for weeks over tropic latitudes, she fascinates the eye with a *Fata-Morgana* revelation, as of human life still subsisting in submarine asylums sacred from the storms that torment our upper air.

Thither, lured by the loveliness of cerulean depths, by the peace of human dwellings privileged from molestation, by the gleam of marble altars sleeping in everlasting sanctity, oftentimes in dreams did I and the Dark Interpreter cleave the watery veil that divided us from her streets. We looked into the belfries, where the pendulous bells were waiting in vain for the summons which should awaken their marriage peals; together we touched the mighty organ-keys, that sang no *jubilates* for the ear of Heaven, that sang no requiems for the ear of human sorrow; together we searched the silent nurseries, where the children were all asleep, and *had* been asleep through five generations. "They are waiting for the heavenly dawn," whispered the Interpreter to himself: "and, when *that* comes, the bells and the organs will utter a *jubilate* repeated by the echoes of Paradise." Then, turning to me, he said,—"This is sad, this is piteous; but less would not have sufficed for the purpose of God. Look here. Put into a Roman clepsydra one hundred drops of water; let these run out as the sands in an hour-glass; every drop measuring the hundredth part of a second, so that each shall represent but the three-hundred-and-sixty-thousandth part of an hour. Now, count the drops as they race along; and, when the fiftieth of the hundred is passing, behold! forty-nine are not, because already they have perished; and fifty are not, because they are yet to come. You see, therefore, how narrow, how incalculably narrow, is the true and actual present. Of that time which we call the present, hardly a hundredth part but belongs either to a past which has fled, or to a future which is still on the wing. It has perished, or it is not born. It was, or it is not. Yet even this approximation to the truth is *infinitely* false. For again subdivide that solitary drop, which only was found to represent the present, into a lower series of similar fractions, and the actual present which you arrest measures now but the thirty-sixth-millionth of an hour; and so by infinite declensions the true and very present, in which only we live and enjoy, will vanish into a mote of a mote, distinguishable only by a heavenly vision. Therefore the present, which only man possesses, offers less capacity for his footing than the slenderest film that ever spider twisted from her womb. Therefore, also, even this incalculable shadow from the narrowest pencil of moonlight is more transitory than geometry can measure, or thought of angel can overtake. The time which *is* contracts into a mathematic point; and even that point perishes a thousand times before we can utter its birth. All is finite in the present; and even that finite is infinite in its velocity of flight towards death. But in God there is nothing finite; but in God there is nothing transitory; but in God there *can* be nothing that tends to death. Therefore, it follows, that for God there can be no present. The future is the present of God, and to the future it is that he sacrifices the human present. Therefore it is that he works by earthquake. Therefore it is that he works by grief. O, deep is the ploughing of earthquake! O, deep" — [and his voice swelled like a *sanctus* rising from the choir of a cathedral] — "O, deep is the ploughing of grief! But oftentimes less would not suffice for the agriculture of God. Upon a night of earthquake he builds a thousand years of pleasant habitations for man. Upon the sorrow of an infant he raises oftentimes from human intellects glorious vintages that could not else have been. Less than these fierce ploughshares would not have stirred the stubborn soil. The one is needed for earth, our planet, — for earth itself as the dwelling-place of man; but the other is needed yet oftener for God's mightiest instrument, — yes" [and he looked solemnly at myself], "is needed for the mysterious children of the earth!"

PART II.

The Oxford visions, of which some have been given, were but anticipations necessary to illustrate the glimpse opened of childhood (as being its reäction). In this Second part, returning from that anticipation, I retrace an abstract of my boyish and youthful days, so far as they furnished or exposed the germs of later experiences in worlds more shadowy.

Upon me, as upon others scattered thinly by tens and twenties over every thousand years, fell too powerfully and too early the vision of life. The horror of life mixed itself already in earliest youth with the heavenly sweetness of life; that grief, which one in a hundred has sensibility enough to gather from the sad retrospect of life in its closing stage, for me shed its dews as a prelibation upon the fountains of life whilst yet sparkling to the morning sun. I saw from afar and from before what I was to see from behind. Is this the description of an early youth passed in the shades of gloom? No; but of a youth passed in the divinest happiness. And if the reader has (which so few have) the passion, without which there is no reading of the legend and superscription upon man's brow, if he is not (as most are) deafer than the grave to every *deep* note that sighs upwards from the Delphic caves of human life, he will know that the rapture of life (or anything which by approach can merit that name) does not arise, unless as perfect music arises, music of Mozart or Beethoven, by the confluence of the mighty and terrific discords with the subtile concords. Not by contrast, or as reciprocal foils, do these elements act, which is the feeble conception of many, but by union. They are the sexual forces in music: "male and female created he them;" and these mighty antagonists do not put forth their hostilities by repulsion, but by deepest attraction.

As "in to-day already walks to-morrow," so in the past experience of a youthful life may be seen dimly the future. The collisions with alien interests or hostile views, of a child, boy, or very young man, so insulated as each of these is sure to be, — those aspects of opposition which such a person *can* occupy, — are limited by the exceedingly few and trivial lines of connection along which he is able to radiate any essential influence whatever upon the fortunes or happiness of others. Circumstances may magnify his importance for the moment; but, after all, any cable which he carries out upon other vessels is easily slipped upon a feud arising. Far otherwise is the state of relations connecting an adult or responsible man with the circles around him, as life advances. The net-work of these relations is a thousand times more intricate, the jarring of these intricate relations a thousand times more frequent, and the vibrations a thousand times harsher which these jarrings diffuse. This truth is felt beforehand misgivingly and in troubled vision, by a young man who stands upon the threshold of manhood. One earliest instinct of fear and horror would darken his spirit, if it could be revealed to itself and self-questioned at the moment of birth: a second instinct of the same nature would again pollute that tremulous mirror, if the moment were as punctually marked as physical birth is marked, which dismisses him finally upon the tides of absolute self-control. A dark ocean would seem the total expanse of life from the first; but far darker and more appalling would seem that interior and second chamber of the ocean which called him away forever from the direct accountability of others. Dreadful would be the morning which should say, "Be thou a human child incarnate;" but more dreadful the morning which should say, "Bear thou henceforth the sceptre of thy self-dominion through life, and the passion of life!" Yes, dreadful would be both; but without a basis of the dreadful there is no perfect rapture. It is a part through the sorrow of life, growing out of dark events, that this basis of awe and solemn darkness slowly accumulates. *That* I have illustrated. But, as life expands, it is more through the *strife* which besets us, strife from conflicting opinions, positions, passions, interests, that the funereal ground settles and deposits itself, which sends upward the dark lustrous brilliancy through the jewel of life, else revealing a pale and superficial glitter. Either the human being must suffer and struggle as the price of a more searching vision, or his gaze must be shallow, and without intellectual revelation.

Through accident it was in part, and, where through no accident but my own nature, not through features of it at all painful to recollect, that constantly in early life (that is, from boyish days until eighteen, when, by going to Oxford, practically I became my own master) I was engaged in duels of fierce continual struggle, with some person or body of persons, that sought, like the Roman *retiarius*, to throw a net of deadly coërcion or constraint over the undoubted rights of my natural freedom. The steady rebellion upon my part in one half was a mere human reäction of justifiable indignation; but in the other half it was the struggle of a conscientious nature, — disdaining to feel it as any mere right or discretional privilege, — no, feeling it as the noblest of duties to resist, though it should be mortally, those that would have enslaved me, and to retort scorn upon those that would have put my head below their feet. Too much, even in later life, I have perceived, in men that pass for good men, a disposition to degrade (and if possible to degrade through self-degradation) those in whom unwillingly they feel any weight of oppression to themselves, by commanding qualities of intellect or character. They respect you: they are compelled to do so, and they hate to do so. Next, therefore, they seek to throw off the sense of this oppression, and to take vengeance for it, by coöperating with any unhappy accidents in your life, to inflict a sense of humiliation upon you, and (if possible) to force you into becoming a consenting party to that humiliation. (O, wherefore is it that those who presume to call themselves the "friends" of this man or that woman are so often those, above all others, whom in the hour of death that man or woman is most likely to salute with the valediction — Would God I had never seen your face?)

In citing one or two cases of these early struggles, I have chiefly in view the effect of these upon my subsequent visions under the reign of opium. And this indulgent reflection should accompany the mature reader through all such records of boyish inexperience. A good-tempered man, who is also acquainted with the world, will easily evade, without needing any artifice of servile obsequiousness, those quarrels which an upright simplicity, jealous of its own rights, and unpractised in the science of worldly address, cannot always evade without some loss of self-respect. Suavity in this manner may, it is true, be reconciled with firmness in the matter; but not easily by a young person who wants all the appropriate resources of knowledge, of adroit and guarded language, for making his good temper available. Men are protected from insult and wrong, not merely by their own skill, but also, in the absence of any skill at all, by the general spirit of forbearance to which society has trained all those whom they are likely to meet. But boys meeting with no such forbearance or training in other boys, must sometimes be thrown upon feuds in the ratio of their own firmness, much more than in the ratio of any natural proneness to quarrel. Such a subject, however, will be best illustrated by a sketch or two of my own principal feuds.

The first, but merely transient and playful, nor worth noticing at all, but for its subsequent resurrection under other and awful coloring in my dreams, grew out of an imaginary slight, as I viewed it, put upon me by one of my guardians. I had four guardians; and the one of these who had the most knowledge and talent of the whole — a banker, living about a hundred miles from my home — had invited me, when eleven years old, to his house. His eldest daughter, perhaps a year younger than myself, wore at that time upon her very lovely face the most angelic expression of character and temper that I have almost ever seen. Naturally, I fell in love with her. It seems absurd to say so; and the more so, because two children more absolutely innocent than we were cannot be imagined, neither of us having ever been at any school; but the simple truth is, that in the most chivalrous sense I was in love with her. And the proof that I was so showed itself in three separate modes: I kissed her glove on any rare occasion when I found it lying on a table; secondly, I looked out for some excuse to be jealous of her; and, thirdly, I did my very best to get up a quarrel. What I wanted the quarrel for was the luxury of a reconciliation; a hill cannot be had, you know, without going to the expense of a valley. And though I hated the very thought of a moment's difference with so truly gentle a girl, yet how, but through such a purgatory, could one win the paradise of her returning smiles? All this, however, came to nothing; and simply because she positively would *not* quarrel. And the jealousy fell through, because there was no decent subject for such a passion, unless it had settled upon an old music-master, whom lunacy itself could not adopt as a rival. The quarrel, meantime, which never prospered with the daughter, silently kindled on my part towards the father. His offence was this. At dinner, I naturally placed myself by the side of M., and it gave me great pleasure to touch her hand at intervals. As M. was my cousin, though twice or even three times removed, I did not feel it taking too great a liberty in this little act of tenderness. No matter if three thousand times removed, I said, my cousin is my cousin; nor had I very much designed to conceal the act; or if so, rather on her account than my own. One evening, however, papa observed my manœuvre. Did he seem displeased? Not at all; he even condescended to smile. But the next day he placed M. on the side opposite to myself. In one respect this was really an improvement, because it gave me a better view of my cousin's sweet countenance. But then there was the loss of the hand to be considered, and secondly there was the affront. It was clear that vengeance must be had. Now, there was but one thing in this world that I could do even decently; but *that* I could do admirably. This was writing Latin hexameters. Juvenal — though it was not very much of him that I had then read — seemed to me a divine model. The inspiration of wrath spoke through him as through a Hebrew prophet. The same inspiration spoke now in me. *Facit indignatio versum,* said Juvenal. And it must be owned that indignation has never made such good verses since as she did in that day. But still, even to me, this agile passion proved a Muse of genial inspiration for a couple of paragraphs; and one line I will mention as worthy to have taken its place in Juvenal himself. I say this without scruple, having not a shadow of vanity, nor, on the other hand, a shadow of false modesty connected with such boyish accomplishments. The poem opened thus:

> "Te nemis austerum sacræ qui fœdera mensæ
> Diruis, insector Satyræ reboante flagello."

But the line which I insist upon as of Roman strength was the closing one of the next sentence. The general effect of the sentiment was, that my clamorous wrath should make its way even into ears that were past hearing:

"——— mea sæva querela
Auribus insidet ceratis, auribus etsi
Non audituris hybernâ nocte procellam."

The power, however, which inflated my verse, soon collapsed; having been soothed, from the very first, by finding, that except in this one instance at the dinner-table, which probably had been viewed as an indecorum, no further restraint, of any kind whatever, was meditated upon my intercourse with M. Besides, it was too painful to lock up good verses in one's own solitary breast. Yet how could I shock the sweet filial heart of my cousin by a fierce lampoon or *stylites* against her father, had Latin even figured amongst her accomplishments? Then it occurred to me that the verses might be shown to the father. But was there not something treacherous in gaining a man's approbation under a mask to a satire upon himself? Or would he have always understood me? For one person, a year after, took the *sacræ mensæ* (by which I had meant the sanctities of hospitality) to mean the sacramental table. And on consideration, I began to suspect that many people would pronounce myself the party who had violated the holy ties of hospitality, which are equally binding on guest as on host. Indolence, which sometimes comes in aid of good impulses as well as bad, favored these relenting thoughts. The society of M. did still more to wean me from further efforts of satire; and, finally, my Latin poem remained a *torso*. But, upon the whole, my guardian had a narrow escape of descending to posterity in a disadvantag ous light, had he rolled down to it through my hexameters.

Here was a case of merely playful feud. But the same talent of Latin verses soon after connected me with a real feud, that harassed my mind more than would be supposed, and precisely by this agency, namely, that it arrayed one set of feelings against another. It divided my mind, as by domestic feud, against itself. About a year after returning from the visit to my guardian's, and when I must have been nearly completing my twelfth year, I was sent to a great public school. Every man has reason to rejoice who enjoys so great an advantage. I condemned, and *do* condemn, the practice of sometimes sending out into such stormy exposures those who are as yet too young, too dependent on female gentleness, and endowed with sensibilities too exquisite. But at nine or ten the masculine energies of the character are beginning to be developed; or if not, no discipline will better aid in their development than the bracing intercourse of a great English classical school. Even the selfish are forced into accommodating themselves to a public standard of generosity, and the effeminate into conforming to a rule of manliness. I was myself at two public schools; and I think with gratitude of the benefit which I reaped from both; as also I think with gratitude of the upright guardian in whose quiet household I learned Latin so effectually. But the small private schools which I witnessed for brief periods, containing thirty to forty boys, were models of ignoble manners as respected some part of the juniors, and of favoritism amongst the masters. Nowhere is the sublimity of public justice so broadly exemplified as in an English school. There is not in the universe such an areopagus for fair play, and abhorrence of all crooked ways, as an English mob, or one of the English time-honored public schools. But my own first introduction to such an establishment was under peculiar and contradictory circumstances. When my "rating," or graduation in the school, was to be settled, naturally my altitude (to speak astronomically) was taken by the proficiency in Greek. But I could then barely construe books so easy as the Greek Testament and the Iliad. This was considered quite well enough for my age; but still it caused me to be placed three steps below the highest rank in the school. Within one week, however, my talent for Latin verses, which had by this time gathered strength and expansion, became known. I was honored as never was man or boy since Mordecai the Jew. Not properly belonging to the flock of the head master, but to the leading section of the second, I was now weekly paraded for distinction at the supreme tribunal of the school; out of which at first grew nothing but a sunshine of approbation delightful to my heart, still brooding upon solitude. Within six weeks this had changed. The approbation, indeed, continued, and the public testimony of it. Neither would there, in the ordinary course, have been any painful reäction from jealousy, or fretful resistance to the soundness of my pretensions; since it was sufficiently known to some of my school-fellows, that I, who had no male relatives but military men, and those in India, could not have benefited by any clandestine aid. But, unhappily, the head master was at that time dissatisfied with some points in the progress of his head form; and, as it soon appeared, was continually throwing in their teeth the brilliancy of my verses at twelve, by comparison with theirs at seventeen, eighteen, and nineteen. I had observed him sometimes pointing to myself; and was perplexed at seeing this gesture followed by gloomy looks, and what French reporters call "sensation," in these young men, whom naturally I viewed with awe as my leaders, boys that were called young men, men that were reading Sophocles — (a name that carried with it the sound of something seraphic to my ears), — and who never had vouchsafed to waste a word on such a child as myself. The day was come, however, when all that would be changed. One of these leaders strode up to me in the public play-grounds, and delivering a blow on my shoulder, which was not intended to hurt me, but as a mere formula of introduction, asked me "What the d—l I meant by bolting out of the course, and annoying other people in that manner? Were other people to have no rest for me and my verses, which, after all, were horribly bad?" There might have been some difficulty in returning an answer to this address, but none was required. I was briefly admonished to see that I wrote worse for the future, or else ——. At this *aposiopesis*, I looked inquiringly at the speaker, and he filled up the chasm by saying that he would "annihilate" me. Could any person fail to be aghast at such a demand? I was to write worse than my own standard, which, by his account of my verses, must be difficult; and I was to write worse than himself, which might be impossible. My feelings revolted, it may be supposed, against so arrogant a demand, unless it had been far otherwise expressed; and on the next occasion for sending up verses, so far from attending to the orders issued, I double-shotted my guns; double applause descended on myself; but I remarked, with some awe though not repenting of what I had done, that double confusion seemed to agitate the ranks of my enemies. Amongst them loomed out in the distance my "annihilating" friend, who shook his huge fist at me, but with something like a grim smile about his eyes. He took an early opportunity of paying his respects to me, saying, "You little devil, do you call this writing your worst?" "No," I replied; "I call it writing my best." The annihilator, as it turned out, was really a good-natured young man; but he soon went off to Cambridge; and with the rest, or some of them, I continued to wage war for nearly a year. And yet, for a word spoken with kindness, I would have resigned the peacock's feather in my cap as the merest of baubles. Undoubtedly praise sounded sweet in my ears also. But that was nothing by comparison with what stood on the other side. I detested distinctions that were connected with mortification to others. And, even if I could have got over *that*, the eternal feud fretted and tormented my nature. Love, that once in childhood had been so mere a necessity to me, *that* had long been a mere reflected ray from a departed sunset. But peace, and freedom from strife, if love were no longer possible (as so rarely it is in this world), was the absolute necessity of my heart. To contend with somebody was still my fate; how to escape the contention I could not see; and yet for itself, and the deadly passions into which it forced me, I hated and loathed it more than death. It added to the distraction and internal feud of my own mind, that I could not *altogether* condemn the upper boys. I was made a handle of humiliation to them. And, in the mean time, if I had an advantage in one accomplishment, which is all a matter of accident, or peculiar taste and feeling, they, on the other hand, had a great advantage over me in the more elaborate difficulties of Greek, and of choral Greek poetry. I could not altogether wonder at their hatred of myself. Yet still, as they had chosen to adopt this mode of conflict with me, I did not feel that I had any choice but to resist. The contest was terminated for me by my removal from the school, in consequence of a very threatening illness affecting my head; but it lasted nearly a year, and it did not close before several amongst my public enemies had become my private friends. They were much older, but they invited me to the houses of their friends, and showed me a respect which deeply affected me, — this respect having more reference, apparently, to the firmness I had exhibited, than to the splendor of my verses. And, indeed, these had rather drooped, from a natural accident; several persons of my own class had formed the practice of asking me to write verses for *them*. I could not refuse. But, as the subjects given out were the same for all of us, it was not possible to take so many crops off the ground without starving the quality of all.

Two years and a half from this time, I was again at a public school of ancient foundation. Now I was myself one of the three who formed the highest class. Now I myself was familiar with Sophocles, who once had been so shadowy a name in my ear. But, strange to say, now, in my sixteenth year, I cared nothing at all for the glory of Latin verse. All the business of school was light and trivial in my eyes. Costing me not an effort, it could not engage any part of my attention; that was now swallowed up altogether by the literature of my native land. I still reverenced the Grecian drama, as always I must. But else I cared little then for classical pursuits. A deeper spell had mastered me; and I lived only in those bowers where deeper passions spoke.

Here, however, it was that began another and more important struggle. I was drawing near to seventeen, and, in a year after *that*, would arrive the usual time for going to Oxford. To Oxford my guardians made no objection; and they readily agreed to make the allowance then universally regarded as the *minimum* for an Oxford student, namely, £200 per annum. But they insisted, as a previous condition, that I should make a positive and definite choice of a profession. Now, I was well aware, that, if I *did* make such a choice, no law existed, nor could any obligation be created through deeds or signature, by which I could finally be compelled into keeping my engagement. But this evasion did not suit me. Here, again, I felt indignantly that the principle of the attempt was unjust. The object was certainly to do me service by saving money, since, if I selected the bar as my profession, it was contended by some persons (misinformed, however), that not Oxford, but a special pleader's office would be my proper destination; but I cared not for arguments of that sort. Oxford I was determined to nake my home; and also to bear my future course utterly untrammelled by promises that I might repent. Soon came the catastrophe of this struggle. A little before my seventeenth birth-day, I walked off, one lovely summer morning, to North Wales, rambled there for months, and, finally, under some obscure hopes of raising money on my personal security, I went up to London. Now I was in my eighteenth year, and during this period it was that I passed through that trial of severe distress, of which I gave some account in my former Confessions. Having a motive, however, for glancing backwards briefly at that period in the present series, I will do so at this point.

I saw in one journal an insinuation that the incidents in the *preliminary* narrative were possibly without foundation. To such an expression of mere gratuitous malignity, as it happened to be supported by no one argument, except a remark, apparently absurd, but certainly false, I did not condescend to answer. In reality, the possibility had never occurred to me that any person of judgment would seriously suspect me of taking liberties with that part of the work, since, though no one of the parties concerned but myself stood in so central a position to the circumstances as to be acquainted with *all* of them, many were acquainted with each separate section of the memoir. Relays of witnesses might have been summoned to mount guard, as it were, upon the accuracy of each particular in the whole succession of incidents; and some of these people had an interest, more or less strong, in exposing any deviation from the strictest *letter* of the truth, had it been in their power to do so It is now twenty-two years since I saw the objection here alluded to; and in saying that I did not condescend to notice it, the reader must not find any reason for taxing me with a blamable haughtiness. But every man is entitled to be haughty when his veracity is impeached; and still more when it is impeached by a dishonest objection, or, if not *that*, by an objection which argues a carelessness of attention almost amounting to dishonesty, in a case where it was meant to sustain an imputation of falsehood. Let a man read carelessly, if he will, but not where he is meaning to use his reading for a purpose of wounding another man's honor. Having thus, by twenty-two years' silence, sufficiently expressed my contempt for the slander,* I now feel myself at liberty to draw it into notice, for the sake, *inter alia*, of showing in how rash a spirit malignity often works. In the preliminary account of certain boyish adventures which had exposed me to suffering of a kind not commonly incident to persons in my station in life, and leaving behind a temptation to the use of opium under certain arrears of weakness, I had occasion to notice a disreputable attorney in London, who showed me some attentions, partly on my

* Being constantly almost an absentee from London, and very often from other great cities, so as to command oftentimes no favorable opportunities for overlooking the great mass of public journals, it is possible enough that other slanders of the same tenor may have existed. I speak of what met my own eye, or was accidentally reported to me ; but, in fact, all of us are exposed to this evil of calumnies lurking unseen, for no degree of energy, and no excess of disposable time, would enable any man to exercise this sort of vigilant police over *all* journals. Better, therefore, tranquilly to leave all such malice to confound itself.

own account as a boy of some expectations, but much more with the purpose of fastening his professional grappling-hooks upon the young Earl of A——t, my former companion, and my present correspondent. This man's house was slightly described, and, with more minuteness, I had exposed some interesting traits in his household economy. A question, therefore, naturally arose in several people's curiosity — Where was this house situated? and the more so because I had pointed a renewed attention to it by saying, that on that very evening (namely, the evening on which that particular page of the Confessions was written) I had visited the street, looked up at the windows, and, instead of the gloomy desolation reigning there when myself and a little girl were the sole nightly tenants, — sleeping, in fact (poor freezing creatures that we both were), on the floor of the attorney's law-chamber, and making a pillow out of his infernal parchments, — I had seen, with pleasure, the evidences of comfort, respectability, and domestic animation, in the lights and stir prevailing through different stories of the house. Upon this, the upright critic told his readers that I had described the house as standing in Oxford-street, and then appealed to their own knowledge of that street whether such a house could be *so* situated. Why not — he neglected to tell us. The houses at the east end of Oxford-street are certainly of too small an order to meet my account of the attorney's house; but why should it be at the east end? Oxford-street is a mile and a quarter long, and, being built continuously on both sides, finds room for houses of *many* classes. Meantime it happens that, although the true house was most obscurely indicated, *any* house whatever in Oxford-street was most luminously excluded. In all the immensity of London there was but one single street that could be challenged by an attentive reader of the Confessions as peremptorily *not* the street of the attorney's house, and *that* one was Oxford-street; for, in speaking of my own renewed acquaintance with the outside of this house, I used some expression implying that, in order to make such a visit of reconnoissance, I had turned *aside* from Oxford-street. The matter is a perfect trifle in itself, but it is no trifle in a question affecting a writer's accuracy. If in a thing so absolutely impossible to be forgotten as the true situation of a house painfully memorable to a man's feelings, from being the scene of boyish distresses the most exquisite, nights passed in the misery of cold, and hunger preying upon him, both night and day, in a degree which very many would not have survived,—he, when retracing his school-boy annals, could have shown indecision, even far more dreaded inaccuracy, in identifying the house,—not one syllable after *that*, which he could have said on any other subject, would have won any confidence, or deserved any, from a judicious reader. I may now mention—the Herod being dead whose persecutions I had reason to fear—that the house in question stands in Greek street on the west, and is the house on that side nearest to Soho-square, but without looking into the square. This it was hardly safe to mention at the date of the published Confessions. It was my private opinion, indeed, that there were probably twenty-five chances to one in favor of my friend the attorney having been by that time hanged. But then this argued inversely; one chance to twenty-five that my friend might be *un*hanged, and knocking about the streets of London; in which case it would have been a perfect god-send to him that here lay an opening (of *my* contrivance, not *his*) for requesting the opinion of a jury on the amount of *solatium* due to his wounded feelings in an action on the passage in the Confessions. To have indicated even the street would have been enough; because there could surely be but one such Grecian in Greek-street, or but one that realized the other conditions of the unknown quantity. There was also a separate danger not absolutely so laughable as it sounds. Me there was little chance that the attorney should meet; but my book he might easily have met (supposing always that the warrant of *Sus. per coll.* had not yet on *his* account travelled down to Newgate). For he was literary; admired literature; and, as a lawyer, he wrote on some subjects fluently; might he not publish *his* Confessions? Or, which would be worse, a supplement to mine, printed so as exactly to match? In which case I should have had the same affliction that Gibbon the historian dreaded so much, namely, that of seeing a refutation of himself, and his own answer to the refutation, all bound up in one and the same self-combating volume. Besides, he would have cross-examined me before the public, in Old Bailey style; no story, the most straightforward that ever was told, could be sure to stand *that*. And my readers might be left in a state of painful doubt, whether *he* might not, after all, have been a model of suffering innocence — I (to say the kindest thing possible) plagued with the natural treacheries of a schoolboy's memory. In taking leave of this case and the remembrances connected with it, let me say that, although really believing in the probability of the attorney's having at least found his way to Australia, I had no satisfaction in thinking of that result. I knew my friend to be the very perfection of a scamp. And in the running account between us (I mean, in the ordinary sense, as to money), the balance could not be in *his* favor; since I, on receiving a sum of money (considerable in the eyes of us both), had transferred pretty nearly the whole of it to *him*, for the purpose ostensibly held out to me (but of course a hoax) of purchasing certain law "stamps;" for he was then pursuing a diplomatic correspondence with various Jews who lent money to young heirs, in some trifling proportion on my own insignificant account, but much more truly on the account of Lord A——t, my young friend. On the other side, he had given to me simply the relics of his breakfast-table, which itself was hardly more than a relic. But in this he was not to blame. He could not give to me what he had not for himself, nor sometimes for the poor starving child whom I now suppose to have been his illegitimate daughter. So desperate was the running fight, yard-arm to yard-arm, which he maintained with creditors fierce as famine and hungry as the grave, — so deep also was his horror (I know not for which of the various reasons supposable) against falling into a prison, — that he seldom ventured to sleep twice successively in the same house. That expense of itself must have pressed heavily in London, where you pay half a crown at least for a bed that would cost only a shilling in the provinces. In the midst of his knaveries, and, what were even more shocking to my remembrance, his confidential discoveries in his rambling conversations of knavish *designs* (not always pecuniary), there was a light of wandering misery in his eye, at times, which affected me afterwards at intervals, when I recalled it in the radiant happiness of nineteen, and amidst the solemn tranquillities of Oxford. That of itself was interesting; the man was worse by far than he had been meant to be; he had not the mind that reconciles itself to evil. Besides, he respected scholarship, which appeared by the deference he generally showed to myself, then about seventeen; he had an interest in literature, — *that* argues something good; and was pleased at any time, or even cheerful, when I turned the conversation upon books; nay, he seemed touched with emotion when I quoted some sentiment noble and impassioned from one of the great poets, and would ask me to repeat it. He would have been a man of memorable energy, and for good purposes, had it not been for his agony of conflict with pecuniary embarrassments. These probably had commenced in some fatal compliance with temptation arising out of funds confided to him by a client. Perhaps he had gained fifty guineas for a moment of necessity, and had sacrificed for that trifle *only* the serenity and the comfort of a life. Feelings of relenting kindness it was not in my nature to refuse in such a case; and I wished to * * * * * *

But I never succeeded in tracing his steps through the wilderness of London until some years back, when I ascertained that he was dead. Generally speaking, the few people whom I have disliked in this world were flourishing people, of good repute. Whereas the knaves whom I have known, one and all, and by no means few, I think of with pleasure and kindness.

Heavens! when I look back to the sufferings which I have witnessed or heard of, even from this one brief London experience, I say, if life could throw open its long suites of chambers to our eyes from some station *beforehand*, — if, from some secret stand, we could look *by anticipation* along its vast corridors, and aside into the recesses opening upon them from either hand, — halls of tragedy or chambers of retribution, simply in that small wing and no more of the great caravanserai which we ourselves shall haunt, — simply in that narrow tract of time, and no more, where we ourselves shall range, and confining our gaze to those, and no others, for whom personally we shall be interested, — what a recoil we should suffer of horror in our estimate of life! What if those sudden catastrophes, or those inexpiable afflictions, which *have* already descended upon the people within my own knowledge, and almost below my own eyes, all of them now gone past, and some long past, had been thrown open before me as a secret exhibition when first I and they stood within the vestibule of morning hopes, — when the calamities themselves had hardly begun to gather in their elements of possibility, and when some of the parties to them were as yet no more than infants! The past viewed not *as* the past but by a spectator who steps back ten years deeper into the rear, in order that he may regard it as a future· the calamity of 1840 contemplated from the station of

1830,— the doom that rang the knell of happiness viewed from a point of time when as yet it was neither feared nor would even have been intelligible,—the name that killed in 1843, which in 1835 would have struck no vibration upon the heart,—the portrait that, on the day of her Majesty's coronation would have been admired by you with a pure disinterested admiration, but which, if seen to-day, would draw forth an involuntary groan,—cases such as these are strangely moving for all who add deep thoughtfulness to deep sensibility. As the hastiest of improvisations, accept, fair reader (for you it is that will chiefly feel such an invocation of the past), three or four illustrations from my own experience.

Who is this distinguished-looking young woman, with her eyes drooping, and the shadow of a dreadful shock yet fresh upon every feature? Who is the elderly lady, with her eyes flashing fire? Who is the downcast child of sixteen? What is that torn paper lying at their feet? Who is the writer? Whom does the paper concern? Ah! if she, if the central figure in the group—twenty-two at the moment when she is revealed to us—could, on her happy birth-day at sweet seventeen, have seen the image of herself five years onwards, just as *we* see it now, would she have prayed for life as for an absolute blessing? or would she not have prayed to be taken from the evil to come—to be taken away one evening, at least, before this day's sun arose? It is true, she still wears a look of gentle pride, and a relic of that noble smile which belongs to *her* that suffers an injury which many times over she would have died sooner than inflict. Womanly pride refuses itself before witnesses to the total prostration of the blow; but, for all *that*, you may see that she longs to be left alone, and that her tears will flow without restraint when she is so. This room is her pretty boudoir, in which, till to-night — poor thing! — she has been glad and happy. There stands her miniature conservatory, and there expands her miniature library; as we circumnavigators of literature are apt (you know) to regard all female libraries in the light of miniatures. None of these will ever rekindle a smile on *her* face; and there, beyond, is her music, which only of all that she possesses will now become dearer to her than ever; but not, as once, to feed a self-mocked pensiveness, or to cheat a half visionary sadness. She will be sad, indeed. But she is one of those that will suffer in silence. Nobody will ever detect *her* failing in any point of duty, or querulously seeking the support in others which she can find for herself in this solitary room. Droop she will not in the sight of men; and, for all beyond, nobody has any concern with *that*, except God. You shall hear what becomes of her, before we take our departure; but now let me tell you what has happened. In the main outline I am sure you guess already, without aid of mine, for we leaden-eyed men, in such cases, see nothing by comparison with you our quick-witted sisters. That haughty-looking lady, with the Roman cast of features, who must once have been strikingly handsome, — an Agrippina, even yet, in a favorable presentation, — is the younger lady's aunt. She, it is rumored, once sustained, in her younger days, some injury of that same cruel nature which has this day assailed her niece, and ever since she has worn an air of disdain, not altogether unsupported by real dignity towards men. This aunt it was that tore the letter which lies upon the floor. It deserved to be torn; and yet she that had the best right to do so would *not* have torn it. That letter was an elaborate attempt on the part of an accomplished young man to release himself from sacred engagements. What need was there to argue the case of *such* engagements? Could it have been requisite with pure female dignity to plead anything, or do more than *look* an indisposition to fulfil them? The aunt is now moving towards the door, which I am glad to see; and she is followed by that pale, timid girl of sixteen, a cousin, who feels the case profoundly, but is too young and shy to offer an intellectual sympathy.

One only person in this world there is who *could* to-night have been a supporting friend to our young sufferer, and *that* is her dear, loving twin-sister, that for eighteen years read and wrote, thought and sang, slept and breathed, with the dividing-door open forever between their bed-rooms, and never once a separation between their hearts; but she is in a far-distant land. Who else is there at her call? Except God, nobody. Her aunt had somewhat sternly admonished her, though still with a relenting in her eye as she glanced aside at the expression in her niece's face, that she must "call pride to her assistance." Ay, true; but pride, though a strong ally in public, is apt in private to turn as treacherous as the worst of those against whom she is invoked. How could it be dreamed, by a person of sense, that a brilliant young man, of merits various and eminent, in spite of his baseness, to whom, for nearly two years, this young woman had given her whole confiding love, might be dismissed from a heart like hers on the earliest summons of pride, simply because she herself had been dismissed from *his*, or seemed to have been dismissed, on a summons of mercenary calculation? Look! now that she is relieved from the weight of an unconfidential presence, she has sat for two hours with her head buried in her hands. At last she rises to look for something. A thought has struck her; and, taking a little golden key which hangs by a chain within her bosom, she searches for something locked up amongst her few jewels. What is it? It is a Bible exquisitely illuminated, with a letter attached by some pretty silken artifice to the blank leaves at the end. This letter is a beautiful record, wisely and pathetically composed, of maternal anxiety still burning strong in death, and yearning, when all objects beside were fast fading from *her* eyes, after one parting act of communion with the twin darlings of her heart. Both were thirteen years old, within a week or two, as on the night before her death they sat weeping by the bedside of their mother, and hanging on her lips, now for farewell whispers and now for farewell kisses. They both knew that, as her strength had permitted during the latter month of her life, she had thrown the last anguish of love in her beseeching heart into a letter of counsel to themselves. Through this, of which each sister had a copy, she trusted long to converse with her orphans. And the last promise which she had entreated on this evening from both was, that in either of two contingencies they would review her counsels, and the passages to which she pointed their attention in the Scriptures; namely first, in the event of any calamity, that, for one sister or for both, should overspread their paths with total darkness; and, secondly, in the event of life flowing in too profound a stream of prosperity, so as to threaten them with an alienation of interest from all spiritual objects. She had not concealed that, of these two extreme cases, she would prefer for her own children the first. And now had that case arrived, indeed, which she in spirit had desired to meet. Nine years ago, just as the silvery voice of a dial in the dying lady's bed-room was striking nine, upon a summer evening, had the last visual ray streamed from her seeking eyes upon her orphan twins, after which, throughout the night, she had slept away into heaven. Now again had come a summer evening memorable for unhappiness; now again the daughter thought of those dying lights of love which streamed at sunset from the closing eyes of her mother; again, and just as she went back in thought to this image, the same silvery voice of the dial sounded nine o'clock. Again she remembered her mother's dying request; again her own tear-hallowed promise, — and with her heart in her mother's grave she now rose to fulfil it. Here, then, when this solemn recurrence to a testamentary counsel has ceased to be a mere office of duty towards the departed, having taken the shape of a consolation for herself, let us pause.

. . . .

Now, fair companion in this exploring voyage of inquest into hidden scenes, or forgotten scenes of human life, perhaps it might be instructive to direct our glasses upon the false, perfidious lover. It might. But do not let us do so. We might like him better, or pity him more, than either of us would desire. His name and memory have long since dropped out of everybody's thoughts. Of prosperity, and (what is more important) of internal peace, he is reputed to have had no gleam from the moment when he betrayed his faith, and in one day threw away the jewel of good conscience, and "a pearl richer than all his tribe." But, however that may be, it is certain that, finally, he became a wreck; and of any *hopeless* wreck it is painful to talk, — much more so, when through him others also became wrecks.

Shall we, then, after an interval of nearly two years has passed over the young lady in the boudoir, look in again upon *her?* You hesitate, fair friend; and I myself hesitate. For in fact she also has become a wreck; and it would grieve us both to see her altered. At the end of twenty-one months she retains hardly a vestige of resemblance to the fine young woman we saw on that unhappy evening, with her aunt and cousin. On consideration, therefore, let us do this.—We will direct our glasses to her room at a point of time about six weeks further on. Suppose this time gone; suppose her now dressed for her grave, and placed in her coffin. The advantage of that is, that though no change can restore the ravages of the past, yet (as often is found to happen with young persons) the expression has revived from her girlish years. The child-like aspect has revolved, and settled back upon her features. The wasting away of the flesh is less apparent in the face; and one might imagine that in this sweet marble countenance was seen the very same upon which, eleven years ago, her mother's darkening eyes had lingered to the last, until clouds had swallowed up the vision of her beloved *twins*. Yet, if that were in part a fancy, this, at least, is no fancy, — that not only much of a child-like truth and simplicity has reinstated itself in the temple of her now reposing features, but also that tranquillity and perfect peace, such as are appropriate to eternity, but which from the *living* countenance had taken their flight forever, on that memorable evening when we looked in upon the impassioned group, — upon the towering and denouncing aunt, the sympathizing but silent cousin, the poor, blighted niece, and the wicked letter lying in fragments at their feet.

Cloud, that hast revealed to us this young creature and her blighted hopes, close up again. And now, a few years later, — not more than four or five, — give back to us the latest arrears of the changes which thou concealest within thy draperies. Once more, "open sesame!" and show us a third generation. Behold a lawn islanded with thickets. How perfect is the verdure; how rich the blossoming shrubberies that screen with verdurous walls from the possibility of intrusion, whilst by their own wandering line of distribution they shape, and umbrageously embay, what one might call lawny saloons and vestibules, sylvan galleries and closets! Some of these recesses, which unlink themselves as fluently as snakes, and unexpectedly as the shyest nooks, watery cells, and crypts, amongst the shores of a forest-lake, being formed by the mere caprices and ramblings of the luxuriant shrubs, are so small and so quiet that one might fancy them meant for *boudoirs*. Here is one that in a less fickle climate would make the loveliest of studies for a writer of breathings from some solitary heart, or of *suspiria* frum some impassioned memory! And, opening from one angle of this embowered study, issues a little narrow corridor, that, after almost wheeling back upon itself, in its playful mazes, finally widens into a little circular chamber; out of which there is no exit (except back again by the entrance), small or great; so that, adjacent to his study, the writer would command how sweet a bed-room, permitting him to lie the summer through, gazing all night long at the burning host of heaven. How silent *that* would be at the noon of summer nights, — how grave-like in its quiet! And yet, need there be asked a stillness or a silence more profound than is felt at this present noon of day? One reason for such peculiar repose, over and above the tranquil character of the day, and the distance of the place from the high-roads, is the outer zone of woods, which almost on every quarter invests the shrubberies, swathing them (as one may express it), belting them and overlooking them, from a varying distance of two and three furlongs, so as oftentimes to keep the winds at a distance. But, however caused and supported, the silence of these fancifu. lawns and lawny chambers is oftentimes oppressive in the depths of summer to people unfamiliar with solitudes, either mountainous or sylvan; and many would be apt to suppose that the villa, to which these pretty shrubberies form the chief dependencies, must be untenanted. But that is not the case. The house is inhabited, and by its own legal mistress, the proprietress of the whole domain; and not at all a silent mistress, but as noisy as most little ladies of five years old, for that is her age. Now, and just as we are speaking, ycu may hear her little joyous clamor, as she issues from the house. This way she comes, bounding like a fawn; and soon she rushes into the little recess which I pointed out as a proper study for any man who should be weaving the deep harmonies of memorial *suspiria.* But I fancy that she will soon dispossess it of that character, for her *suspiria* are not many at this stage of her life. Now she comes dancing into sight; and you see that, if she keeps the promise of her infancy, she will be an interesting creature to the eye in after life. In other respects, also, she is an engaging child, — loving, natural, and wild as any one of her neighbors for some miles round namely, leverets, squirrels, and ring-doves. But what will surprise you most is, that, although a child of pure English blood, she speaks very little English; but more Bengalee than perhaps you will find it convenient to construe. That is her ayah, who comes up from behind, at a pace so different from her youthful mistress's. But, if their paces are different, in other things they agree most cordially; and dearly they love each other. In reality, the child has passed her whole life in the arms of this ayah. She remembers nothing elder than *her;* eldest of things is the ayah in her eyes; and, if the ayah should insist on her worshipping herself as the goddess Railroadina or Steamboatina, that made England, and the sea, and Bengal, it is certain that the little thing would do so, asking no question but this, — whether kissing would do for worshipping.

Every evening at nine o'clock, as the ayah sits by the little creature lying awake in bed, the silvery tongue of a dial tolls the hour. Reader, you know who she is She is the grand-daughter of her that faded away about sunset in gazing at her twin orphans. Her name is Grace. And she is the niece of that elder and once happy Grace, who spent so much of her happiness in this very room, but whom, in her utter desolation, we saw in the boudoir, with the torn letter at her feet. She is the daughter of that other sister, wife to a military officer who died abroad. Little Grace never saw her grandmamma, nor her lovely aunt, that was her namesake, nor consciously her mamma. She was born six months after the death of the elder Grace; and her mother saw her only through the mists of mortal suffering, which carried her off three weeks after the birth of her daughter.

This view was taken several years ago; and since then the younger Grace, in her turn, is under a cloud of affliction. But she is still under eighteen; and of her there may be hopes. Seeing such things in so short a space of years, for the grandmother died at thirty-two, we say, — Death we can face: but knowing, as some of us do, what is human life, which of us is it that without shuddering could (if consciously we were summoned) face the hour of birth?

www.ingramcontent.com/pod-product-compliance
Lightning Source LLC
LaVergne TN
LVHW010226110826
845151LV00004B/1191
9781425526597